F1
2004

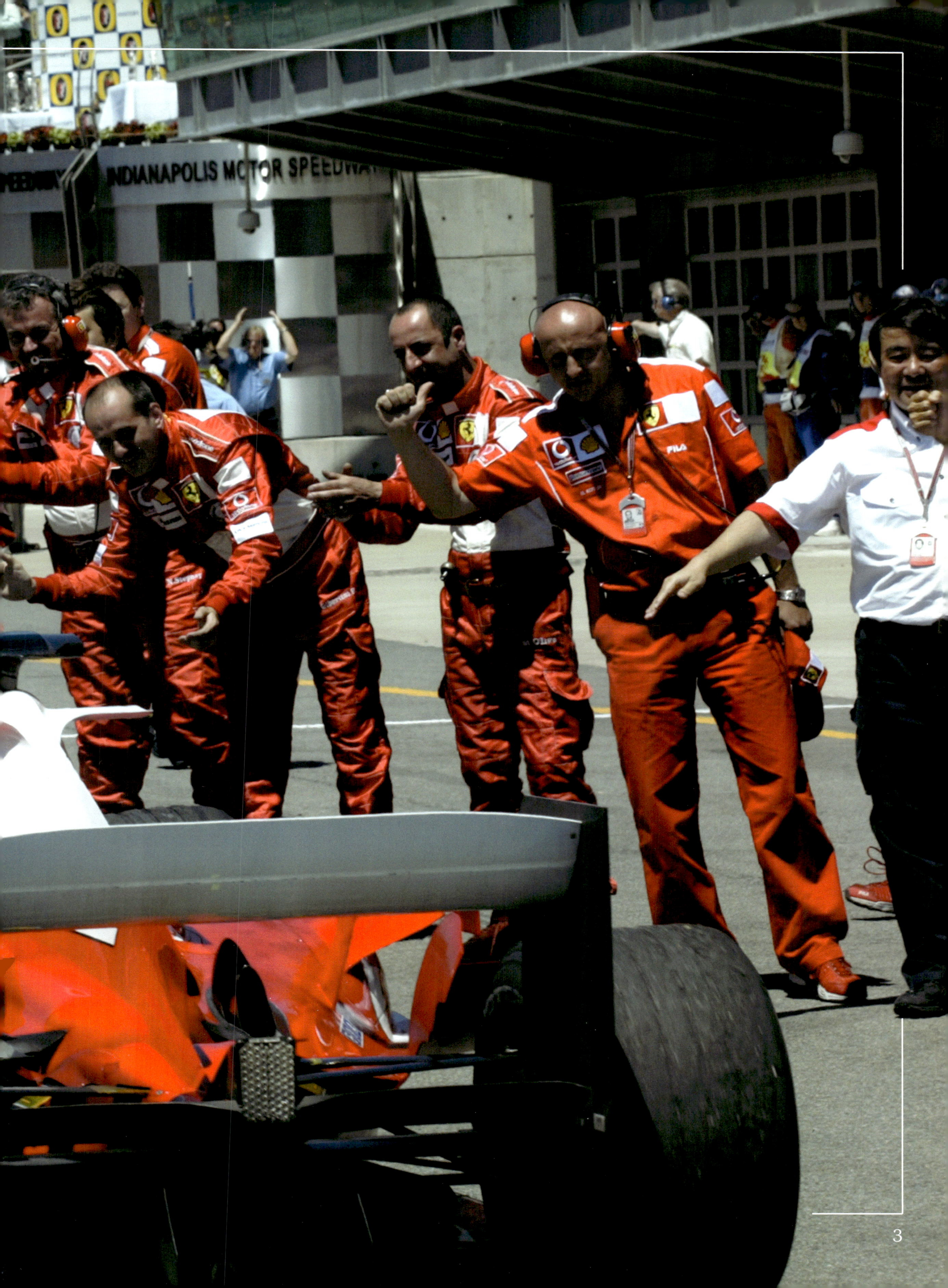
INDIANAPOLIS MOTOR SPEEDWAY

4

Marlboro
Marlboro
vodafone
vodafone
Marlboro
SKF
brembo
MAHLE

vodafone

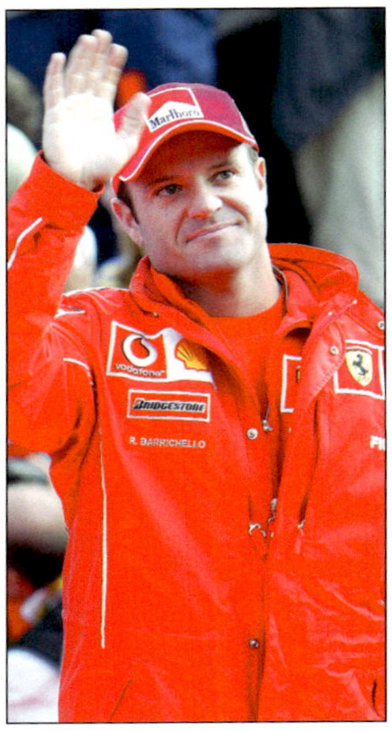

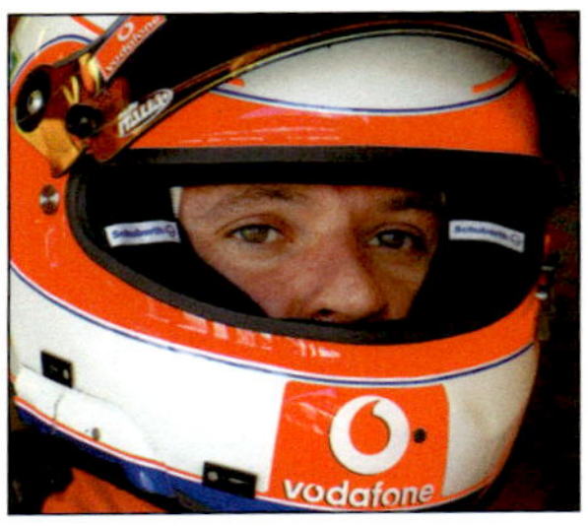
vodafone

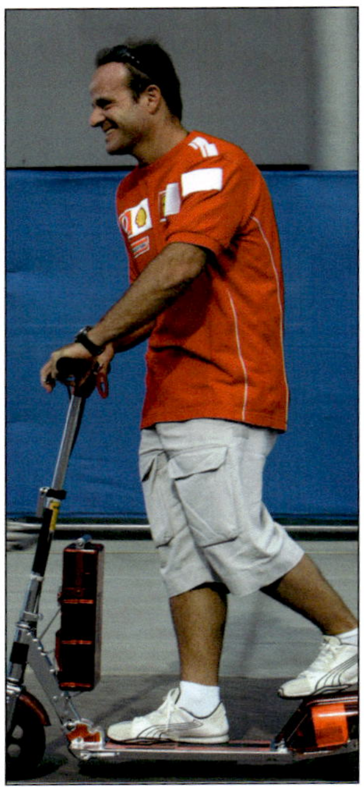

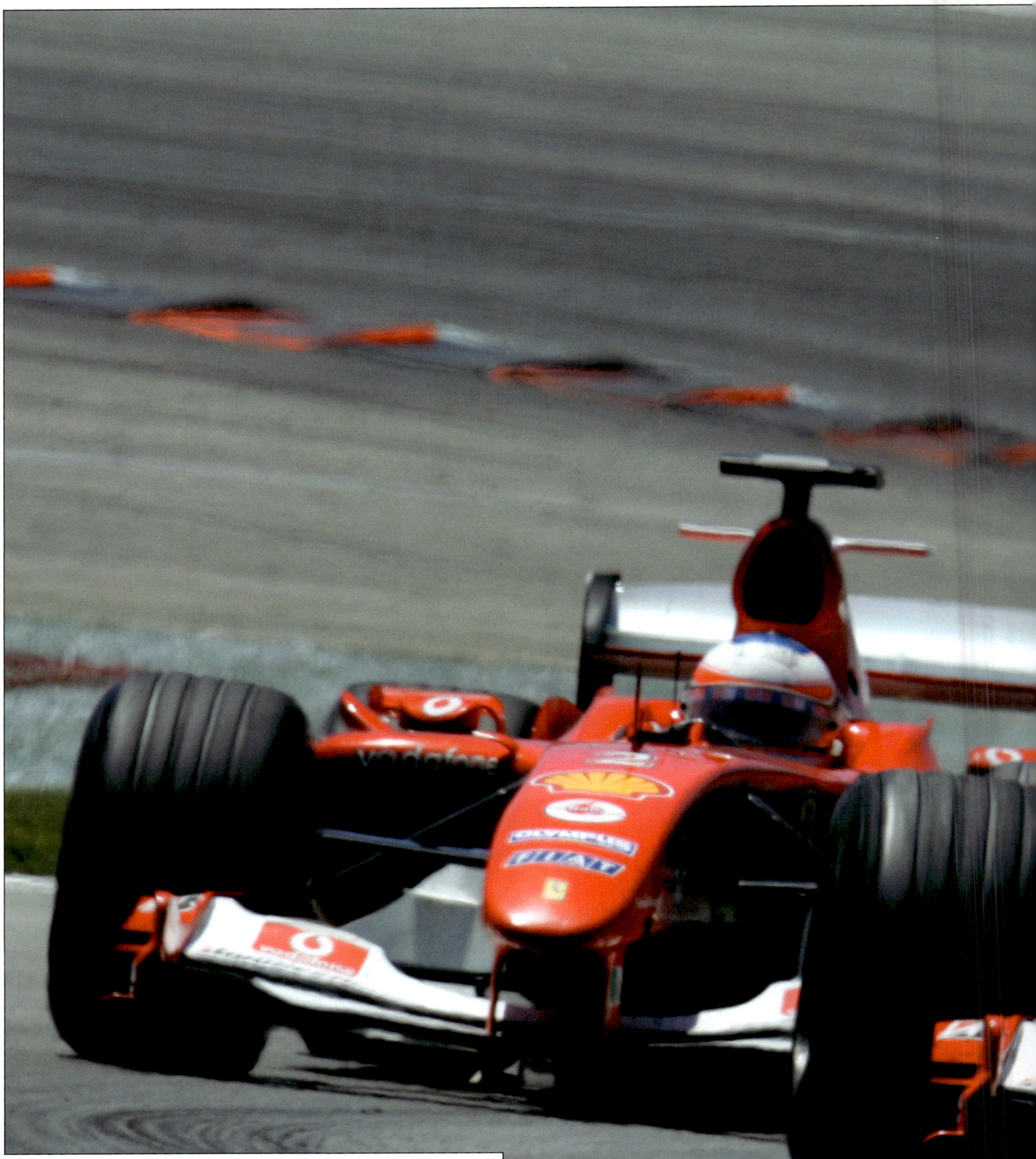
vodafone
OLYMPUS

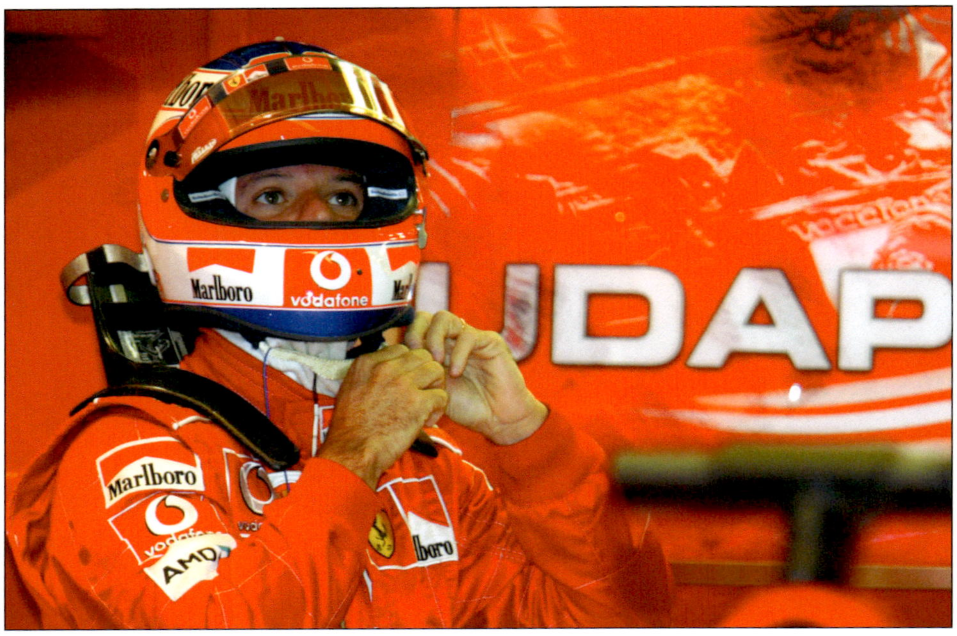
Marlboro
vodafone
UDAP
AMD

7

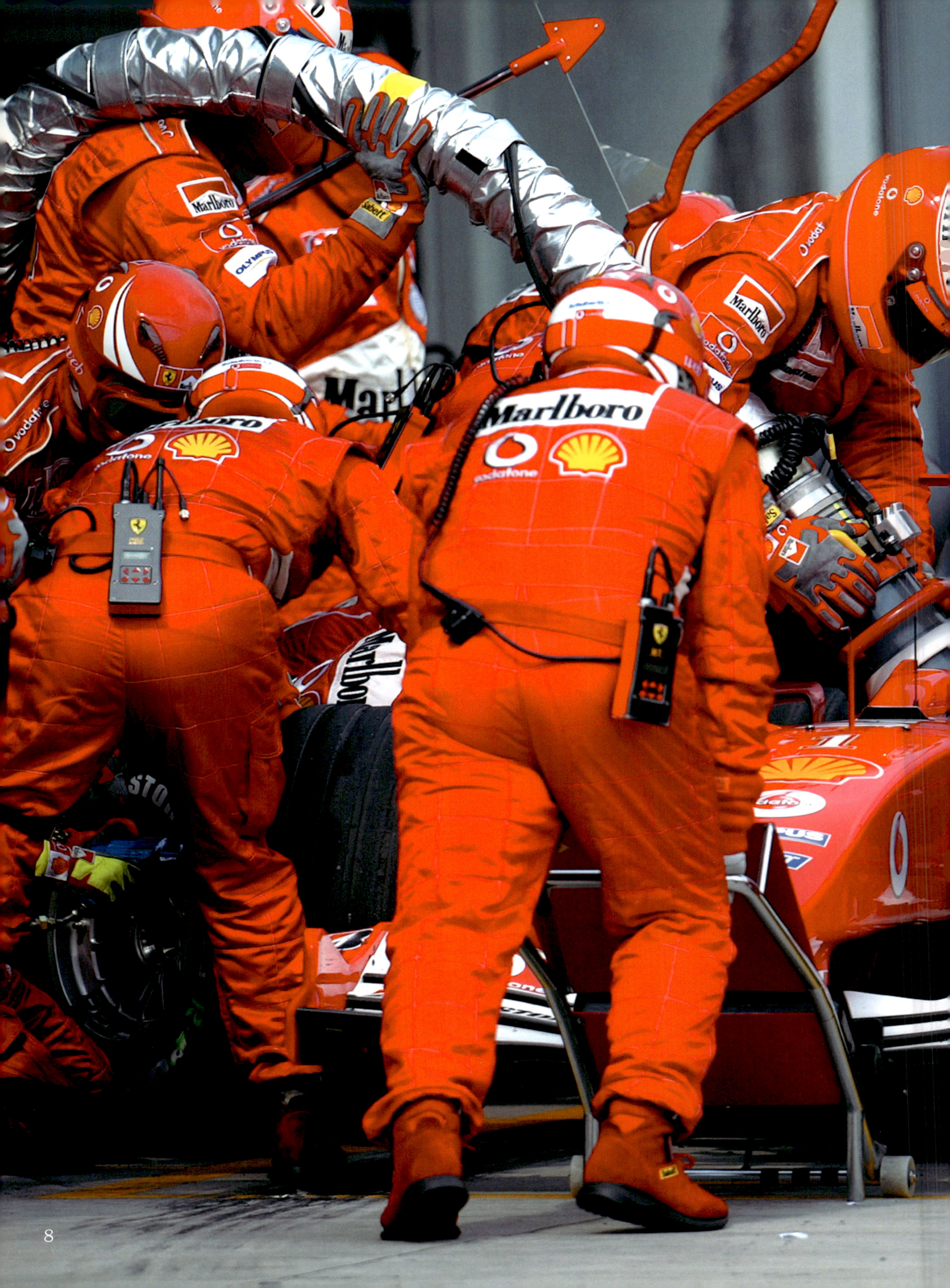
Marlboro
vodafone

9

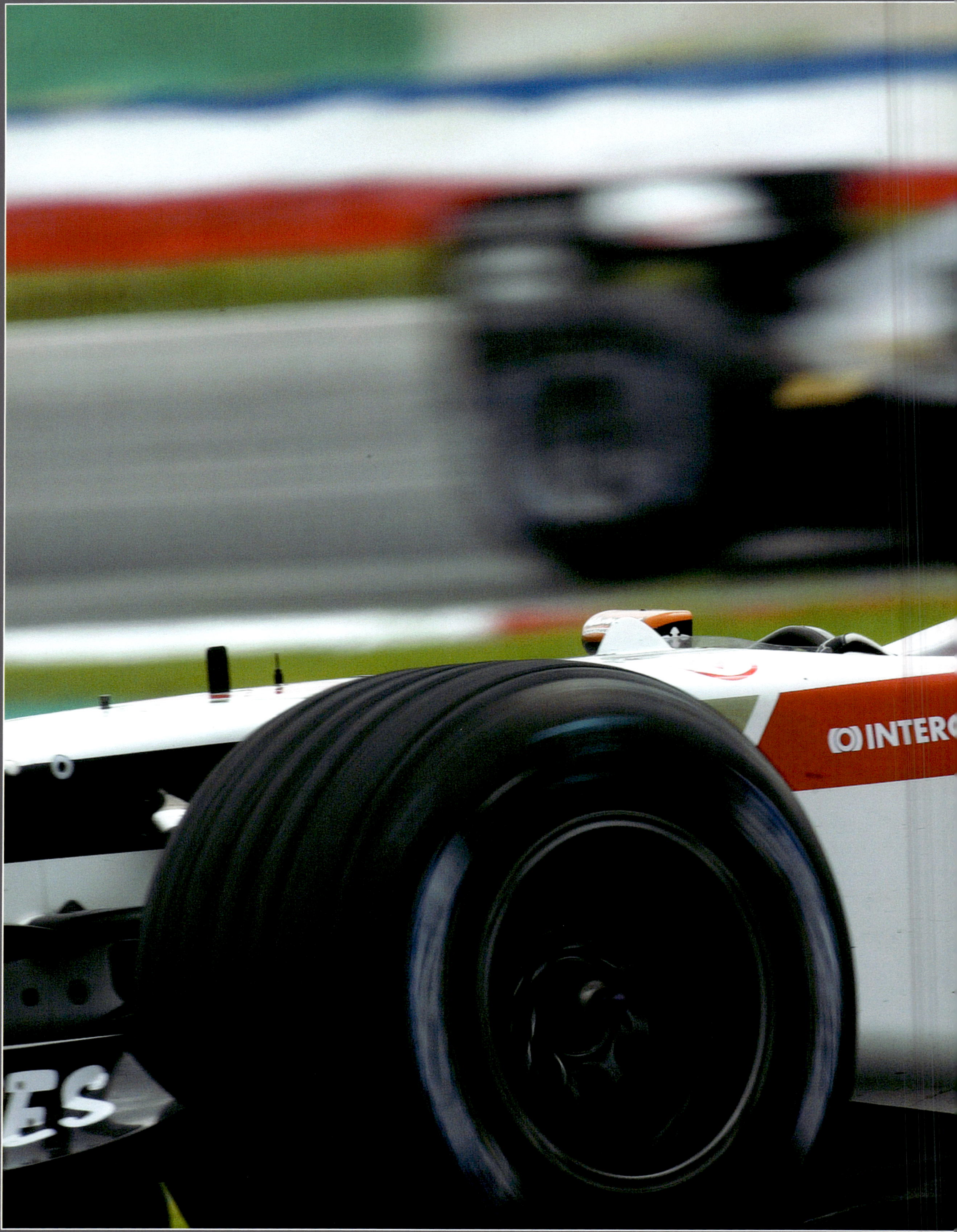
INTERC

11

LUCKY STRIKE
555
WORLD RACING
J.BUTTON
BARf1.com
HONDA
LUCKY STRIKE

13

LUCKY STRIKE
LUCKY STRIKE
Ray-Ban
www.takumasato.com
BRUNOTTI
SPORTSWEAR
T.SATO
LUCKY

INTERCOND

16

17

18

19

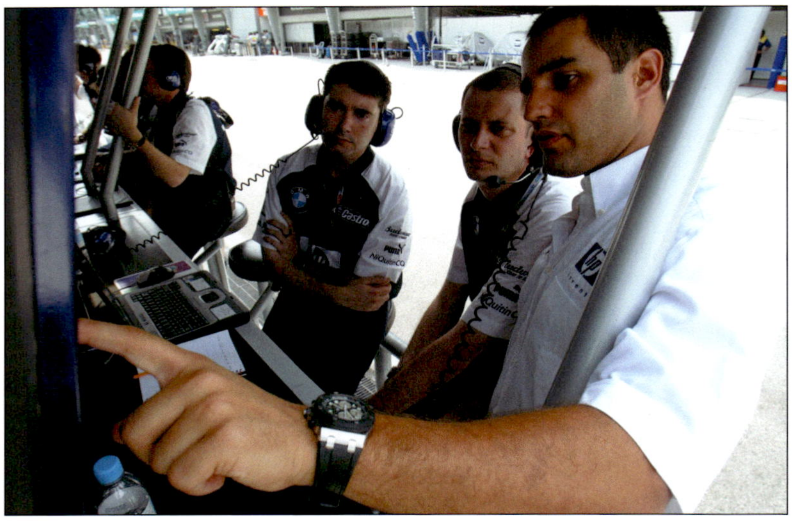

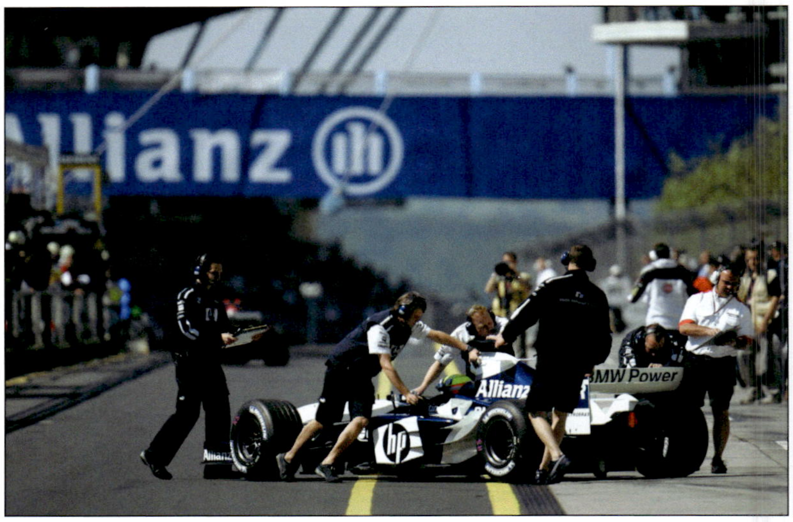
Allianz
Allianz

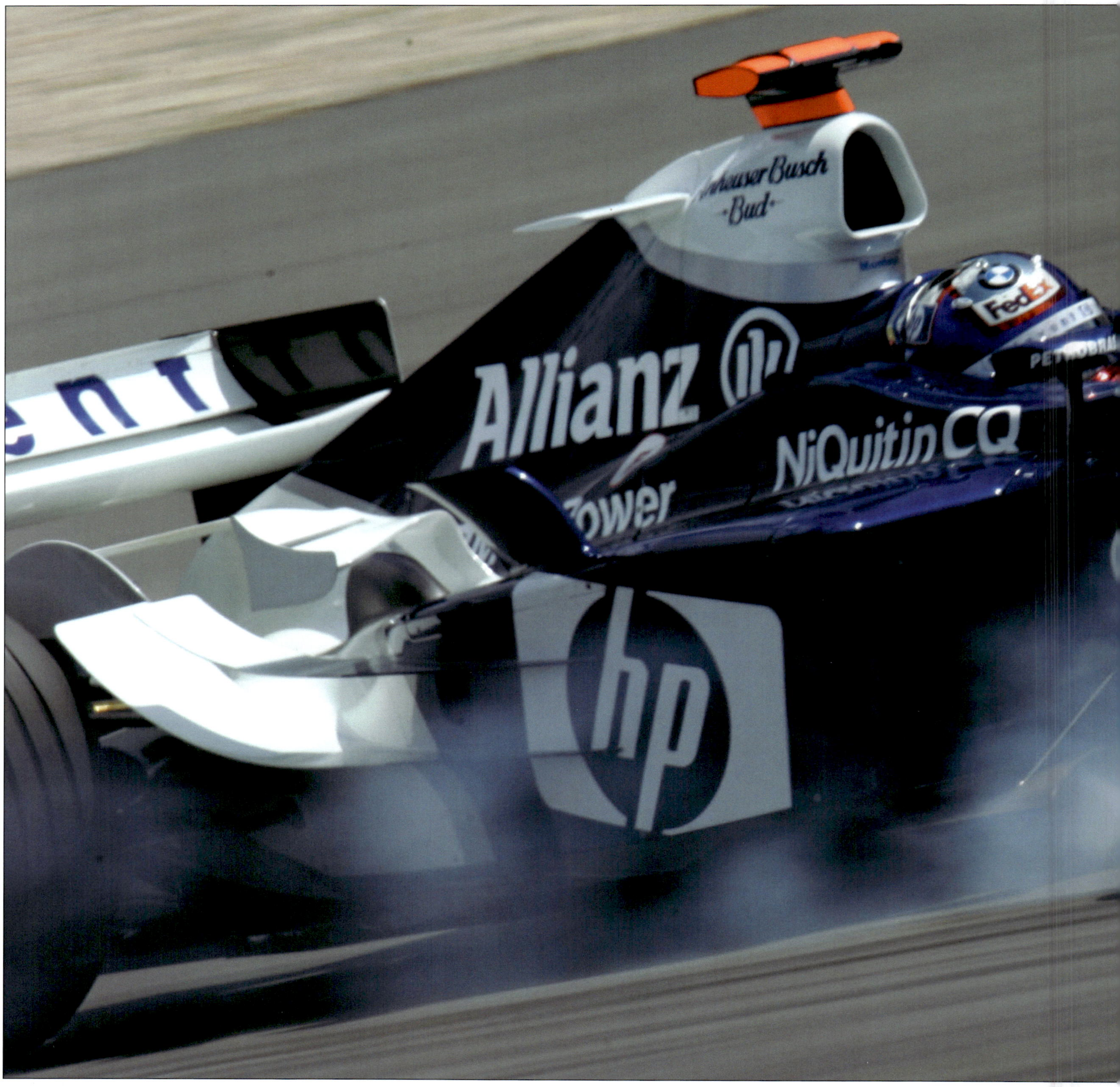
Bud
Allianz
NiQuitin CQ
hp

21

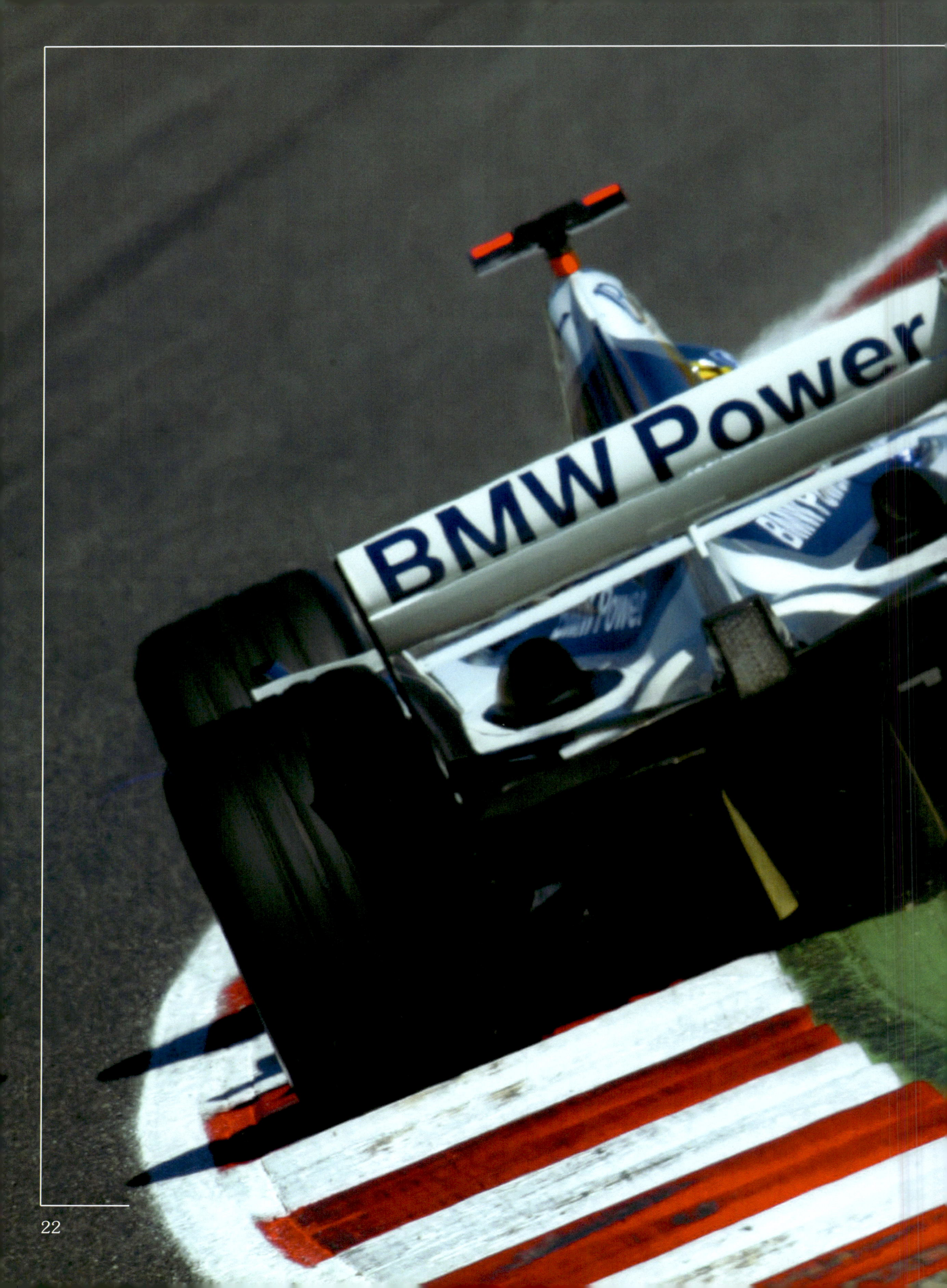
BMW Power

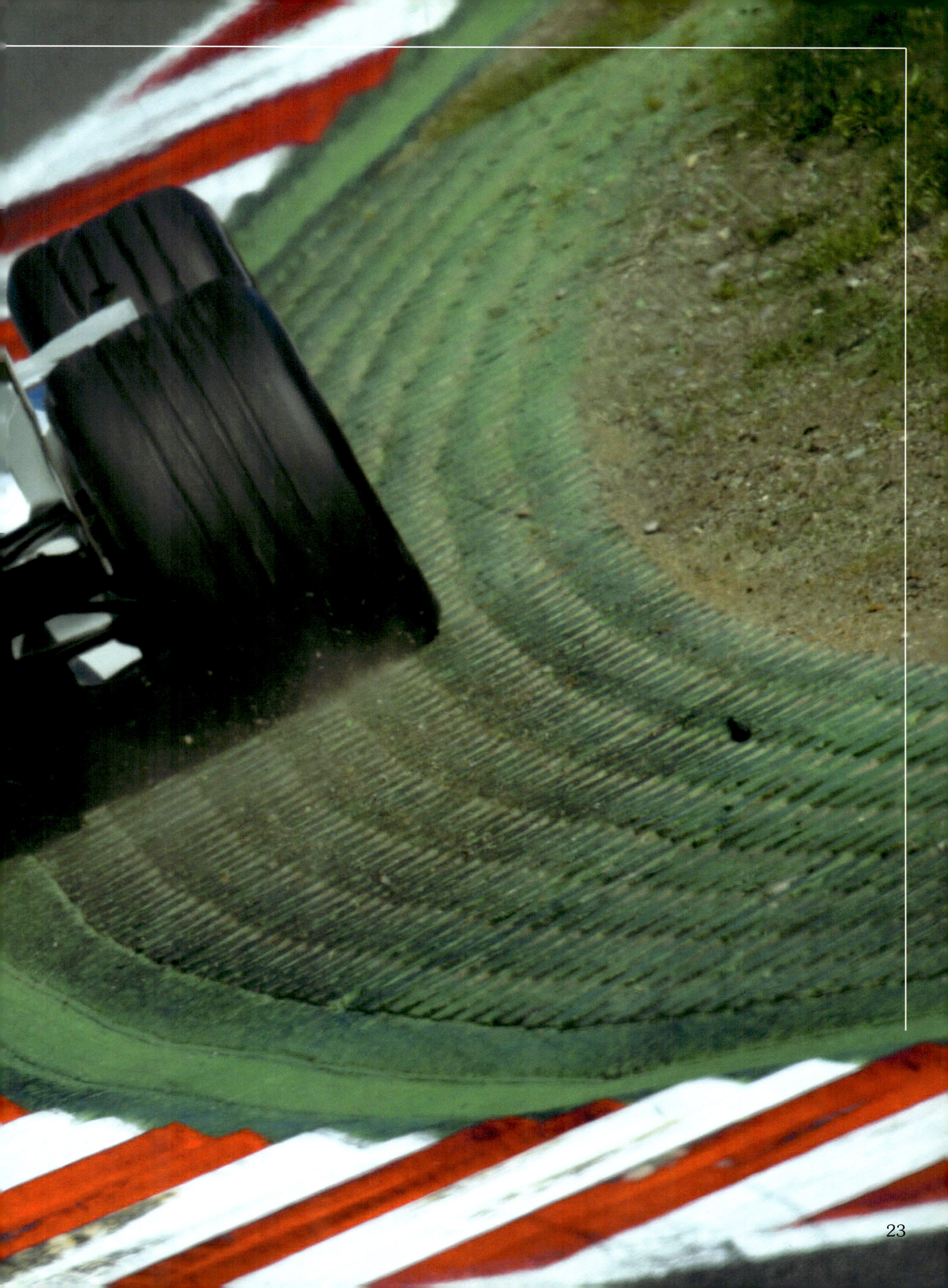

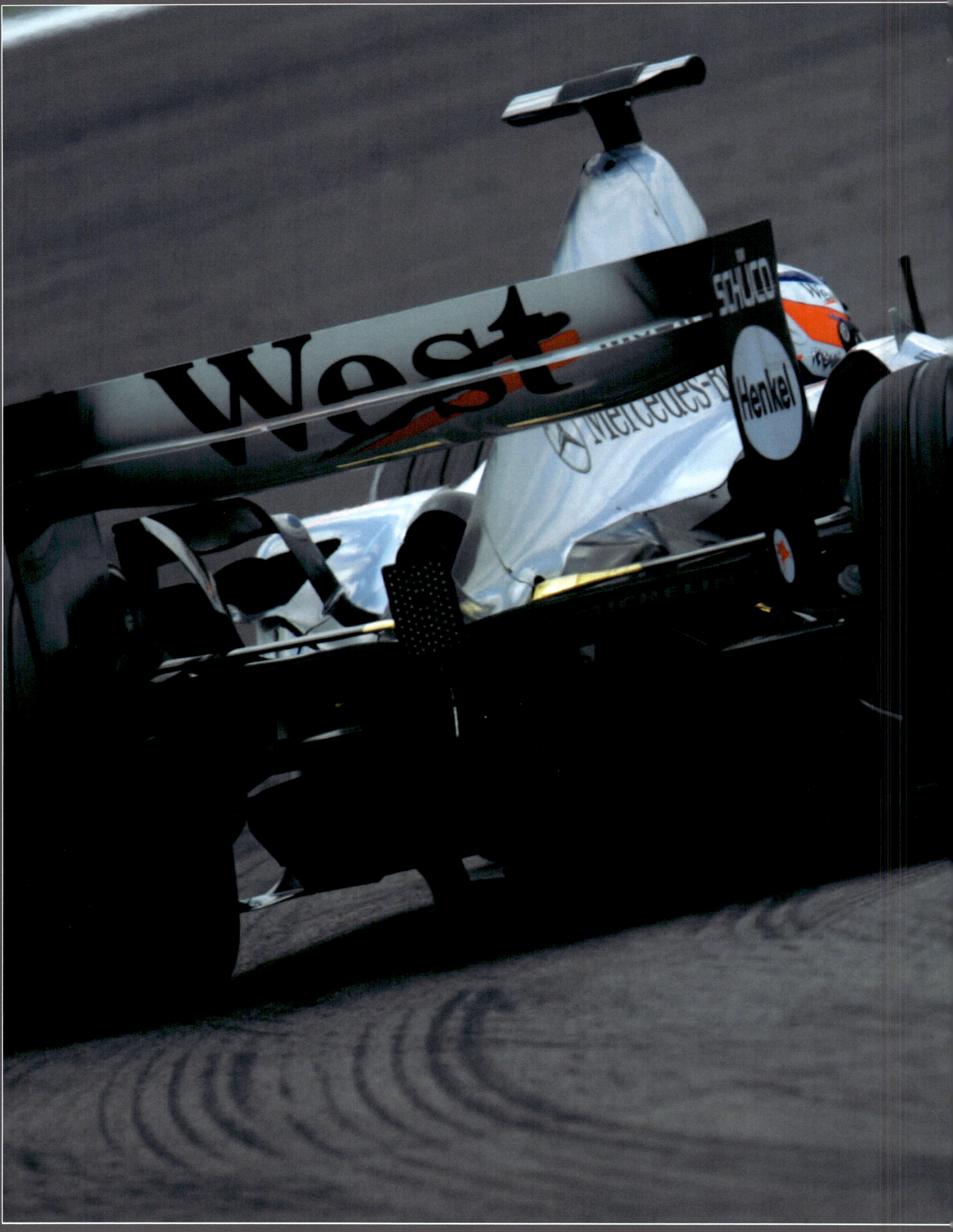
West
SCHÜCO
Henkel

25

West
Coulthard
BOSS
West
Computer Associates
SIEMENS
BOSS
West
Sun
SIEMENS

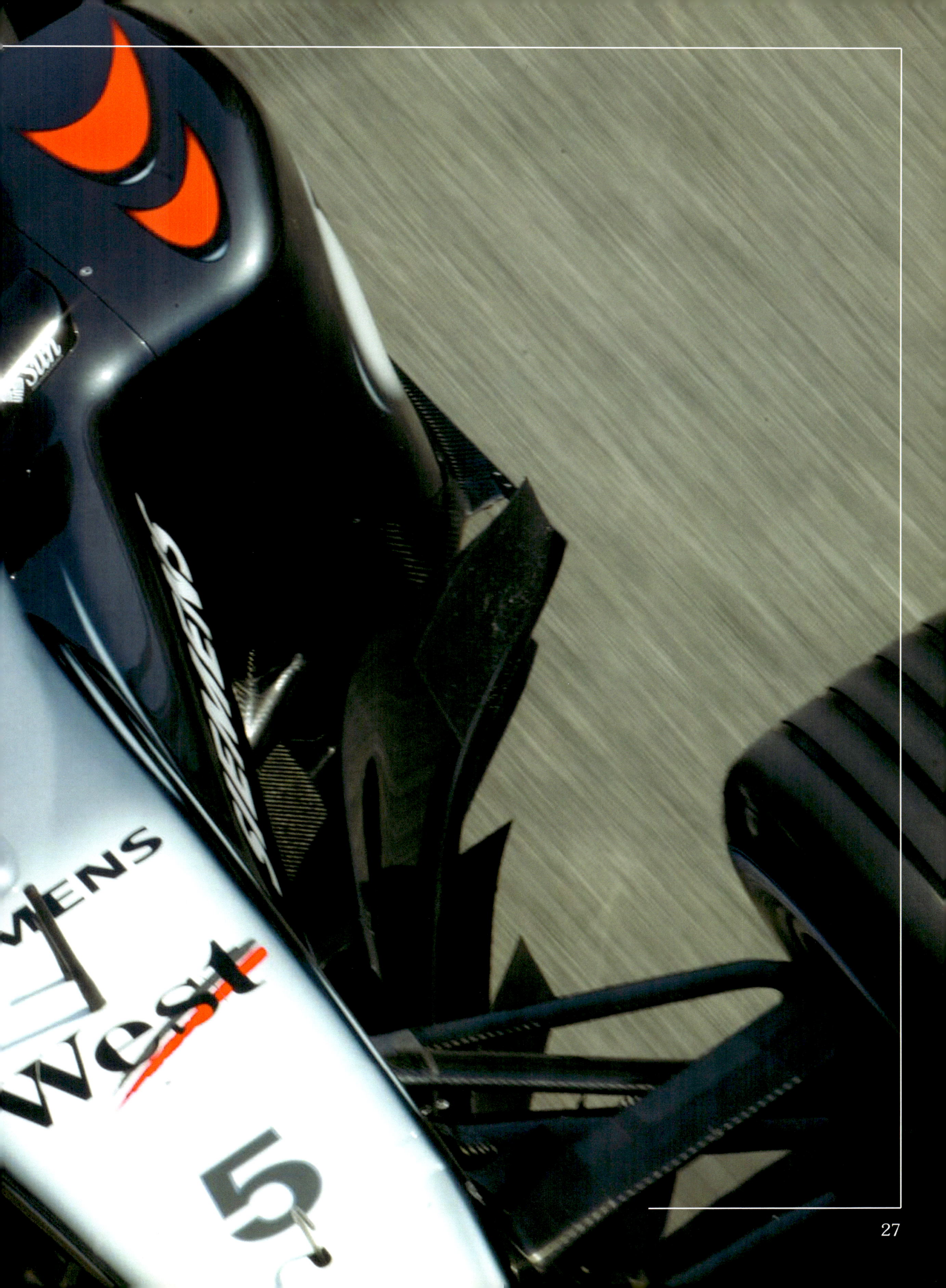
MENS
West
5

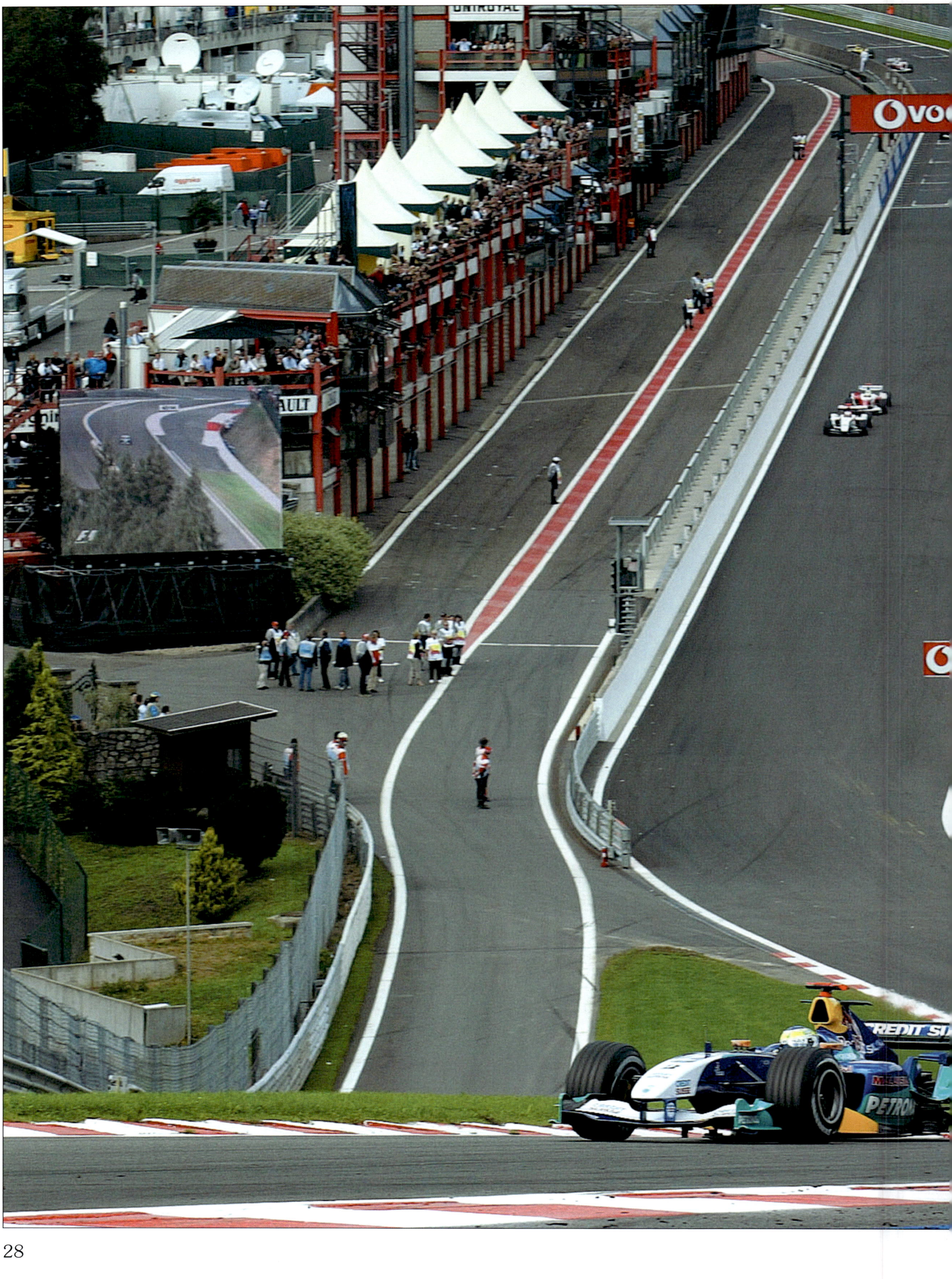

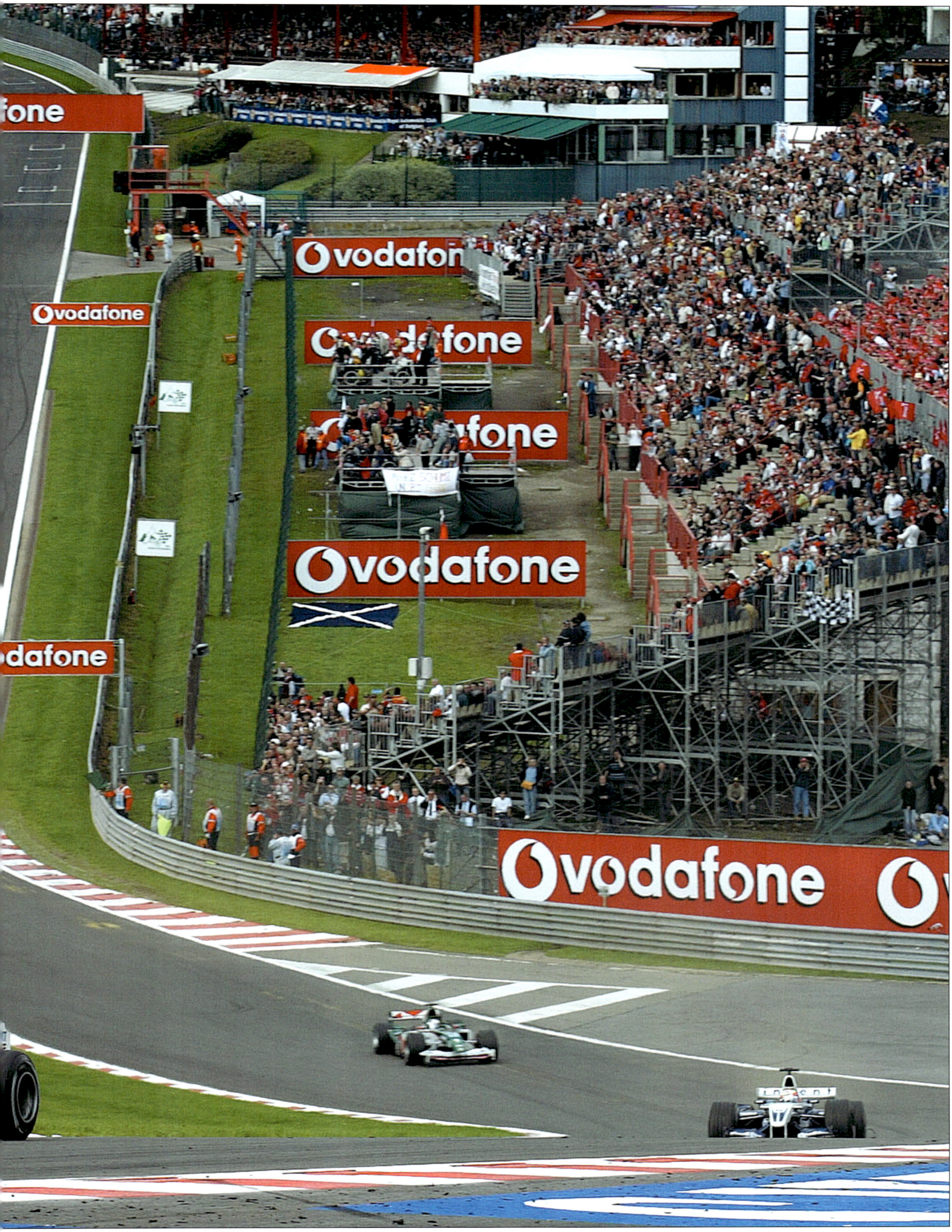
fone
vodafone
vodafone
vodafone
vodafone
vodafone
vodafone
odafone
vodafone

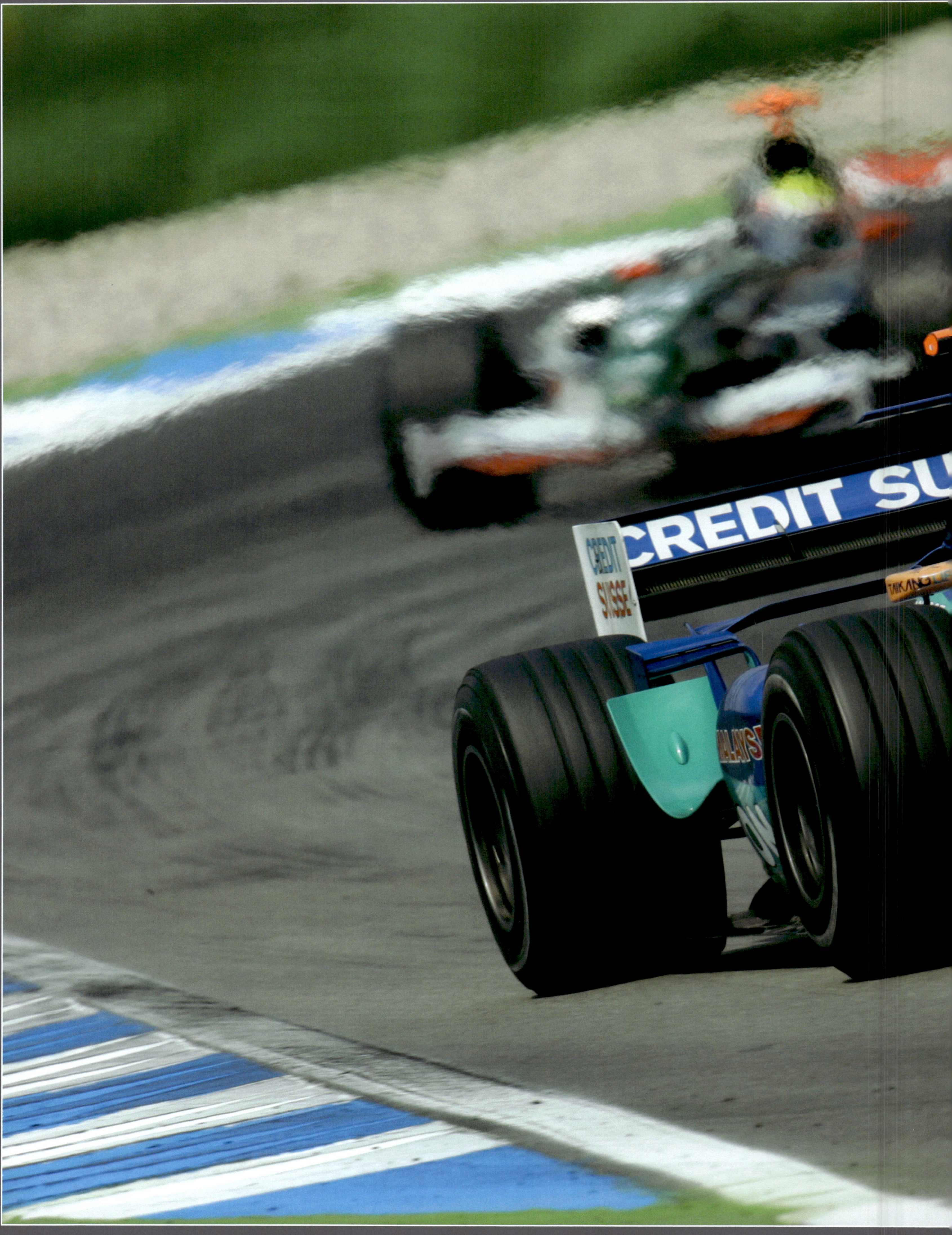
CREDIT SU
CREDIT SUISSE

VIDAL
CREDIT SUISSE
CREDIT SUISSE
CREDIT SUISSE
CREDIT SUISSE

32

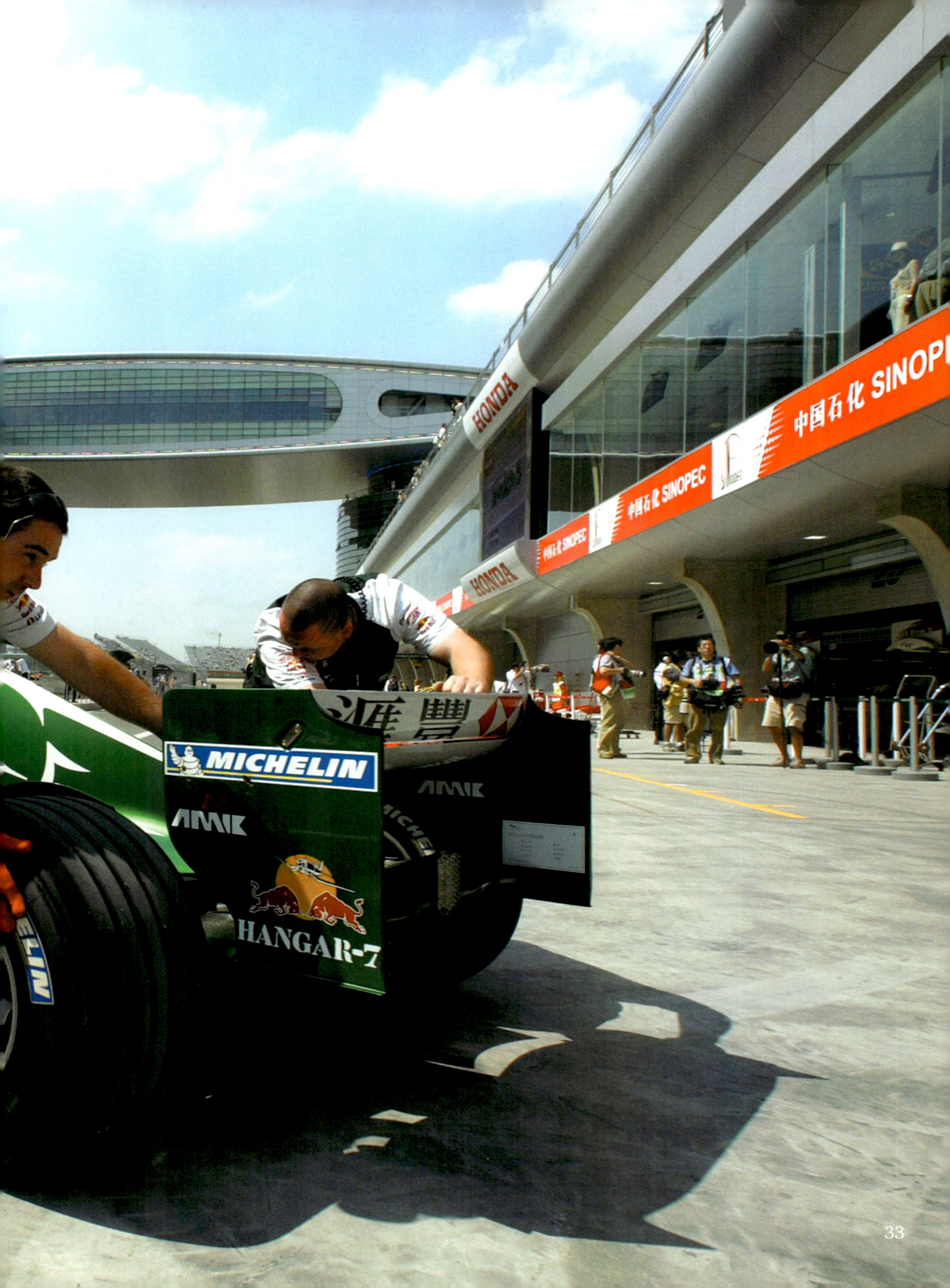
HONDA
中国石化 SINOPEC
中国石化 SINOPEC
HONDA
MICHELIN
HANGAR-7

Pioneer
Castrol
HSBC
AT&T
BECK'S
JAGUAR
TOM TAILOR
MICHELIN
14
YTL
DUPONT
UGS

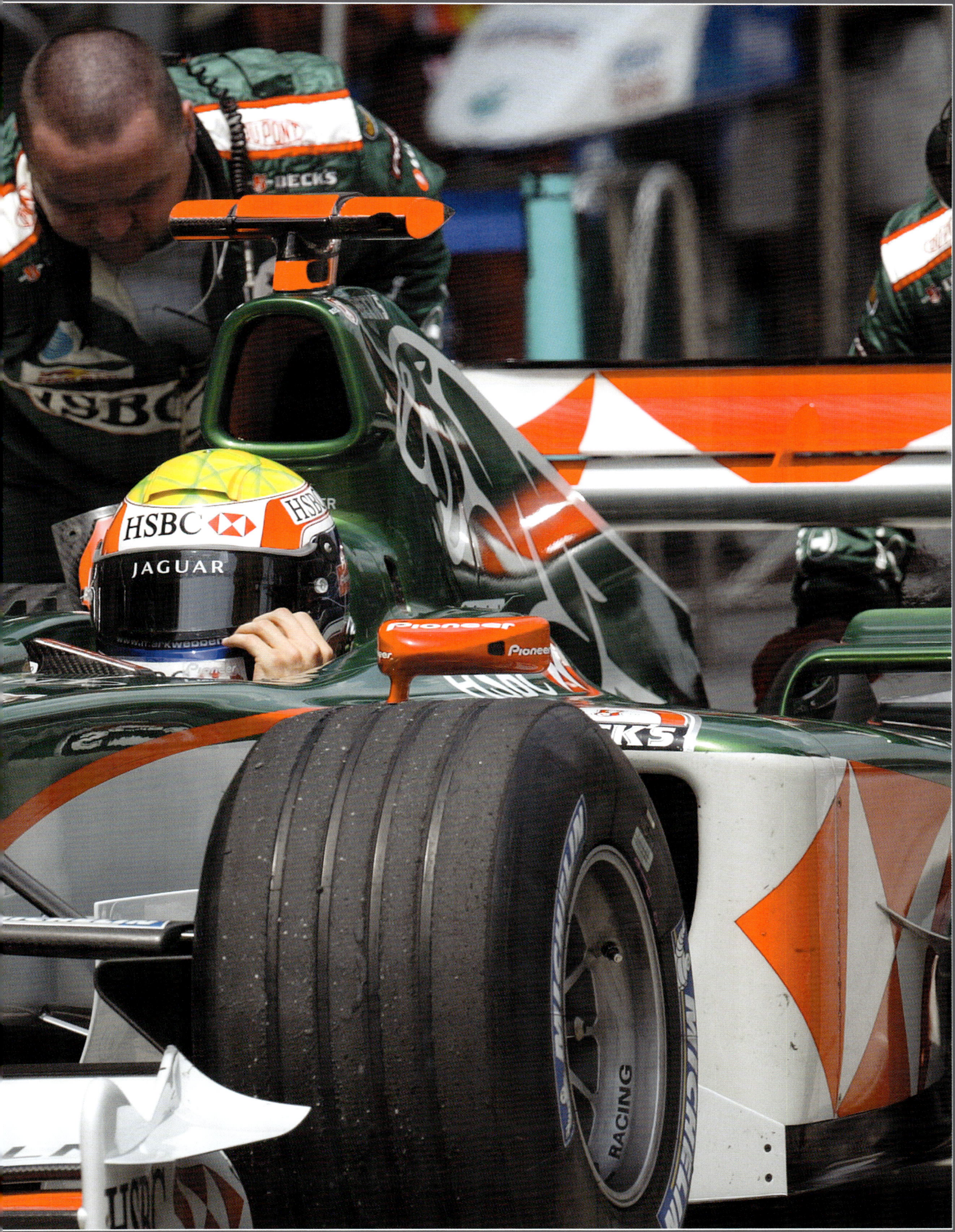
HSBC
JAGUAR
Pioneer
RACING

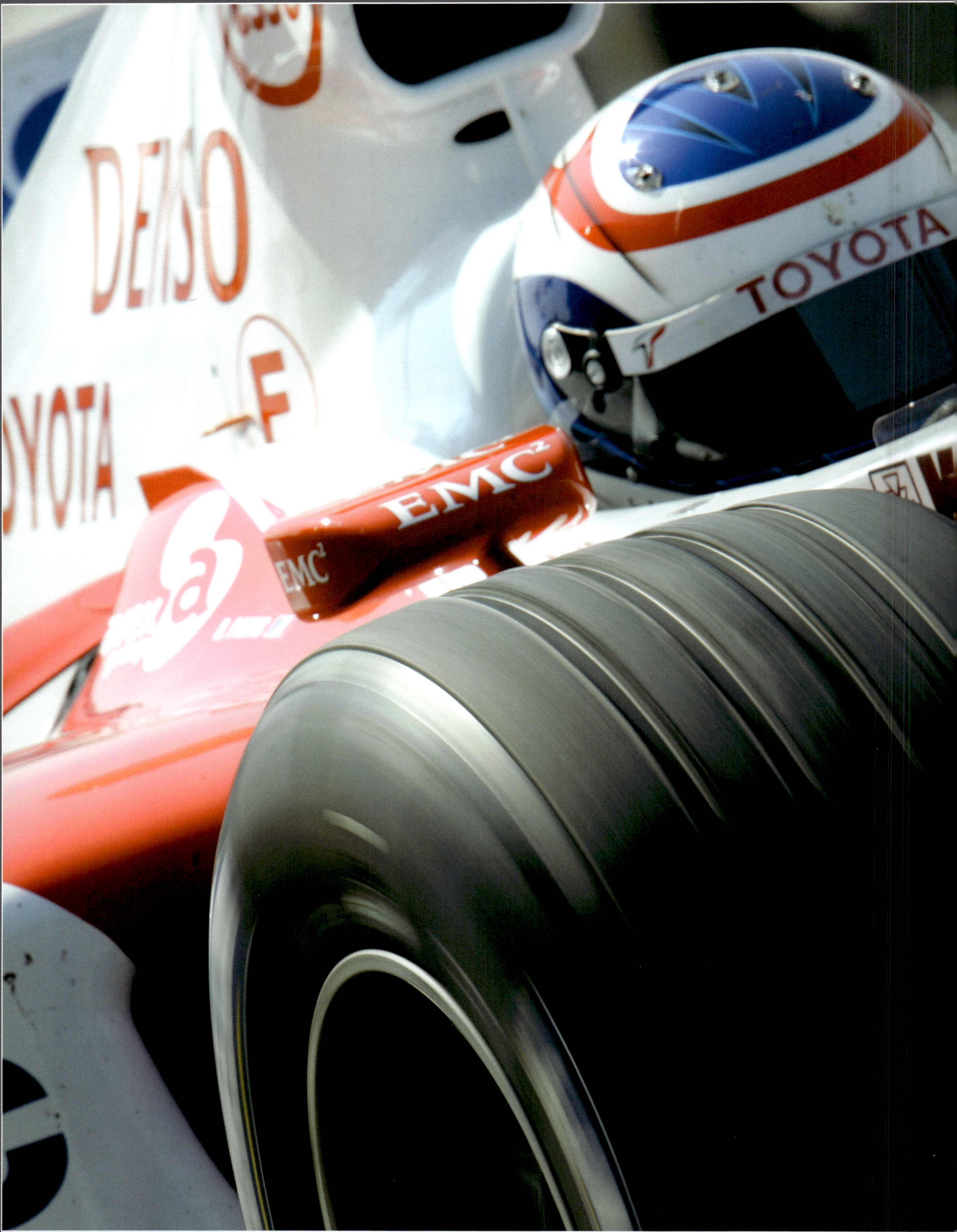
DENSO
TOYOTA
EMC
EMC
TOYOTA

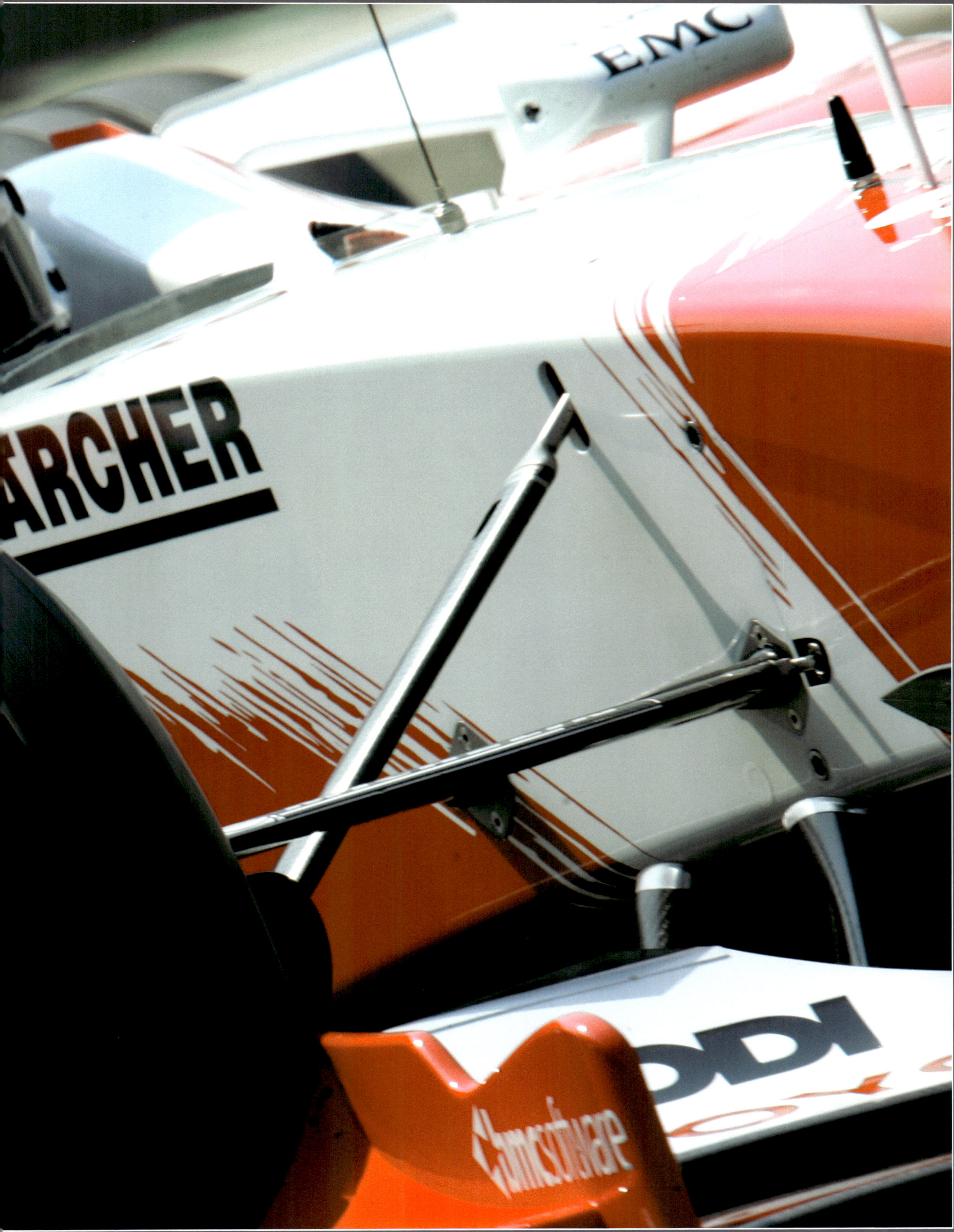
EMC
ARCHER

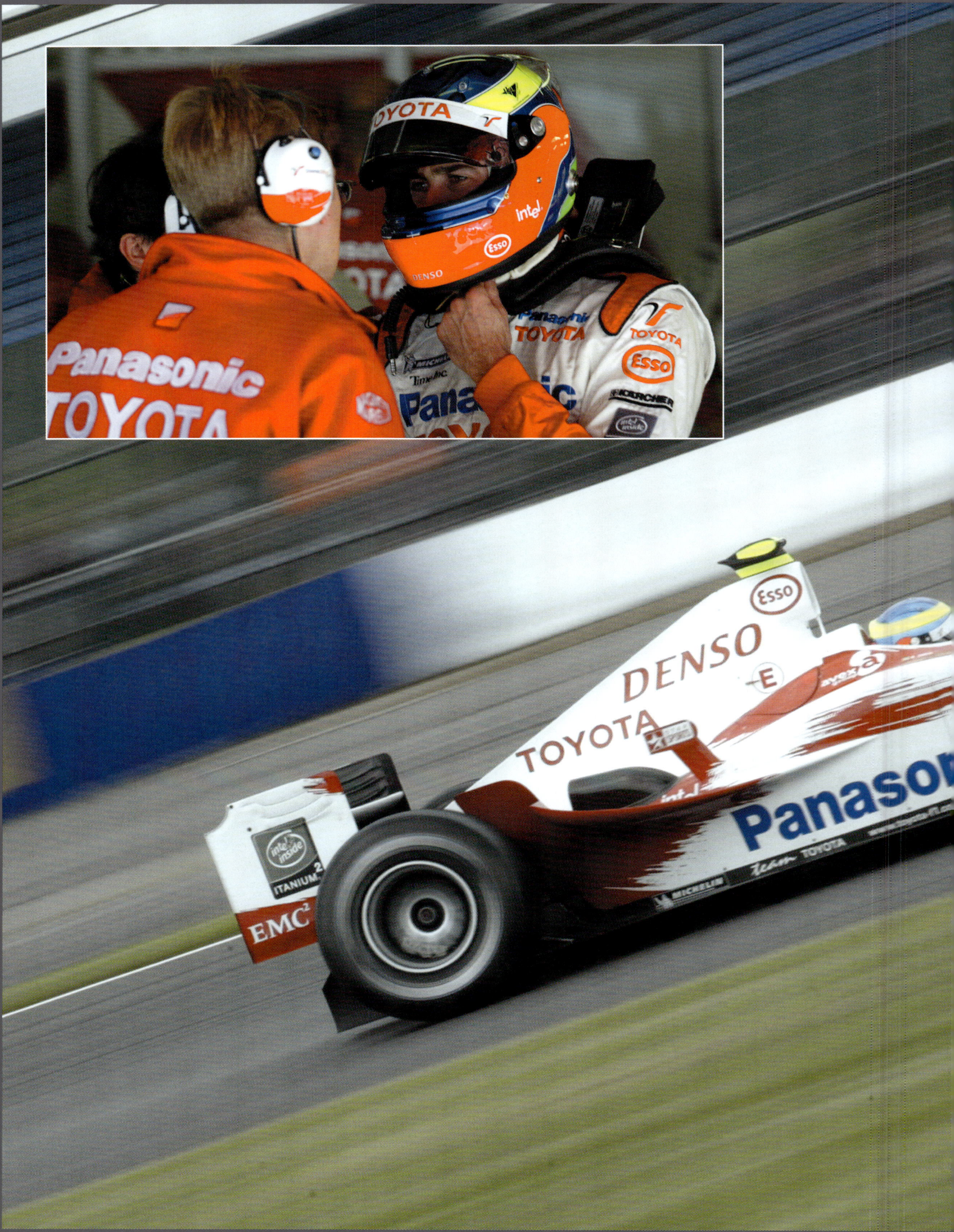
TOYOTA
Panasonic
Esso
intel
DENSO
EMC²
ITANIUM 2

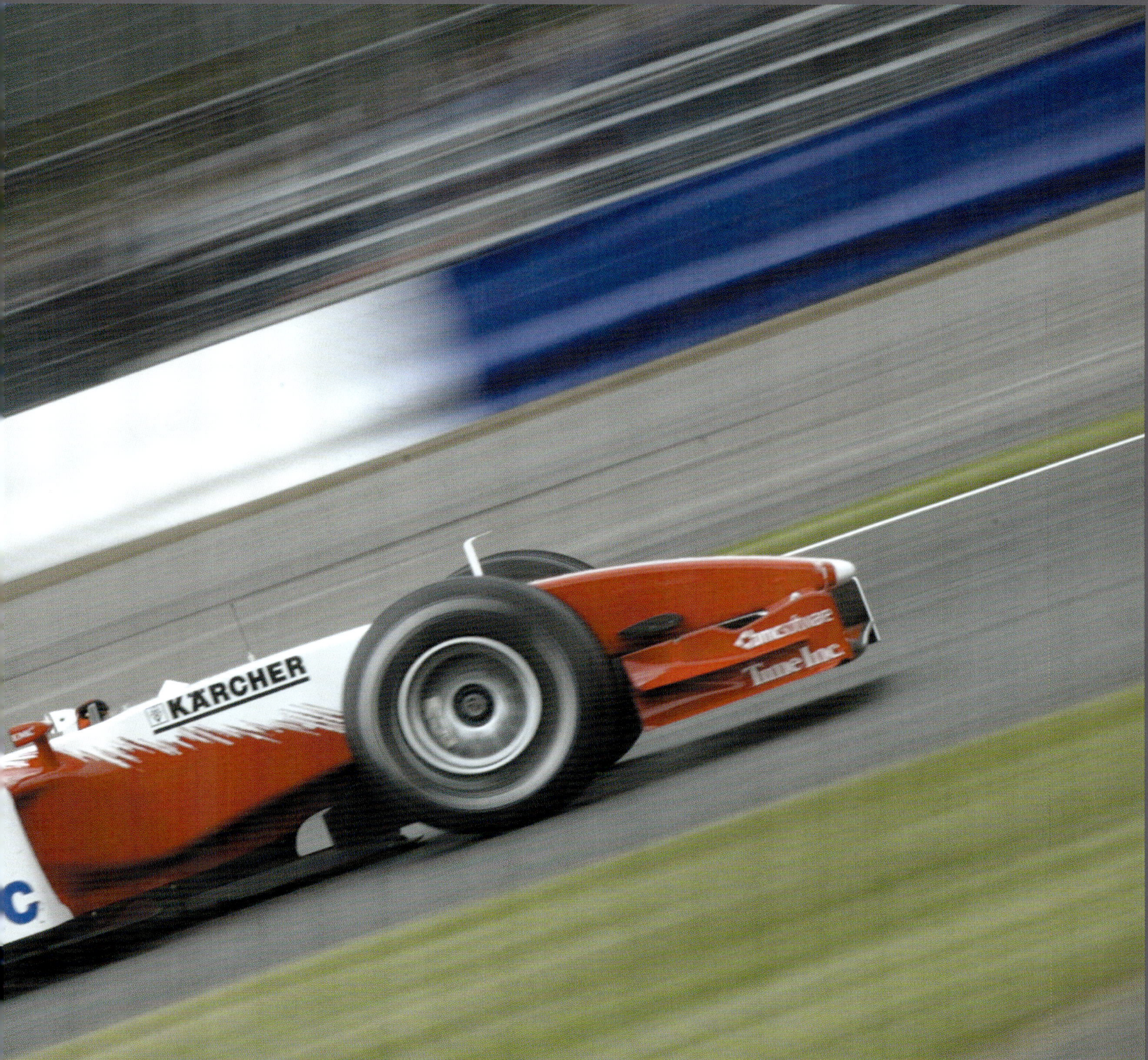
KÄRCHER
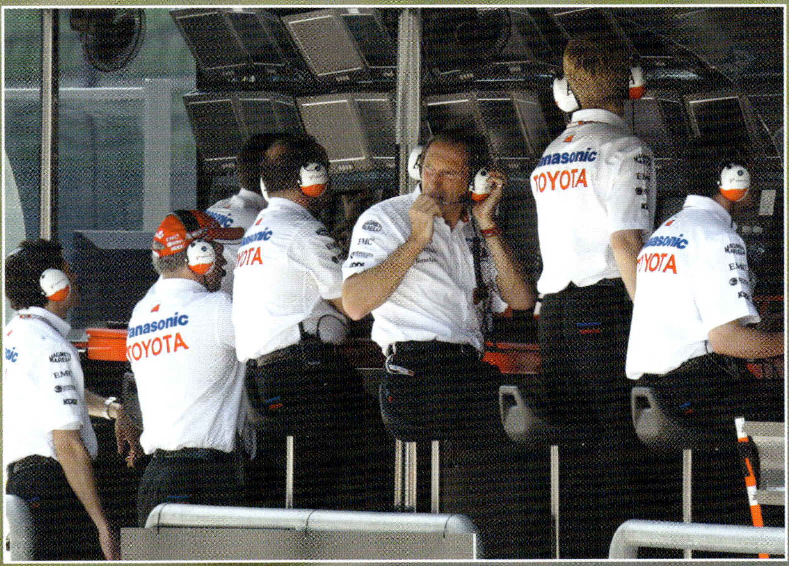
TOYOTA
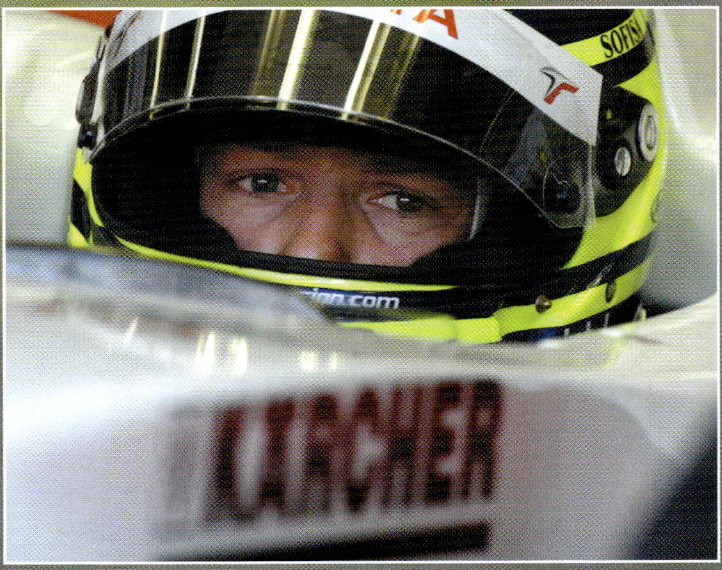
KÄRCHER

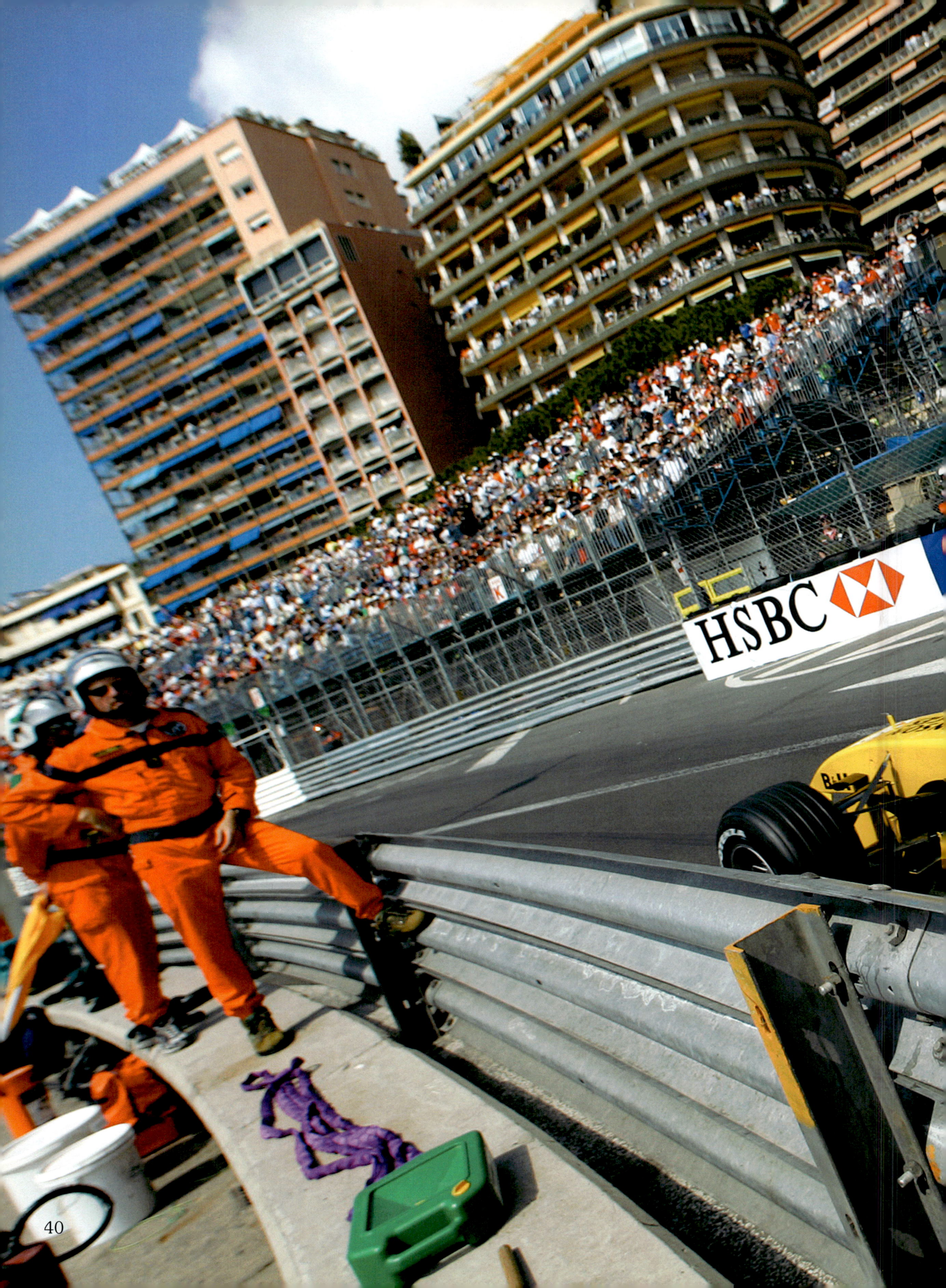
HSBC

41

42

43

GOLDEN PALACE
.COM
wilux
TOSINVEST

B.Leinders

POTENZA
wilux
UNIQA
CIB
LIZING
STANDOX
BRIDGESTONE

45

58
SUPERFUND
THE FUTURE OF INVESTING
www.superfund.com
wilux
CONNECT
Santogal
WWW.MINARDI.IT
Beta
Cimatron
3D SYSTEMS

47

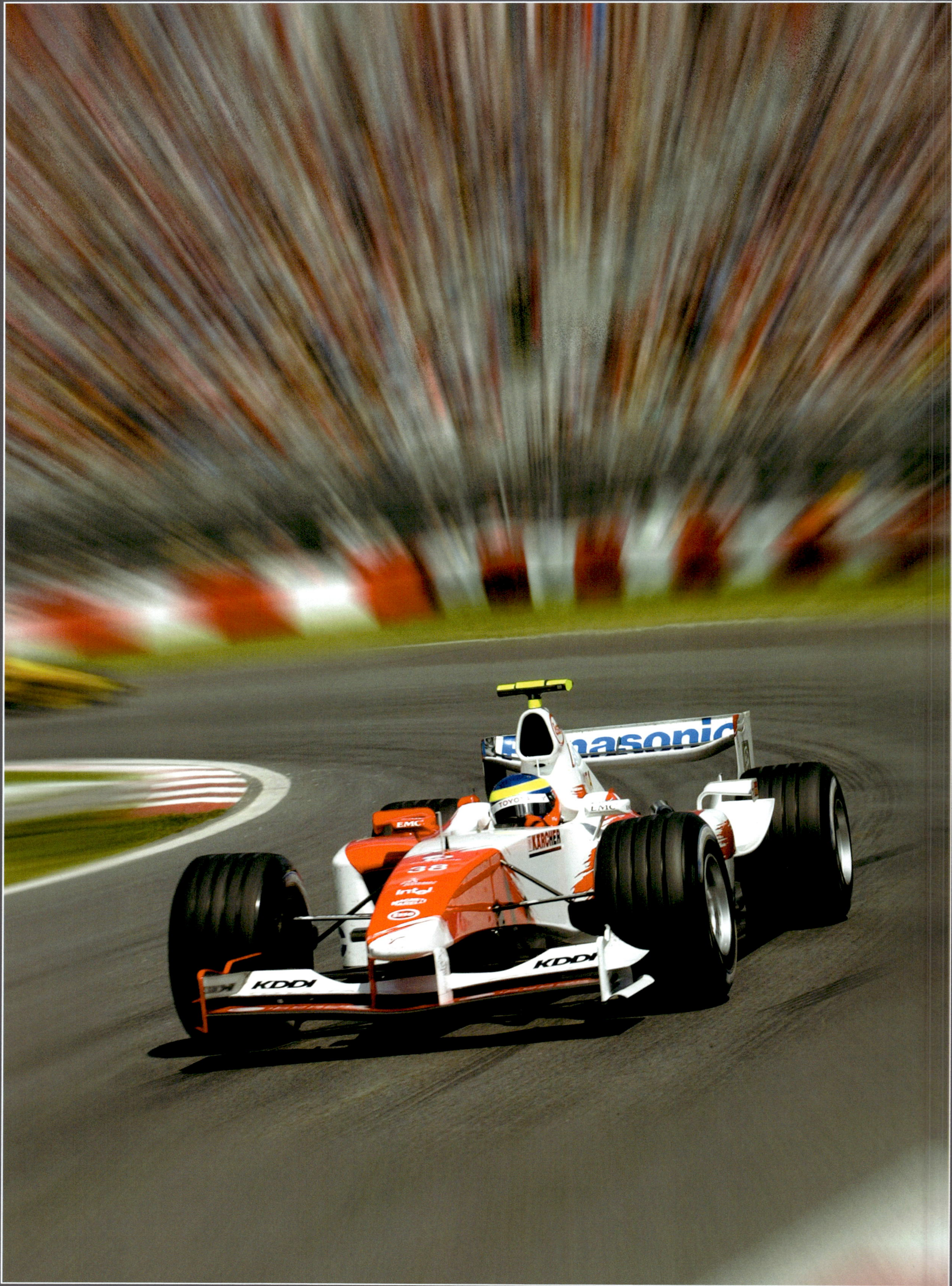
EMC
KÄRCHER
38
KDDI
KDDI

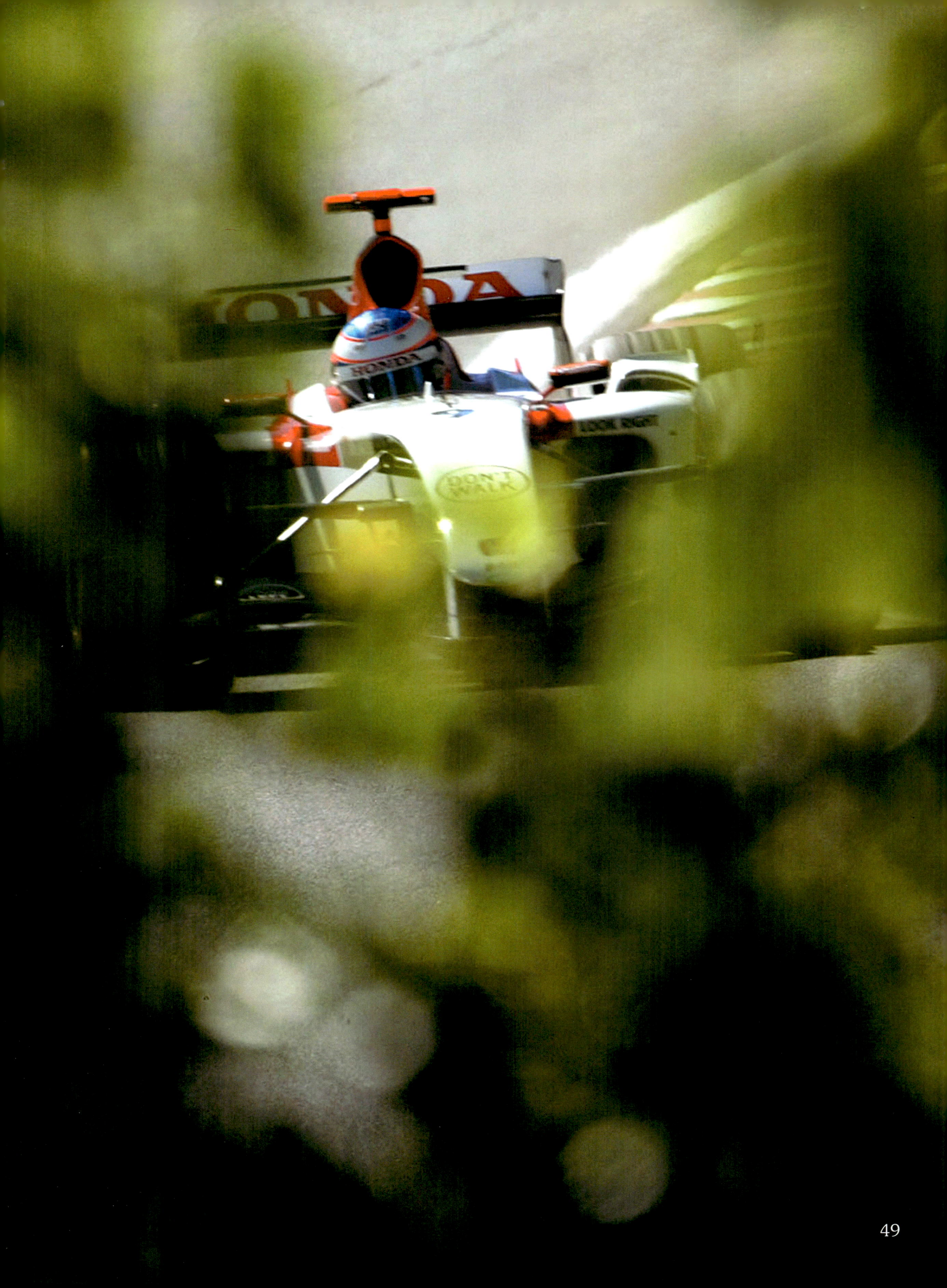
HONDA
DON'T WALK
LOOK RIGHT

50

51

52

53

UGS
The PLM Company
WEBBER
UGS
The PLM Company
SIEMENS
HSBC
BECK'S
BECK'S
DU PONT
UGS
PERFORMANCE
PERFORMANCE
14
MICHELIN
MICHELIN
UGS
UGS
DU PONT
Pioneer

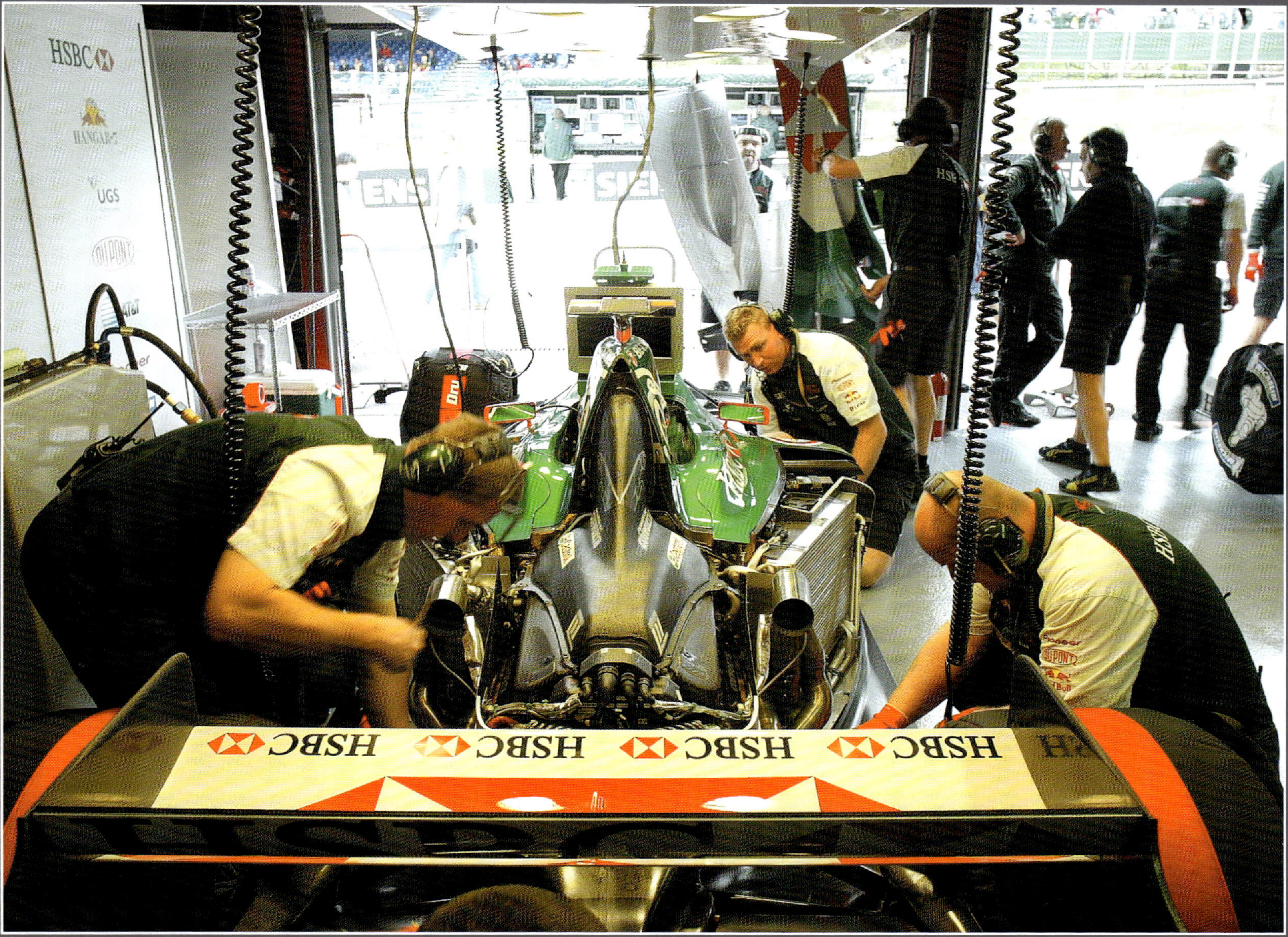
HSBC
HANGAR-7
UGS

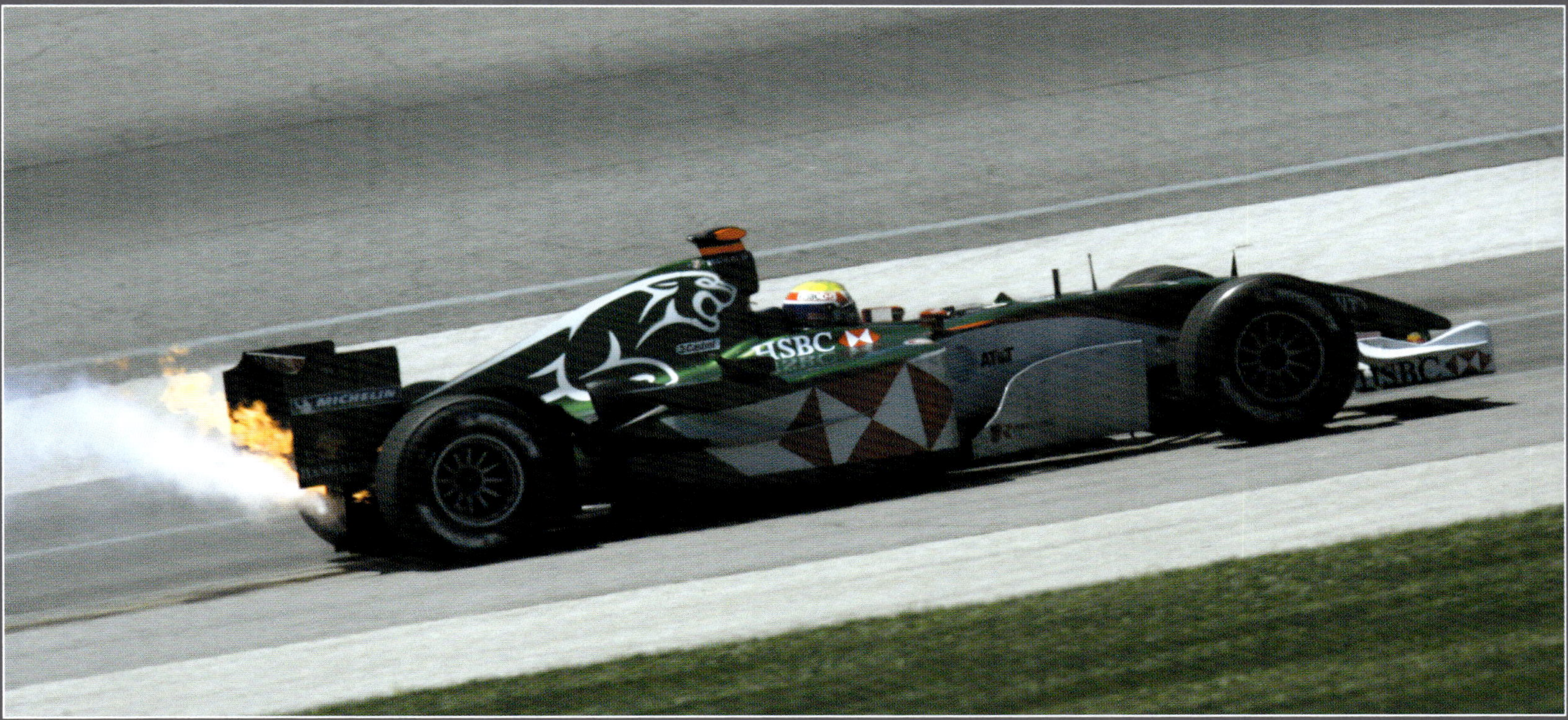
HSBC
MICHELIN
AT&T

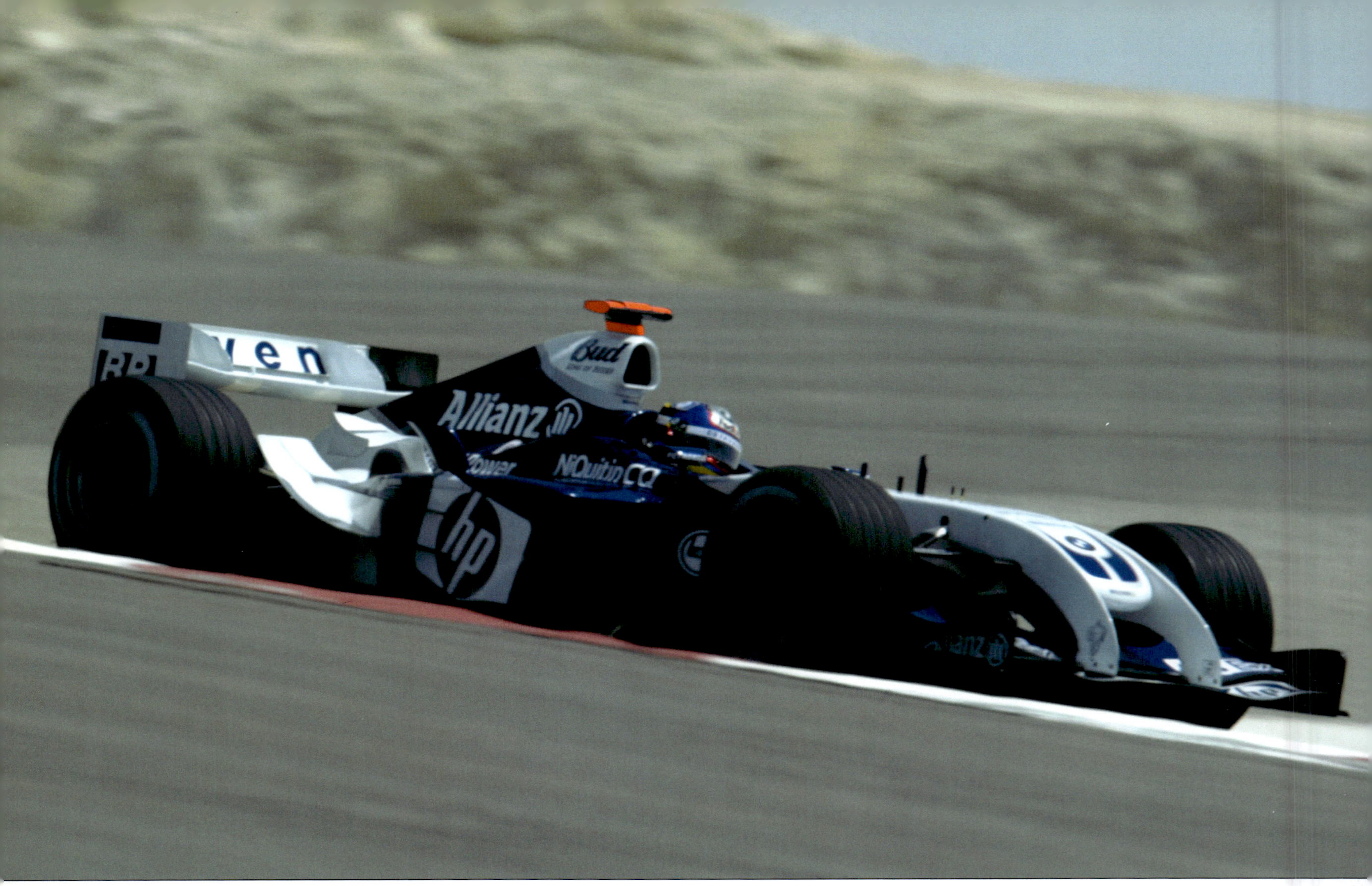
Bud
Allianz
NiQuitin CQ
hp

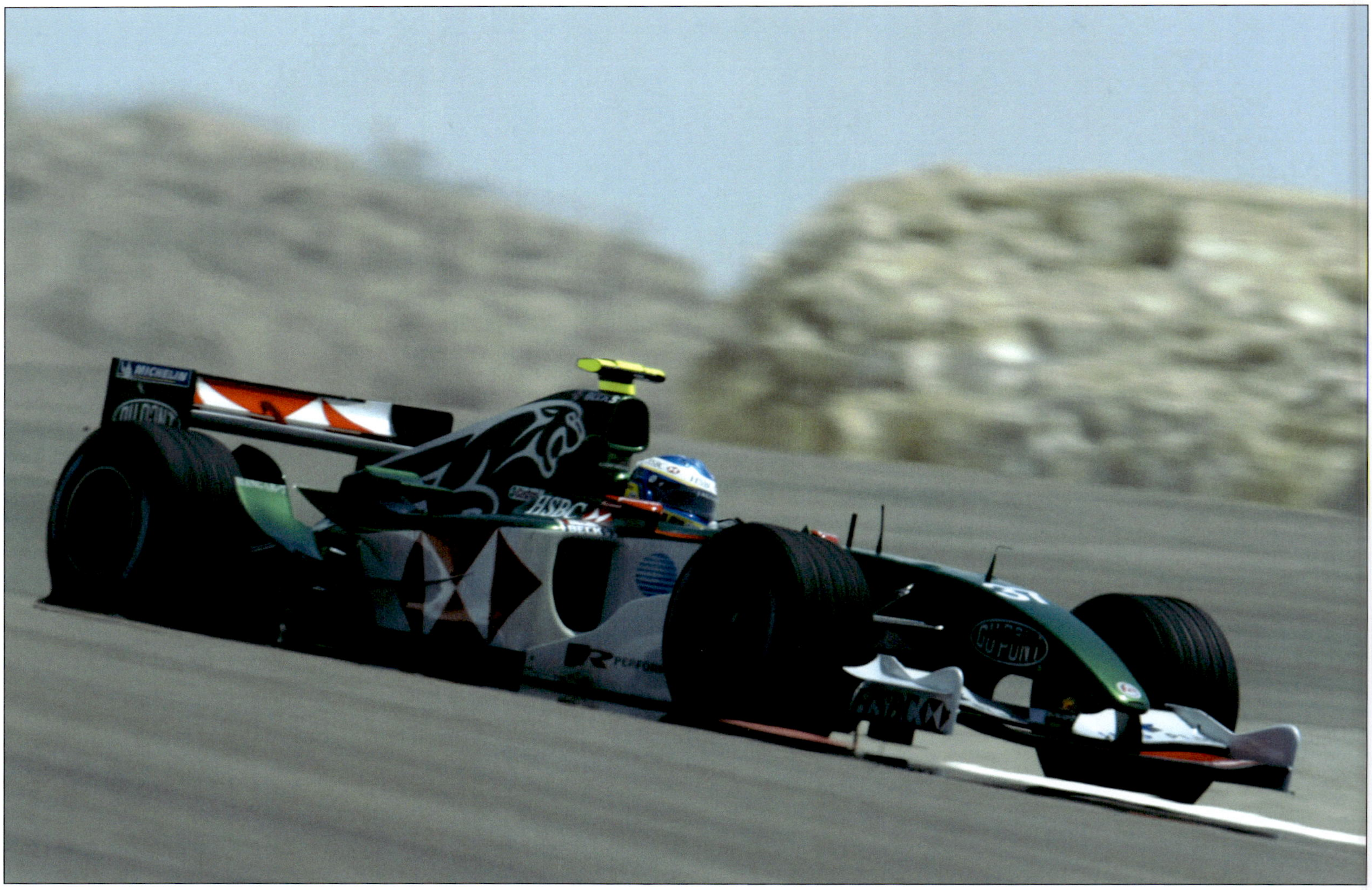
MICHELIN
HSBC
DUPONT

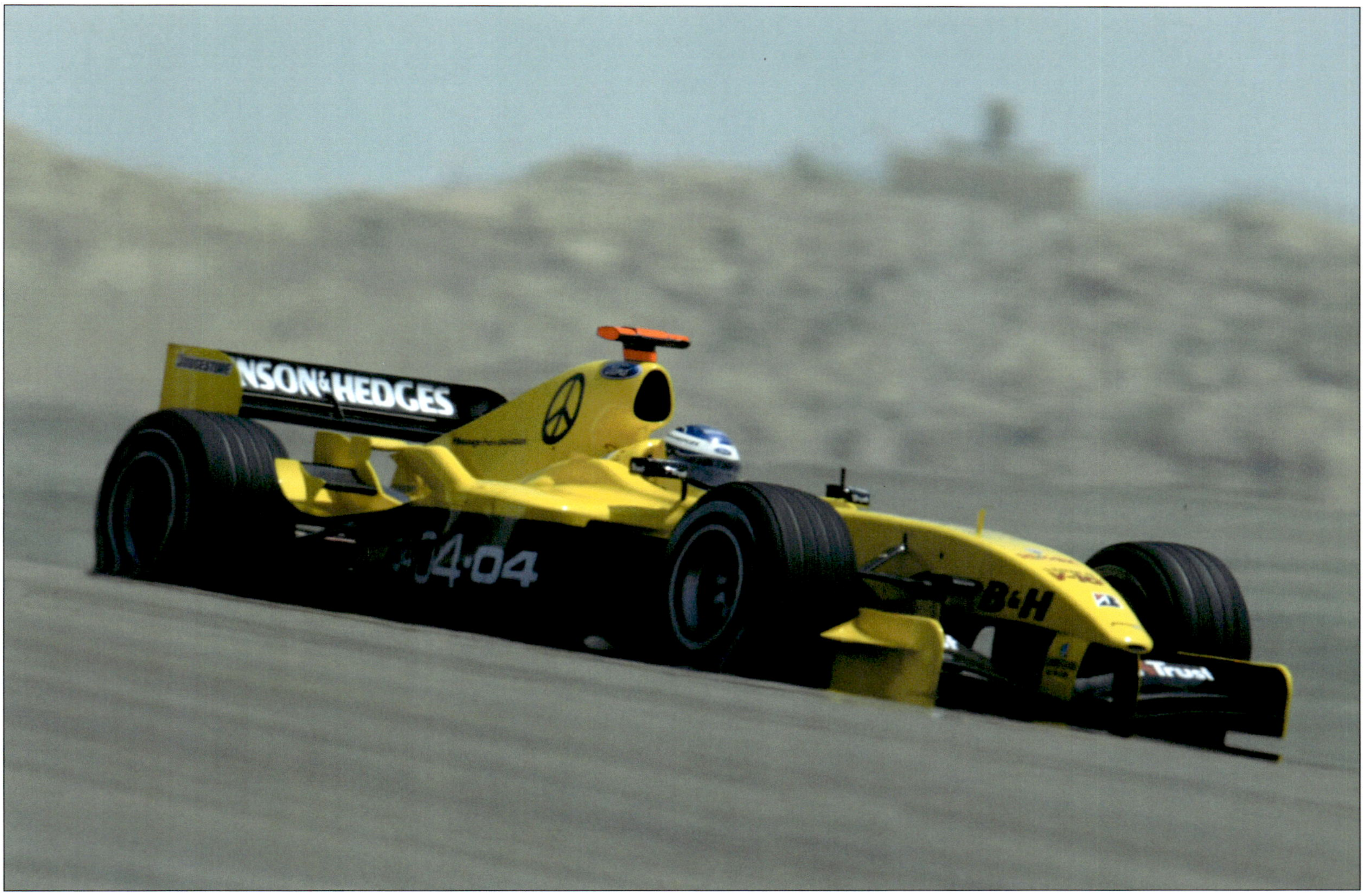
NSON&HEDGES
B&H

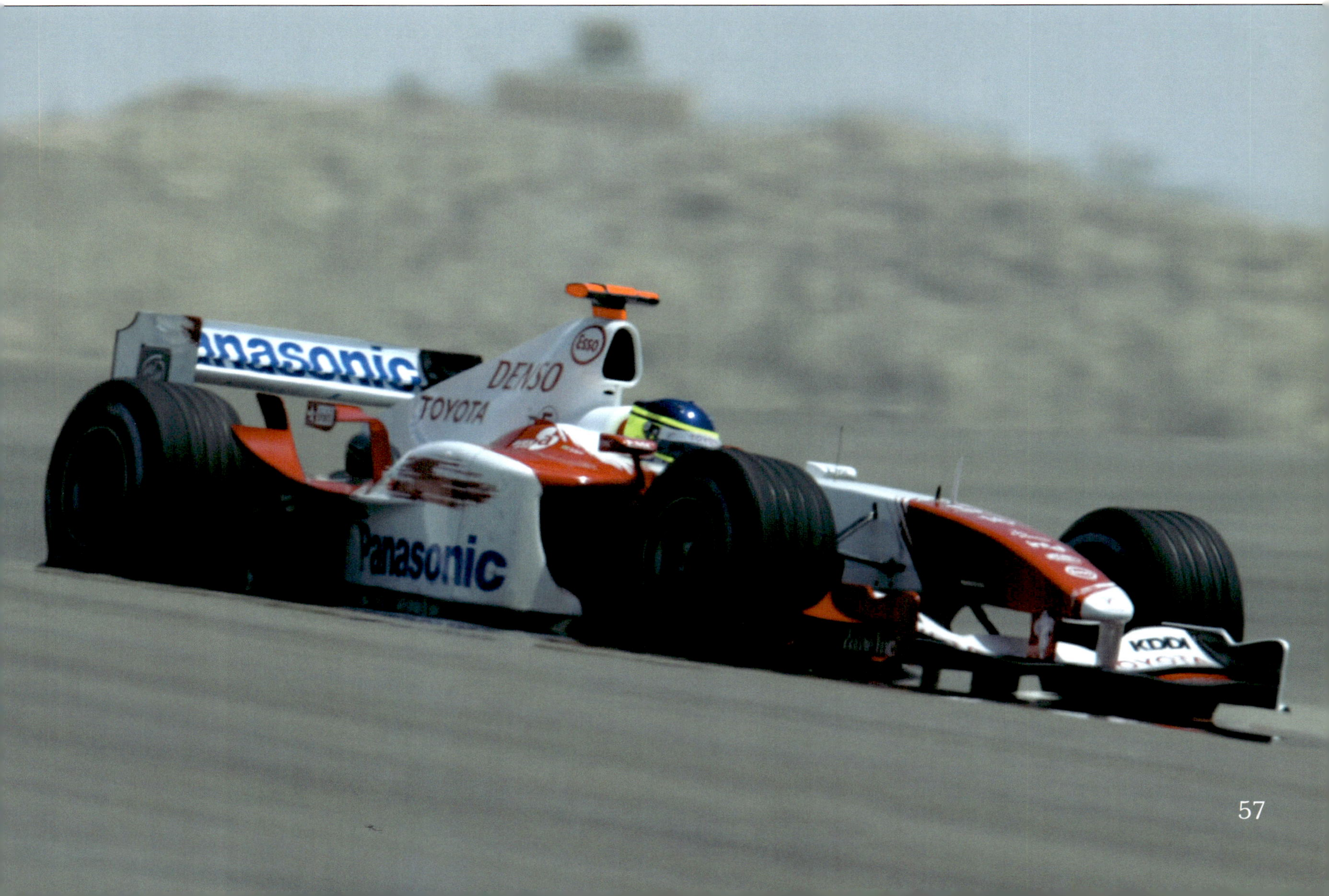
anasonic
DENSO
TOYOTA
Esso
Panasonic
KDDI

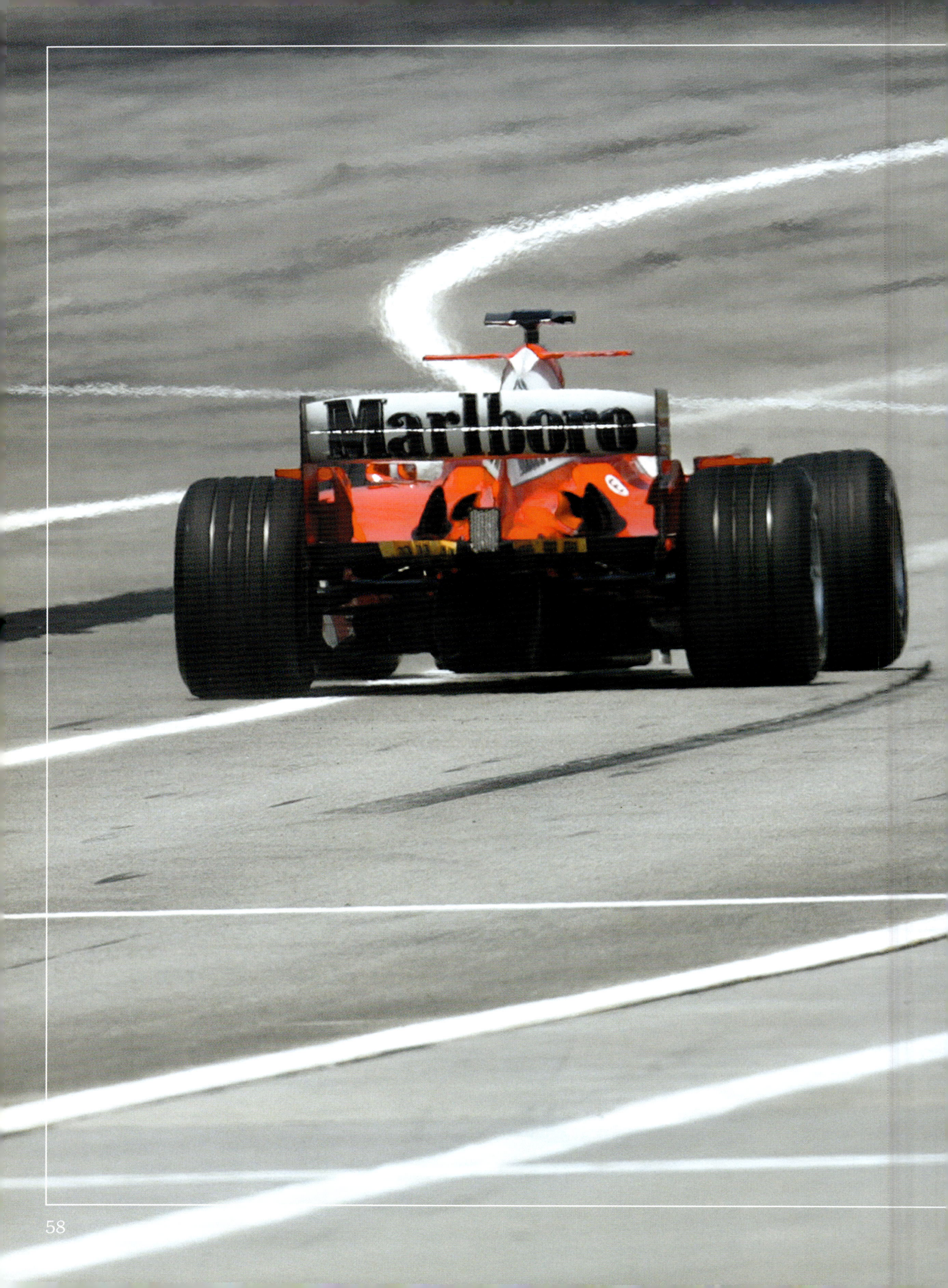
Marlboro

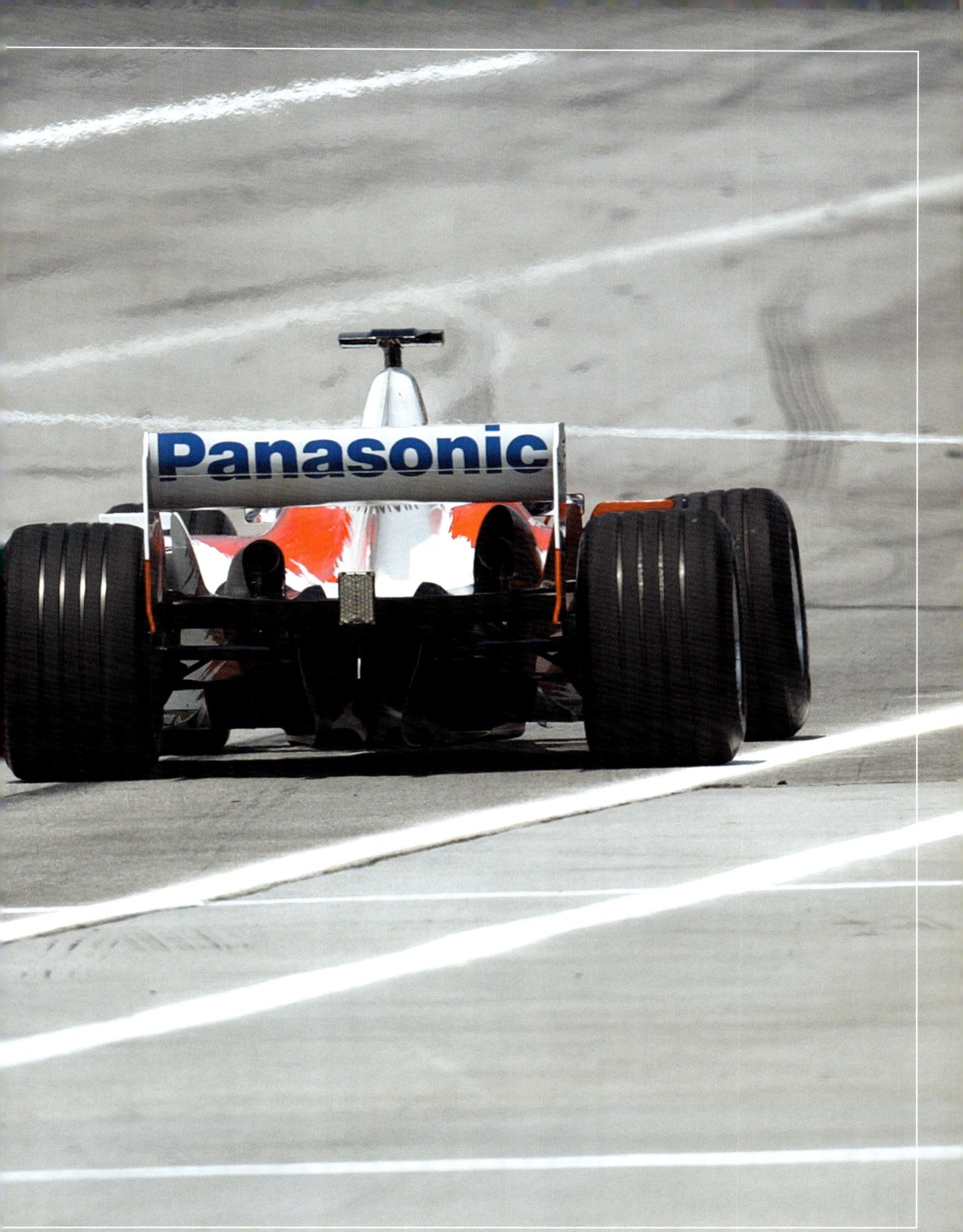
Panasonic

SOBRANIE
B&Q 百安居
SOBRANIE
RE/MAX
SOBRANIE
Trust
Beijing Château
北京公館
Beijing Château

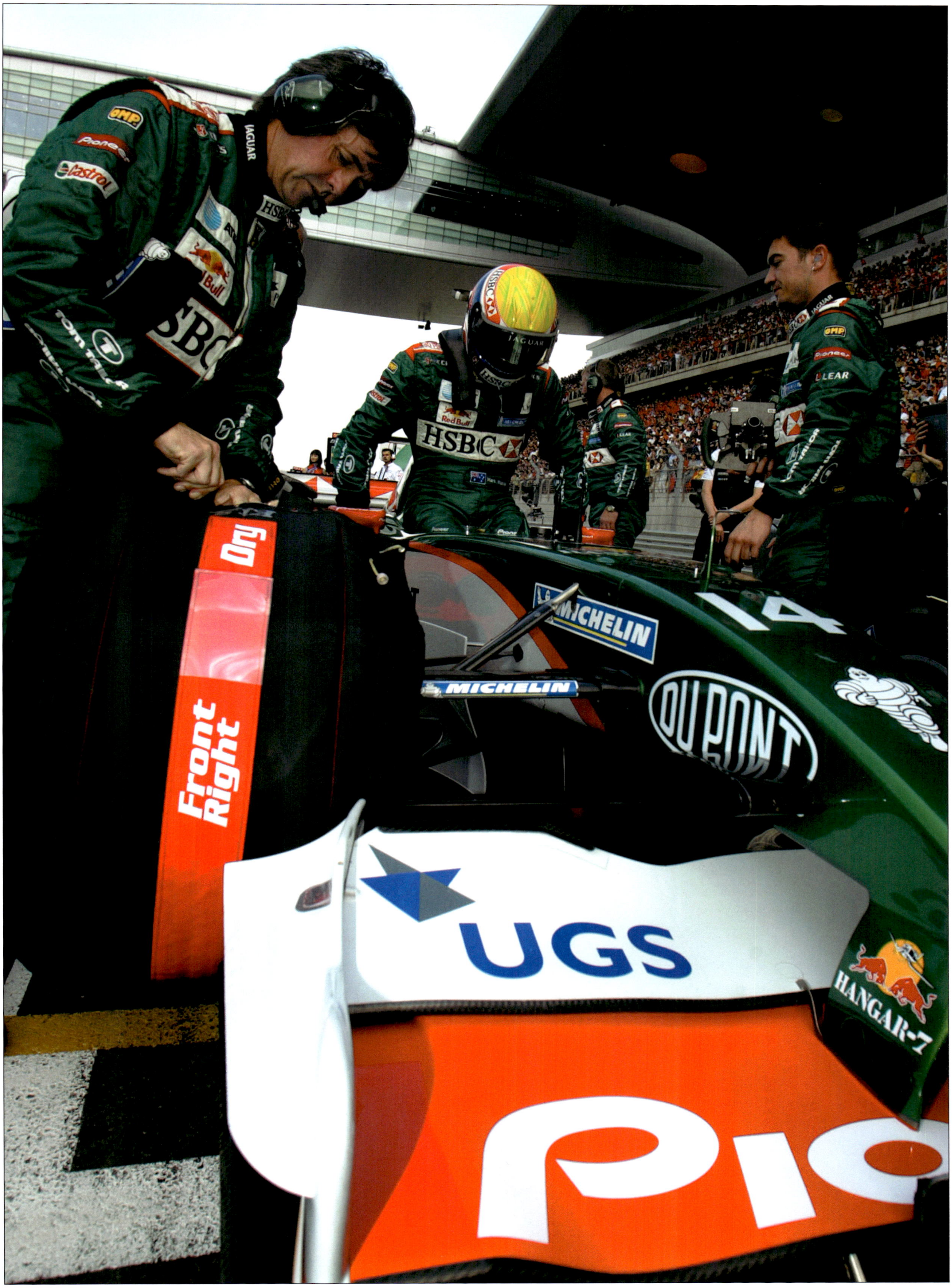

Dry
Front Right
MICHELIN
14
DU PONT
UGS
HANGAR-7
HSBC

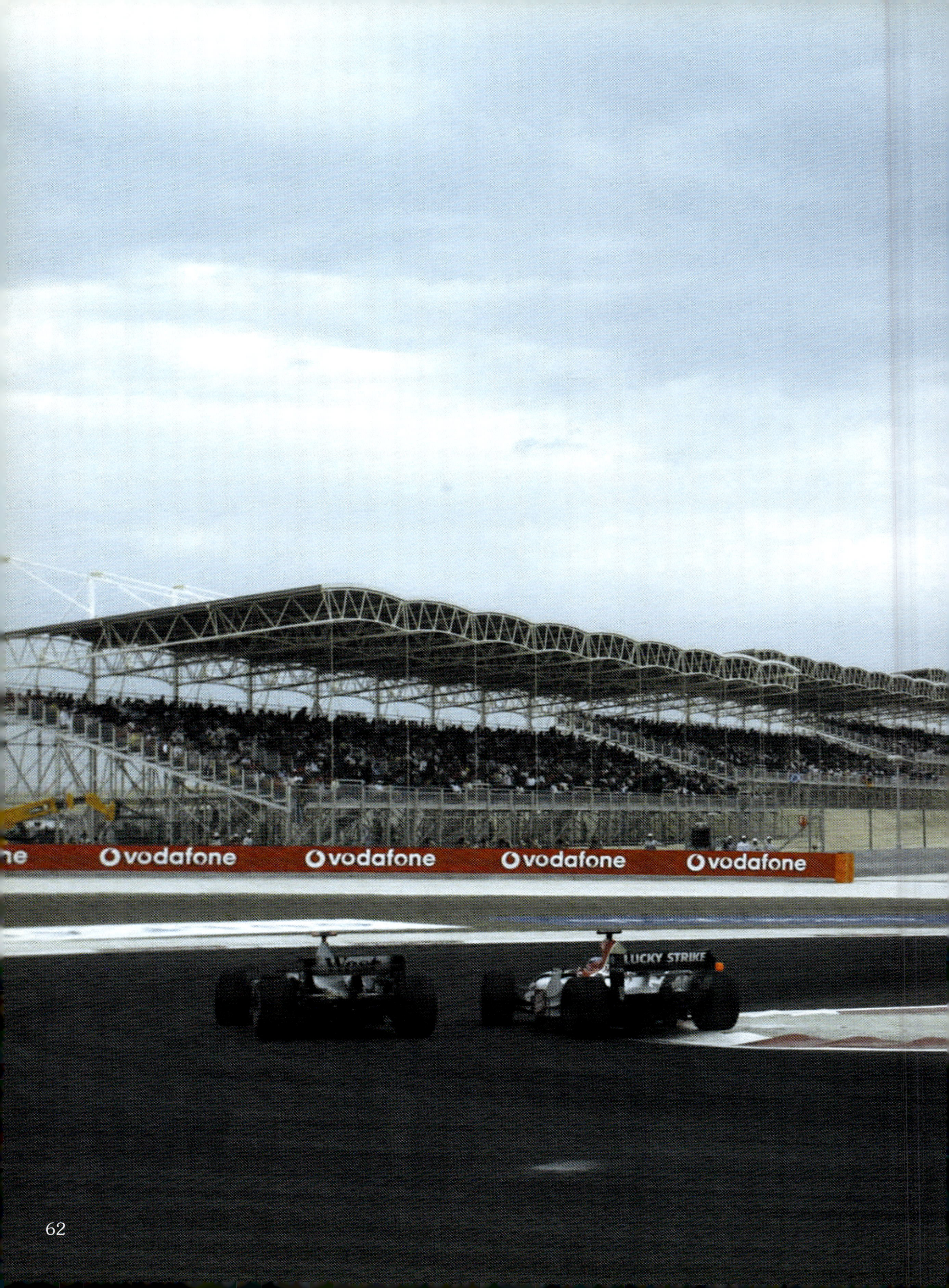
vodafone
vodafone
vodafone
vodafone
LUCKY STRIKE

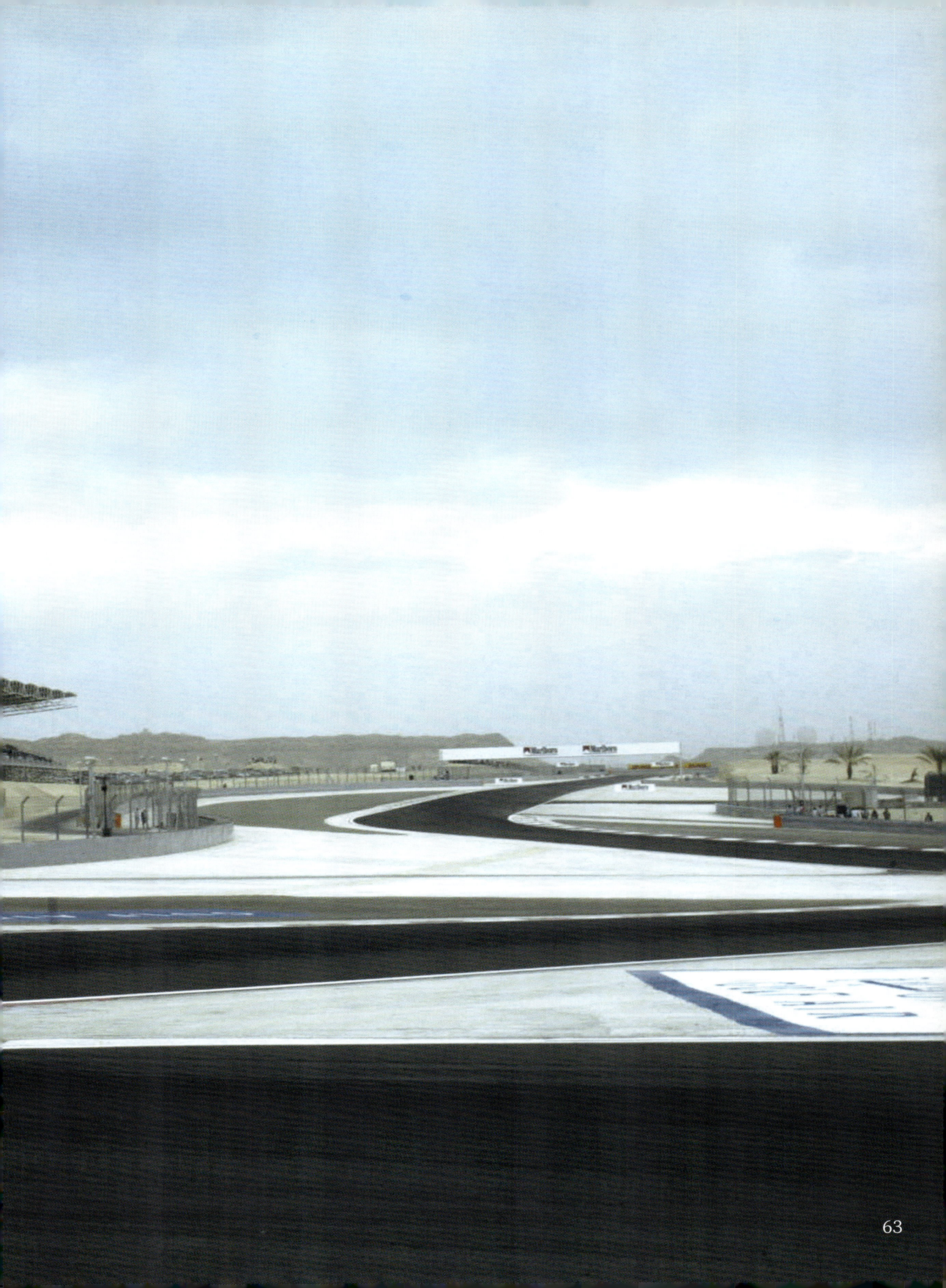

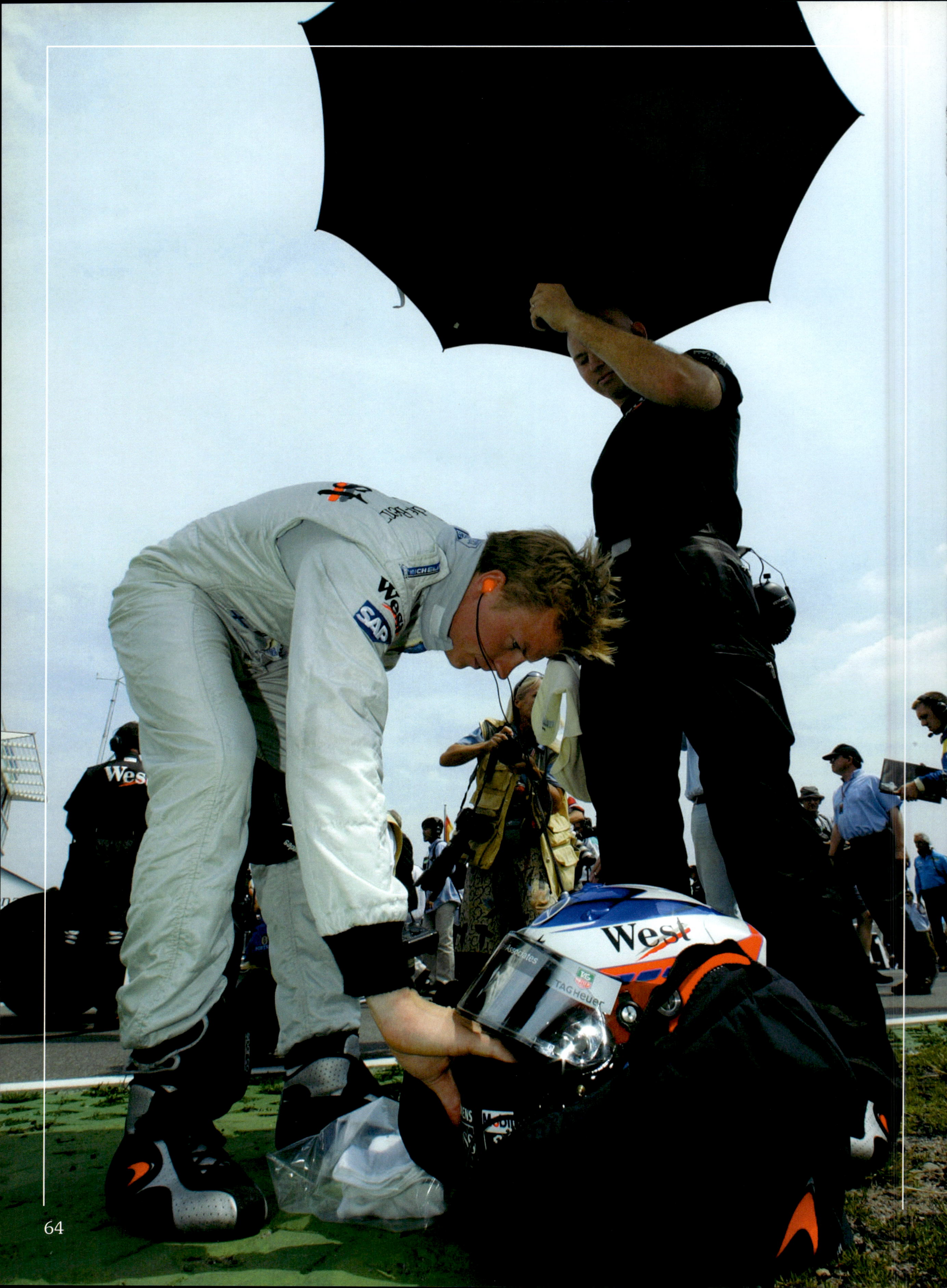
SAP
West
TAG Heuer
West

SCHUMACHER, OH DEAR!

by Giorgio STIRANO

It's that man Schumacher again! There was nothing new under the sun in Formula 1 in 2004. After 2003, when the German diced for the title to the very end with Raikkonen, this year he got to grips with his rivals right from the start so as not to run any risks later in the season. Schumacher was quite simply in a class of his own, winning almost all the races, and setting numerous pole positions and fastest laps on his way to taking his seventh world title. He left the crumbs for his rivals on his way to a fifth successive crown and helped Ferrari take its sixth successive Constructors' title. He also smashed all existing records, leaving behind the Argentinean champion and legend Juan Manuel Fangio, who won five titles, including four on the run.

We would risk boring our readers if we were to list all the other records that have been smashed by the Kerpen-born champion, but maybe it's worth mentioning that Michael Schumacher also holds the record for being the highest-paid racing driver of all time. We are not in a position to have a look at his tax return form, but the figure is probably not far from 100 million Euro. However Schumacher is not the highest-paid sportsman because that honour belongs to golfer Tiger Woods.

Whichever way you look at it, the Ferrari driver is a phenomenon.

But what qualities does the German champion possess?

Schumacher has a remarkable talent and an extraordinary ability to manage all the situations that emerge during a weekend, not only during the race, but also during testing, free practice and qualifying. He also has an unbridled hunger to win in every situation and at all costs.

There is a total integration with the team with which he works, and he has a willingness to share working methods, technologies and ways of thinking.

Add to this his total enthusiasm, his enthusiasm to race, to be on the track at the wheel of a Formula 1 car, the passion to drive for Ferrari.

This enthusiasm and passion lead him to enter into a state of total satisfaction for the things he does every day, without distraction and without boredom.

Boredom is the worst enemy of any sportsman or sportswoman, boredom at having to repeat mechanically the things that they do every day, when they have an opportunity to do anything they want thanks to the wealth accumulated in their particular sport.

For example, Michael is a driver who dialogs with his engineers when he is on his way back to the pits after a practice session so they can get an early idea of what changes and modifications can be made to the car.

Moreover, his lucidity behind the wheel allows the team's wizards on the pit wall to modify their race strategy.

This year's French Grand Prix will go down in Formula 1 history after Ross Brawn altered Michael's pit stop strategy to short, qualifying-style stints to compensate for Alonso's record pace in the Renault. A light fuel load, soft tyres and away he went. The mixed look of surprise and frustration on the face of Flavio Briatore when he realised that the German and the British engineer were playing games with him, will remain one of the lasting images of this world championship. It was an extraordinary performance,

vodafone
vodafone
vodafone
Marlboro
BRIDGESTONE
Marlboro
Marlboro

one brought about by a rapid analysis and decision-making process put into act by Ferrari that was equally extraordinary.

One must never forget that Michael's legend is intrinsically linked to Ferrari's ability to constantly make available a winning car, which helps to add to the legend as well.

Ferrari is, by definition, a legend in itself, but before the German arrived, it was losing much of its glossy appeal: results since 1979 had been poor but the German put things back on track in 1999 by helping Ferrari to win the Constructors' title before he really stamped his authority on F1 in the following years. Now the legend shines once again, thanks to the German and the team that has been created around him.

The successful team was created at the start of the 1990s when an Italian entrepreneur by the name of Luca Cordero di Montezemolo took control of Ferrari. Di Montezemolo was the man who reinvented the Ferrari legend when he took over as the company's leader and guiding beacon, a role that until 1988 had been played by the company founder Enzo Ferrari, a man of extraordinary personality and authority. Luca Montezemolo was intelligent and sensible enough not to mimic the irreplaceable Enzo, but instead he concentrated on the difficult task of putting back together the building blocks of a company that had appeared to be heading for a long and inexorable decline.

Today all one has to do is visit the Ferrari factory to get an idea of the extraordinary 'imperial' vision that has been imposed on the company by Luca Montezemolo, even on an architectural level. As a result Ferrari has abandoned all traces of the provincialism that had been with it since it was founded. Today we can safely say that the Maranello company has reached maturity and that Formula 1 has been a vital part of this project, as a laboratory of men and ideas.

The Ferrari team is an amalgamation of different experiences and nationalities, but this has not come about by chance. It takes a miracle to put together two drivers from Germany (Michael Schumacher) and Brazil (Rubens Barrichello) with a general manager from France (Jean Todt), a technical director from England (Ross Brawn) and a chief engineer from Italy (Paolo Martinelli).

That's all there is to it even though the story doesn't end here. The victorious experience accumulated in racing, as well as the extraordinary positive image that has been obtained, has made a fundamental contribution to the overall quality of the Ferrari trademark.

But back to Michael Schumacher ... and the question of whether or not he has any defects. Remember the world title he lost against Villeneuve, when their violent contact aroused controversy and long-lasting enmity between the two champions?

That was the year when Villeneuve appeared to be on the road to an ultra-successful career, but the world title he won was the start of a sad and inexorable decline, the exact opposite to Michael's rising parabola.

For sure Michael Schumacher hates to lose! Those with good memories can remember a similar contact in 1994 with Damon Hill, which enabled the German to win the world title. Maybe his only defect is that he is unable to accept defeat, but in the past few years the number of defeats he has suffered have been so rare as to be almost negligible.

And the way things are going at the moment, it hardly seems to be the right time to worry.

F1 CALENDAR - 2004

January 5 - Valencia

The new Williams BMW FW26 was presented in Valencia. The car sports an unusual 'walrus-shaped' front nose. It is the work of the young Italian designer Antonia Terzi, who used to be in charge of aerodynamics in Ferrari, and who has worked in Williams for three years. The car also has a new seven-speed gearbox.

January 17 - Cologne

The Toyota TF104, which is intended to be the Japanese manufacturer's winning card after the encouraging results of 2003, was presented in Germany. The drivers, Da Matta and Panis, are the same as last year, while Mike Gascoyne joins the team from Renault as Technical Director. Toyota's third driver for the season is Ricardo Zonta.

January 18 Barcelona

The Jaguar R5, denoting the Ford-owned team's fifth season in Formula 1, was launched in Spain. Australian Mark Webber is joined by the 21-year-old Austrian Christian Klien. The season looks to be a tough one for Jaguar after the drastic cut in the budget by the parent company. The only ace up their sleeve is Webber, who had some superb drives in 2003.

January 26 - Maranello

The Ferrari F 2004, the 50th single-seater Formula 1 car to come from the Maranello factory, was presented at Maranello. In the presence of top management and authorities, the car was unveiled by Schumacher and Barrichello, in their fifth season together, and by test-driver Luca Badoer, in his seventh season with Ferrari.

Photo archives Ferrari S.p.A.

January 29 Palermo

Flavio Briatore chose the Teatro Massimo in Palermo, Sicily for the launch of the new Renault R24. A brand-new engine and an extremely sophisticated and refined aerodynamics package are the main features of the new French car, which will be driven by expert Jarno Trulli and F1's rising star, Fernando Alonso from Spain. The Renault test-driver is 26-year-old Frenchman Franck Montagny.

February 1 - Barcelona

Jenson Button and Takuma Sato launched the new BAR-Honda 006, now fitted with Michelin tyres, directly at the Spanish track. In 2003 BAR finished fifth in the Constructors' standings and for 2004 David Richards promised that more was to come from the Anglo-Japanese car.

February 7 - Silverstone

Finally the 2004 Jordan, the EJ14, took to the track with new signing, Nick Heidfeld from Germany, the only driver confirmed at the time. It seemed certain that the number 2 driver would be Italian Giorgio Pantano, while the position of test-driver will probably go to the young German Timo Glock.

February 12 - Salzburg

Paying homage to sponsor Red Bull, Sauber launched its 2004 car, the C23, in Salzburg Airport's futuristic hangar. Starting in 2004, the Swiss car will be equipped with the current season's Ferrari engine, not the previous year's version as before. The gearbox also comes from Ferrari. The team's new driver line-up is Italian Giancarlo Fisichella and Brazilian Felipe Massa, while test-driver will be Neel Jani from Switzerland.

March 3 - Melbourne

Ever since Australian Paul Stoddart took over Minardi, the new Faenza-built car is traditionally launched in Australia, just before the GP. The main sponsor of the new (or rather updated) Minardi PS 04B, is Dutch bathroom and shower fittings company, Willux.

March 3 - Melbourne

Minardi announced that its third driver will be 28-year-old Bas Leinders from Belgium.

March 7 - Melbourne

With a 1-2 in the Australian GP, Ferrari finished first and second in a GP for the 62nd time in its history.

March 21 Sepang

For the first time in his career Mark Webber (Jaguar) started from the front row of the grid, alongside Ferrari champion Schumacher. He would ruin everything however with a disastrous race, strewn with errors.

21 Marzo
Sepang

In his fifth F1 season and with 67 GPs to his name despite his young age, 24 year-old British driver Jenson Button scored the first podium finish of his career in Malaysia. During qualifying he had already demonstrated the competitiveness of the new BAR with sixth place on the grid.

April 21
Fiorano-Mugello

Surrounded by the utmost secrecy, Valentino Rossi lapped Ferrari's private test-track at Fiorano in Michael Schumacher's Ferrari. Valentino had just returned from his triumphant win in South Africa on his debut with the Yamaha. It was the first time ever in a Formula 1 car for the reigning MotoGP world champion and he completed around 40 laps, setting some respectable times.

April 21/25 - Imola

A number of events were organised to commemorate the death of Ayrton Senna at the Italian circuit ten years before during the week leading up to Imola. On Wednesday the Drivers' football squad took on a Brazilian All-Star team of 1994 World Cup winners at Forlì, just down the road from Imola. The Drivers' squad included Schumacher, Barrichello, Alonso, Massa and Max Biaggi in its line-up.
At Imola the inauguration of a photography exhibition dedicated to Ayrton was followed by a lap of honour by Gerhard Berger with the Lotus 97T. This was the car driven by Ayrton in 1985 with which he won his first-ever Formula 1 race. Finally the circuit's main grandstand was named after the Brazilian champion in a ceremony.

April 24

Trust returned to Formula 1 in a big way as sponsor of the Jordan Team. The announcement was made by Michel Perridon and Eddie Jordan and put an end to a dispute that started months ago involving Dutch driver Jos Verstappen, a friend of the chairman of Trust and testimonial for the Dutch company, who sponsored him in 2003 on the Minardi.

June 11 - Montreal

Jordan driver Giorgio Pantano fails to take part in Canadian GP qualifying due to problems with his F1 management company. Currently in the middle of financial troubles, Jordan temporarily suspends its agreement with Pantano and replaces him with the team's third driver, the young German Timo Glock.

June 11 - Montreal

Timo Glock makes his Formula 1 debut in the Canadian GP. The 22 year-old German was appointed official tester for the Jordan team for 2004 and comes from the German Formula BMW Championship, which he won in 2001, and the European Formula 3 Championship, in which he won three races in 2003.

June 20 - Indianapolis

Olivier Panis, one of the veterans of Formula 1, notches up the 150 GP mark at Indianapolis. Born on September 2, 1966 in Lyons, Panis made his debut in the 1994 Australian GP for Ligier. In 1996 he won the rain-affected Monaco GP for Ligier, a race in which only four cars reached the finish-line.

July 4 - Magny-Cours

Spain's Marc Genè took the place of Ralf Schumacher at Williams with an unimpressive performance. After setting eighth-quickest time in qualifying, Genè finished the race in tenth position, a result considered to be unsatisfactory by the British team.

July 6
London

A massive crowd turns out in the streets of central London to watch a display of Formula 1 cars. Nigel Mansell, 1992 World Champion with Williams, drives a Jordan, while Ferrari are also present with test-driver Luca Badoer, Minardi with Baumgartner, Montoya with a Williams, David Coulthard with a McLaren and Da Matta with a Toyota. Everyone is enthusiastic about the idea of a future street-circuit GP in the centre of London.

July 7

Toyota officially announce that Ralf Schumacher will be the number one driver for the Japanese team in 2005. Ralf, currently recovering from his horrific crash against the Indianapolis wall, is 29 years of age and has raced in F1 since 1997, when he made his debut for Jordan in the Australian GP. After two years in Jordan he moved to Williams, where so far he has scored six wins.

July 25

Antonio Pizzonia took Marc Genè's place at Williams, after a poor race by the Spanish test-driver. The Brazilian immediately proved to be much quicker than his team-mate, confirming the ability he showed in 2003 for Jaguar.

August 5

Jenson Button's manager informed David Richards, the boss of BAR, that their contract would come to an end at the end of the 2004 season. At the same time Williams communicated that it had signed up the young British driver for 2005 alongside the already confirmed Mark Webber. David Richards immediately sent all the documentation to the Contract Recognition Board in Geneva to prove that Button is under contract with BAR and that the agreement cannot be rescinded. A legal battle is now underway between the two teams.

August 13 - Budapest

Ricardo Zonta returned to Formula in place of Cristiano da Matta at Toyota. The Brazilian's last race in F1 was in 2001 for Jordan and his absence from top-class racing was soon felt. Fifteenth quickest in qualifying, and never competitive in the race, Zonta had to stop on lap 31 with an electronics problem.

August 29

Ferrari took part in its 700th GP at the Spa-Francorchamps circuit and celebrated its 400th podium.

September 16

Toyota announced that Jarno Trulli and Ralf Schumacher will be the team's two drivers for the 2005 championship. Ricardo Zonta will remain as third driver and Olivier Panis will be the test-driver.

September 23
Shanghai

Jordan replaced Italian Giorgio Pantano with Timo Glock, who had already taken part in the Canadian GP for the team, finishing seventh. The return of Jacques Villeneuve to F1 at the wheel of the Renault was clearly followed by the media for the fact that the Canadian is an intelligent driver, capable of thrilling the crowds.
Another return saw Ralf Schumacher back at Williams after the Indianapolis crash that forced him to miss six GPs.

September 17

Jaguar, the subsidiary of the Ford Group, announced that it will be retiring from Formula 1 at the end of the season after five years. In 2000 the British marque took over from Team Stewart, which already had an engine supply from Ford Cosworth.

September 30

Jarno Trulli, dumped by Renault in favour of Jacques Villeneuve, will make his debut at Suzuka in the Japanese GP for Toyota in place of Brazilian Ricardo Zonta, who however had a deal to take part in the final GP of the season, his home race at San Paolo.

The Rookies

Gianmaria (Gimmi) Bruni, is Minardi's number 1 driver for 2004, after earning his place as tester for the Faenza-based team during the second half of last year. Bruni, 23 years old from Rome, is the 41st Italian driver in Formula 1. In 1999 he won the European Formula Renault Championship, while in 2003 he finished runner-up in the Euro 3000 series.

Timo Glock, the 22-year-old from Lindenfels, Germany made his debut in the Canadian GP at the wheel of the ex-Giorgio Pantano Jordan. Glock comes through the ranks of karting and in 2003 he took part in the Formula 3 Euro Series, scoring three wins.

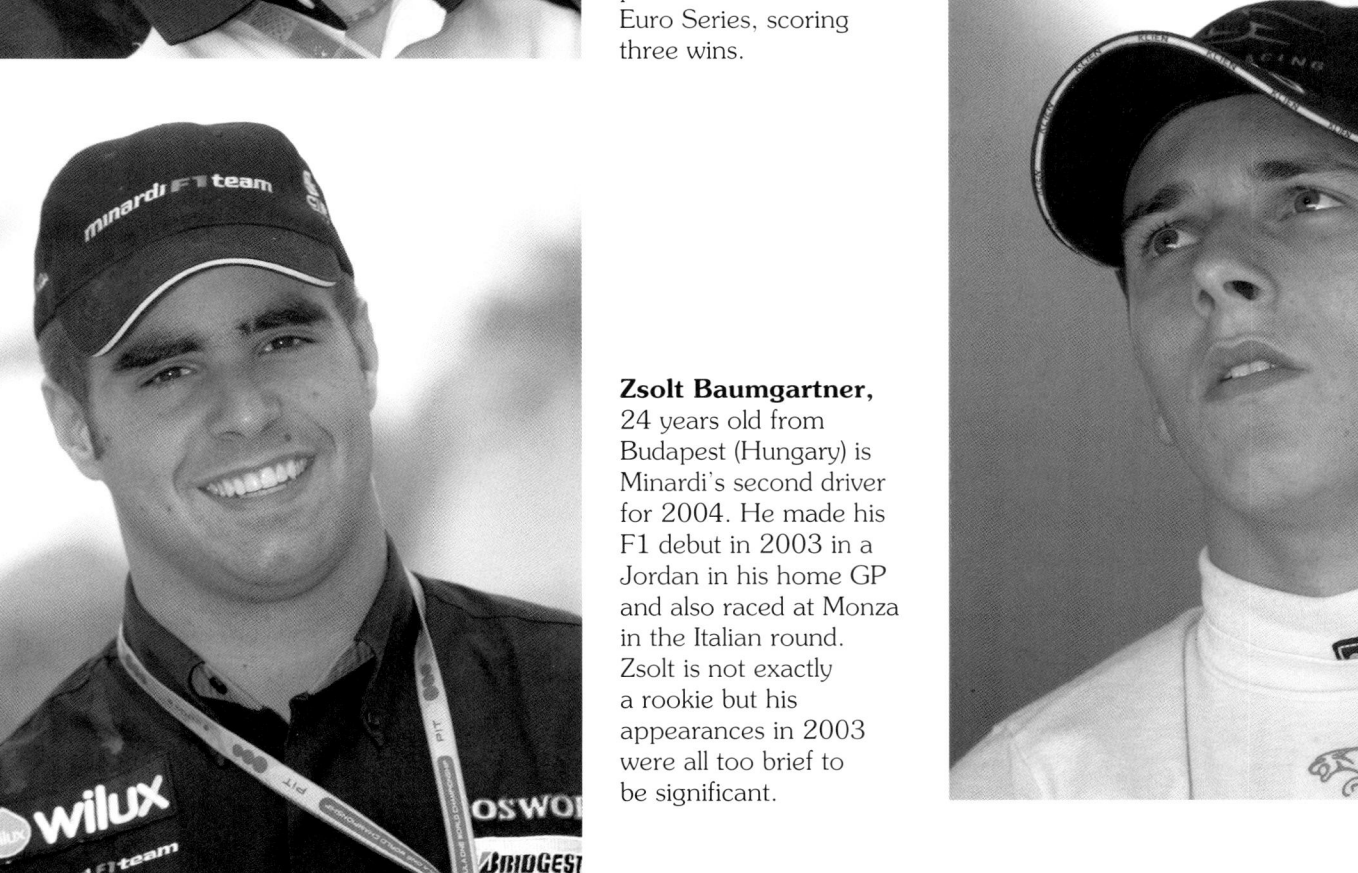

Zsolt Baumgartner, 24 years old from Budapest (Hungary) is Minardi's second driver for 2004. He made his F1 debut in 2003 in a Jordan in his home GP and also raced at Monza in the Italian round. Zsolt is not exactly a rookie but his appearances in 2003 were all too brief to be significant.

25-year-old **Giorgio Pantano** from Padua, Italy is Jordan's number 2 driver for 2004. After testing for Benetton, Williams and McLaren in previous years, which had led the young Italian to believe that he was about to enter Formula 1, his big break has come with Jordan. Eddie Jordan's team is not one of the top outfits, but is probably good enough to display his talents. Pantano was World Junior Karting Champion in 1993 and 1994.

Christian Klien, from Hohenems in Austria, was born on February 7, 1983. His magic moment came last year in the Marlboro Masters at Zandvoort in Holland and he comes to Jaguar with the backing of his personal sponsor, Red Bull.

Michael Schumacher

Date of birth: 3 January 1969
Hurt-Hermulheim (Germany)
F1 debut: Belgian GP 1991

Year	Team	GP	Points	Pole	Victories
1991	Jordan/Benetton-Ford	6	4	-	-
1992	Benetton-Ford	16	53	-	1
1993	Benetton-Ford	16	52	-	1
1994	Benetton-Ford	14	92	6	8
1995	Benetton-Renault	17	102	4	9
1996	Ferrari	15	59	4	3
1997	Ferrari	17	78	3	5
1998	Ferrari	16	86	3	6
1999	Ferrari	9	44	3	2
2000	Ferrari	17	108	9	9
2001	Ferrari	17	123	11	9
2002	Ferrari	17	144	7	11
2003	Ferrari	16	93	5	6

Rubens Barrichello

Date of birth: 23 May 1972
Sao Paulo (Brazil)
F1 debut: Brazilian GP 1993

Year	Team	GP	Points	Pole	Victories
1991					
1992					
1993	Jordan-Hart	16	2	-	-
1994	Jordan-Hart	15	19	1	-
1995	Jordan-Peugeot	17	11	-	-
1996	Jordan-Peugeot	16	14	-	-
1997	Stewart-Ford	17	6	-	-
1998	Stewart-Ford	15	4	-	-
1999	Stewart-Ford	16	21	1	-
2000	Ferrari	17	62	1	1
2001	Ferrari	17	56	-	-
2002	Ferrari	17	77	3	4
2003	Ferrari	16	65	3	2

Juan Pablo Montoya

Date of birth: 20 September 1975
Bogotá (Colombia)
F1 debut: Australian GP 2001

Year	Team	GP	Points	Pole	Victories
1991					
1992					
1993					
1994					
1995					
1996					
1997					
1998					
1999					
2000					
2001	Williams-BMW	17	31	1	1
2002	Williams-BMW	17	50	7	-
2003	Williams-BMW	16	82	1	2

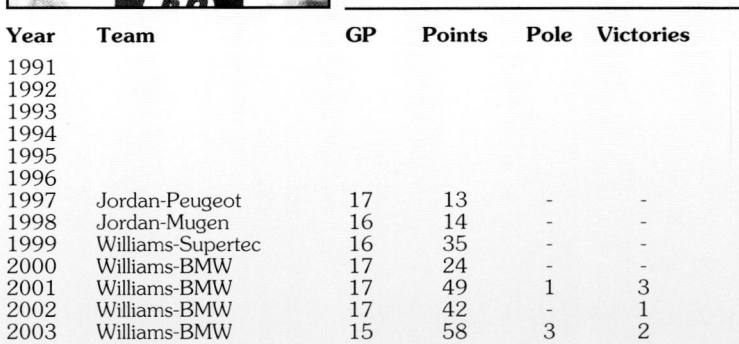

Ralf Schumacher

Date of birth: 30 June 1975
Hurt-Hermulheim (Germany)
F1 debut: Australian GP 1997

Year	Team	GP	Points	Pole	Victories
1991					
1992					
1993					
1994					
1995					
1996					
1997	Jordan-Peugeot	17	13	-	-
1998	Jordan-Mugen	16	14	-	-
1999	Williams-Supertec	16	35	-	-
2000	Williams-BMW	17	24	-	-
2001	Williams-BMW	17	49	1	3
2002	Williams-BMW	17	42	-	1
2003	Williams-BMW	15	58	3	2

David Coulthard

Date of birth: 27 March 1971
Twynholm (Scotland)
F1 debut: Spanish GP 1994

Year	Team	GP	Points	Pole	Victories
1991					
1992					
1993					
1994	Williams-Renault	8	14	-	-
1995	Williams-Renault	17	49	5	1
1996	McLaren-Mercedes	16	18	-	-
1997	McLaren-Mercedes	17	36	-	2
1998	McLaren-Mercedes	16	56	3	1
1999	McLaren-Mercedes	16	48	-	2
2000	McLaren-Mercedes	17	73	2	3
2001	McLaren-Mercedes	17	65	2	2
2002	McLaren-Mercedes	17	41	-	1
2003	McLaren-Mercedes	16	51	-	1

Kimi Raikkonen

Date of birth: 17 October 1979
Espoo (Finland)
F1 debut: Australian GP 2001

Year	Team	GP	Points	Pole	Victories
1991					
1992					
1993					
1994					
1995					
1996					
1997					
1998					
1999					
2000					
2001	Sauber-Petronas	16	9	-	-
2002	McLaren-Mercedes	17	24	-	-
2003	McLaren-Mercedes	16	91	2	1

Jarno Trulli

Date of birth: 13 July 1974
Pescara (Italy)
F1 debut: Australian GP 1997

Year	Team	GP	Points	Pole	Victories
1991					
1992					
1993					
1994					
1995					
1996					
1997	Minardi-Prost	14	3	-	-
1998	Prost-Peugeot	16	1	-	-
1999	Prost-Peugeot	15	7	-	-
2000	Jordan-Mugen	17	6	-	-
2001	Jordan-Honda	17	12	-	-
2002	Renault	17	9	-	-
2003	Renault	16	33	-	-

Fernando Alonso

Date of birth: 29 July 1981
Oviedo (Spain)
F1 debut: Australian GP 2001

Year	Team	GP	Points	Pole	Victories
1991					
1992					
1993					
1994					
1995					
1996					
1997					
1998					
1999					
2000					
2001	Minardi	-	-	-	-
2002					
2003	Renault	16	55	2	1

Jenson Button

Date of birth: 19 January 1980
Frome, Somerset (England)
F1 debut: Australian GP 2000

Year	Team	GP	Points	Pole	Victories
1991					
1992					
1993					
1994					
1995					
1996					
1997					
1998					
1999					
2000	Williams-BMW	17	12	-	-
2001	Benetton-Renault	17	2	-	-
2002	Renault	17	14	-	-
2003	BAR-Honda	15	17	-	-

Takuma Sato

Date of birth: 28 January 1977
Tokyo (Japan)
F1 debut: Australian GP 2002

Year	Team	GP	Points	Pole	Victories
1991					
1992					
1993					
1994					
1995					
1996					
1997					
1998					
1999					
2000					
2001					
2002	Jordan	17	2	-	-
2003	BAR-Honda	1	3	-	-

Giancarlo Fisichella

Date of birth: 14 January 1973
Roma (Italy)
F1 debut: Australian GP 1996

Year	Team	GP	Points	Pole	Victories
1991					
1992					
1993					
1994					
1995					
1996	Minardi-Ford	8	-	-	-
1997	Jordan-Peugeot	17	20	-	-
1998	Benetton-Playlife	16	16	1	-
1999	Benetton-Playlife	16	13	-	-
2000	Benetton-Playlife	17	18	-	-
2001	Benetton-Renault	17	8	-	-
2002	Jordan	16	7	-	-
2003	Sauber	16	12	-	1

Felipe Massa

Date of birth: 25 April 1981
Sao Paulo (Brazil)
F1 debut: Australian GP 2002

Year	Team	GP	Points	Pole	Victories
1991					
1992					
1993					
1994					
1995					
1996					
1997					
1998					
1999					
2000					
2001					
2002	Sauber-Petronas	16	4	-	-
2003					

Mark Webber

Date of birth: 27 August 1976
Queanbeyan (Australia)
F1 debut: Australian GP 2002

Year	Team	GP	Points	Pole	Victories
1991					
1992					
1993					
1994					
1995					
1996					
1997					
1998					
1999					
2000					
2001					
2002	Minardi	16	2	-	-
2003	Jaguar	16	17	-	-

Christian Klien

Date of birth: 7 February 1983
Hohenems (Austria)
F1 debut: Australian GP 2004

Olivier Panis

Date of birth: 2 September 1966
Lione (France)
F1 debut: Brazilian GP 1994

Year	Team	GP	Points	Pole	Victories
1991					
1992					
1993					
1994	Ligier-Renault	16	9	-	-
1995	Ligier-Mugen	17	16	-	-
1996	Ligier-Mugen	16	13	-	1
1997	Prost-Mugen	10	16	-	-
1998	Prost-Peugeot	15	-	-	-
1999	Prost-Peugeot	16	2	-	-
2000					
2001	BAR-Honda	17	5	-	-
2002	BAR-Honda	17	3	-	-
2003	Toyota	16	6	-	-

Cristiano Da Matta

Date of birth: 19 September 1973
Belo Horizonte (Brazil)
F1 debut: Australian GP 2003

Year	Team	GP	Points	Pole	Victories
1991					
1992					
1993					
1994					
1995					
1996					
1997					
1998					
1999					
2000					
2001					
2002					
2003	Toyota	16	10	-	-

Nick Heidfeld

Date of birth: 10 May 1977
Monchengladbach (Germany)
F1 debut: Australian GP 2000

Year	Team	GP	Points	Pole	Victories
1991					
1992					
1993					
1994					
1995					
1996					
1997					
1998					
1999					
2000	Prost-Peugeot	16	-	-	-
2001	Sauber-Petronas	17	12	-	-
2002	Sauber-Petronas	17	7	-	-
2003	Sauber-Petronas	16	6	-	-

Giorgio Pantano

Date of birth: 4 February 1979
Conselve (Italy)
F1 debut: Australian GP 2004

Zsolt Baumgartner

Date of birth: 1 January 1981
Budapest (Hungary)
F1 debut: Hungarian GP 2003

Year	Team	GP	Points	Pole	Victories
1991					
1992					
1993					
1994					
1995					
1996					
1997					
1998					
1999					
2000					
2001					
2002					
2003	Jordan	2	-	-	-

Gianmaria Bruni

Date of birth: 30 May 1981
Roma (Italy)
F1 debut: Australian GP 2004

Riccardo Zonta

Date of birth: 23 March 1976
Curitiba (Brazil)
F1 debut: Australian GP 1999

Year	Team	GP	Points	Pole	Victories
1991					
1992					
1993					
1994					
1995					
1996					
1997					
1998					
1999	BAR-Supertec	13	-	-	-
2000	BAR-Honda	17	3	-	-
2001	Jordan-Honda	2	-	-	-
2002					
2003					

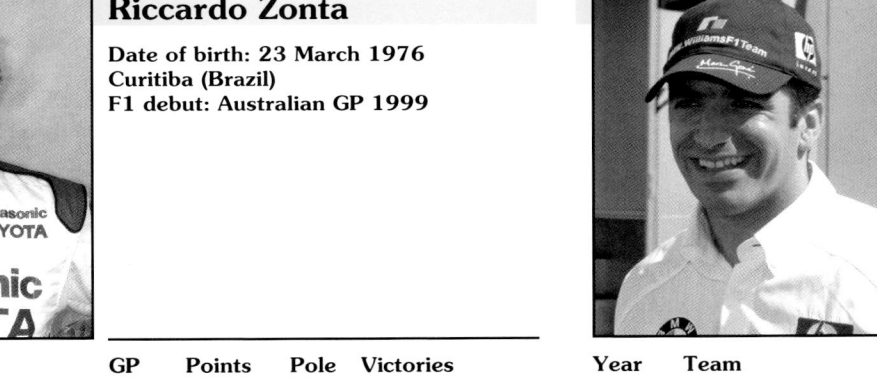

Mark Genè

Date of birth: 29 March 1974
Sabadell (Spain)
F1 debut: Australian GP 1999

Year	Team	GP	Points	Pole	Victories
1991					
1992					
1993					
1994					
1995					
1996					
1997					
1998					
1999	Minardi	16	1	-	-
2000	Minardi	17	-	-	-
2001					
2002					
2003	Williams-BMW	1	4	-	-

Jacques Villeneuve

Date of birth: 9 April 1971
St. Jean-sur-Richelieu (Canada)
F1 debut: Australian GP 1996

Year	Team	GP	Points	Pole	Victories
1991					
1992					
1993					
1994					
1995					
1996	Williams-Renault	16	78	3	4
1997	Williams-Renault	17	81	10	7
1998	Williams-Mecachrome	16	21	-	-
1999	BAR-Supertec	16	-	-	-
2000	BAR-Honda	17	17	-	-
2001	BAR-Honda	17	12	-	-
2002	BAR-Honda	17	4	-	-
2003	BAR-Honda	15	6	-	-

Timo Glock

Date of birth: 18 March 1982
Lindenfels (Germany)
F1 debut: Canadian GP 2004

Antonio Pizzonia

Date of birth: 11 September 1980
Manaus (Brazil)
F1 debut: Australian GP 2003

THE BEATING HEART OF FORMULA 1

HP, as exclusive IT- supplier, is the worldwide sponsor and technology partner of the BMW WilliamsF1 team. The partnership between BMW WilliamsF1 and HP has proved to be a fruitful one. That is largely explained by the similarities: dynamics, technology, speed, innovation, design and durability are of overriding importance to them both. And Formula 1 racing lends itself ideally to testing new developments – where would we be without the combination of technology and cars?

These days, information technology forms the beating heart of a Formula 1 team. Speed, reliability, hi-tech solutions and team spirit form the cutting edge of the world's most popular sport: Formula 1. The commitment of technology supplier HP to the BMW Williams Formula 1 team not only involves providing a technology platform for the future design of the cars and their performance, but also the analysis of races and training sessions and the correct tuning of the cars. And it also extends to Internet technologies that make it possible to take split-second decisions precisely when they are needed. These aspects are all vital to maintaining a team's optimum performance. HP server systems form the heart of the communications network on the circuit. The speed and power of these systems really come into their own in a design and aerodynamics environment. And all BMW WilliamsF1 team members use notebooks and handhelds supplied by HP so that they always have the latest information at their fingertips, wherever they are on the circuit.

Aerodynamics
In today's Formula 1 racing, the off-circuit competition to improve the cars and optimise the aerodynamics is just as important as the race itself. That is why Formula 1 teams continuously work on improving the design processes using the latest technologies. Aerodynamics is one of the most important factors that affects the performance of a Formula 1 car. Technicians study a car's aerodynamics by ascertaining how the airflows pass over, under and around the car. The car performs best – drives fastest – when there is an absolute minimum of air displacement. Other aspects that are comprehensively studied include the response to weather conditions, different track surfaces and the downward pressure and air resistance affecting the various parts of the car. Computer software is used to make calculations that are used for analyses in the design and testing process. And since the search for hundredths of seconds never ends, the Formula 1 teams apply advanced IT technology to improve racing performance even further.

The effect of technology on Formula 1 is that the mutual differences between the teams are becoming smaller and smaller. That results in cutthroat competition, and makes the races even more exciting. But needless to say, all of this stands or falls on the skill of the driver: despite all the technology, it is ultimately drivers who win races.

You'll find more information about this 'partnership for invention' between HP and the BMW WilliamsF1 Team at www.hp.nl/f1

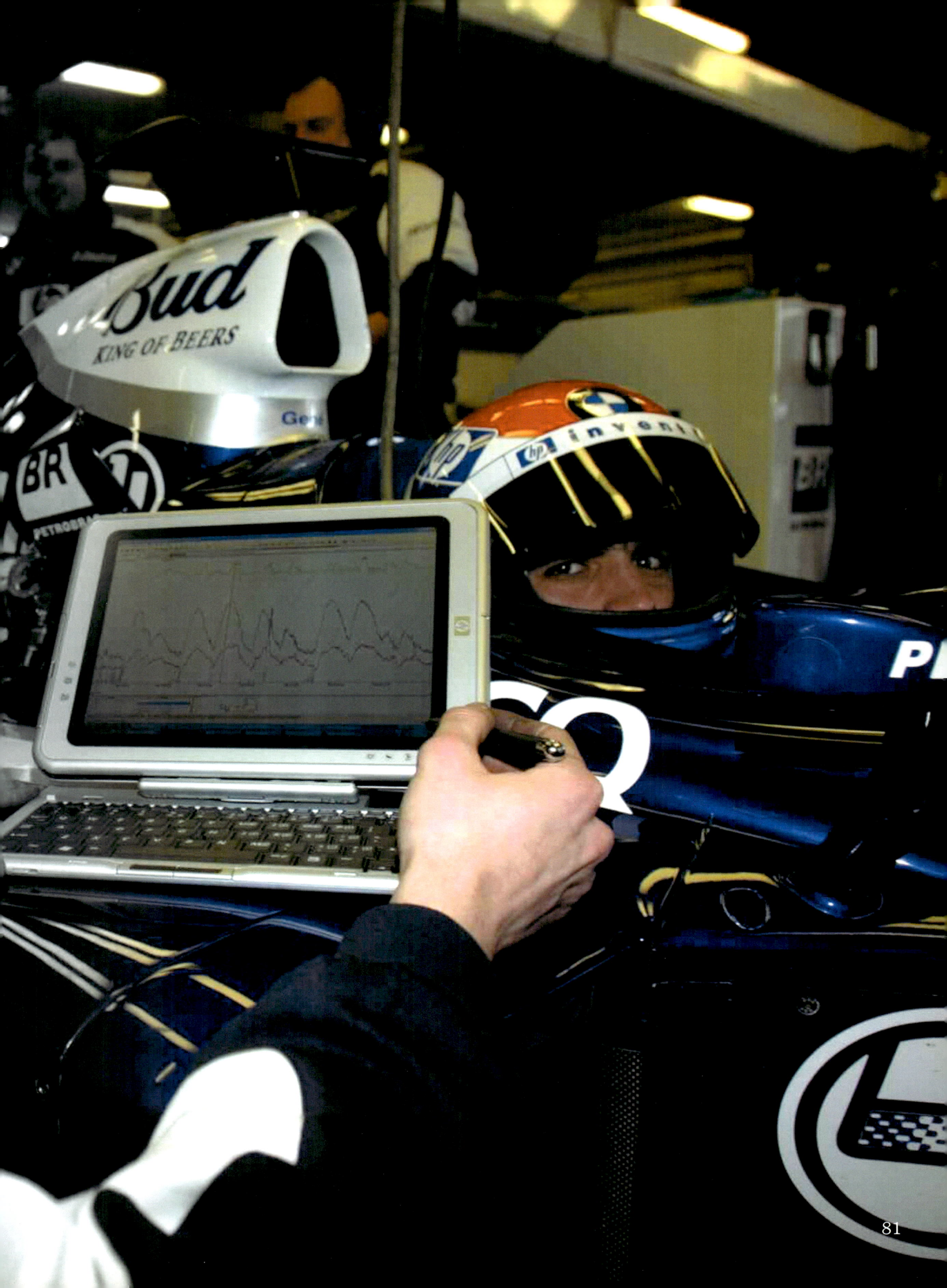
Bud
KING OF BEERS

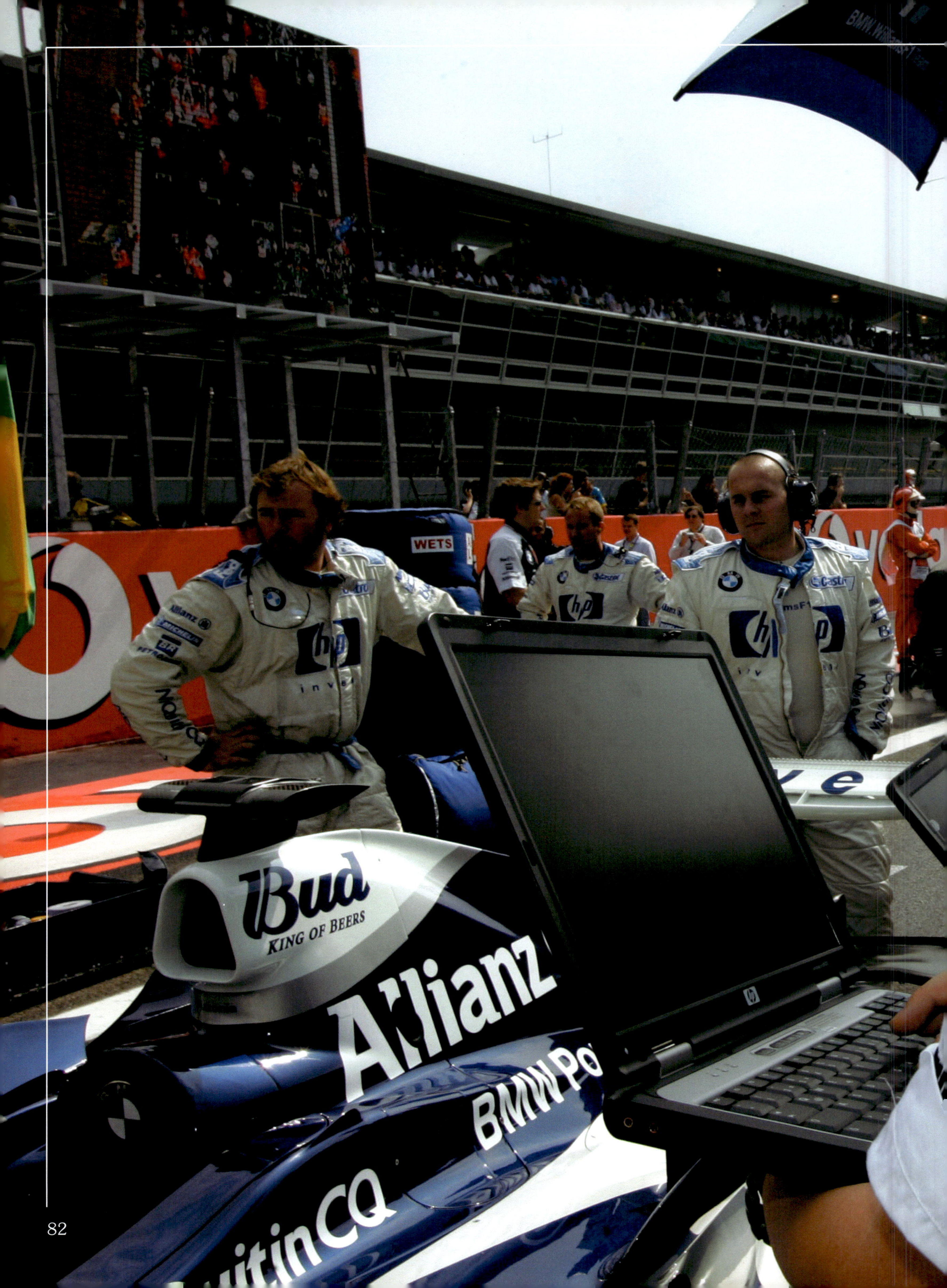
WETS
Bud
KING OF BEERS
Allianz

83

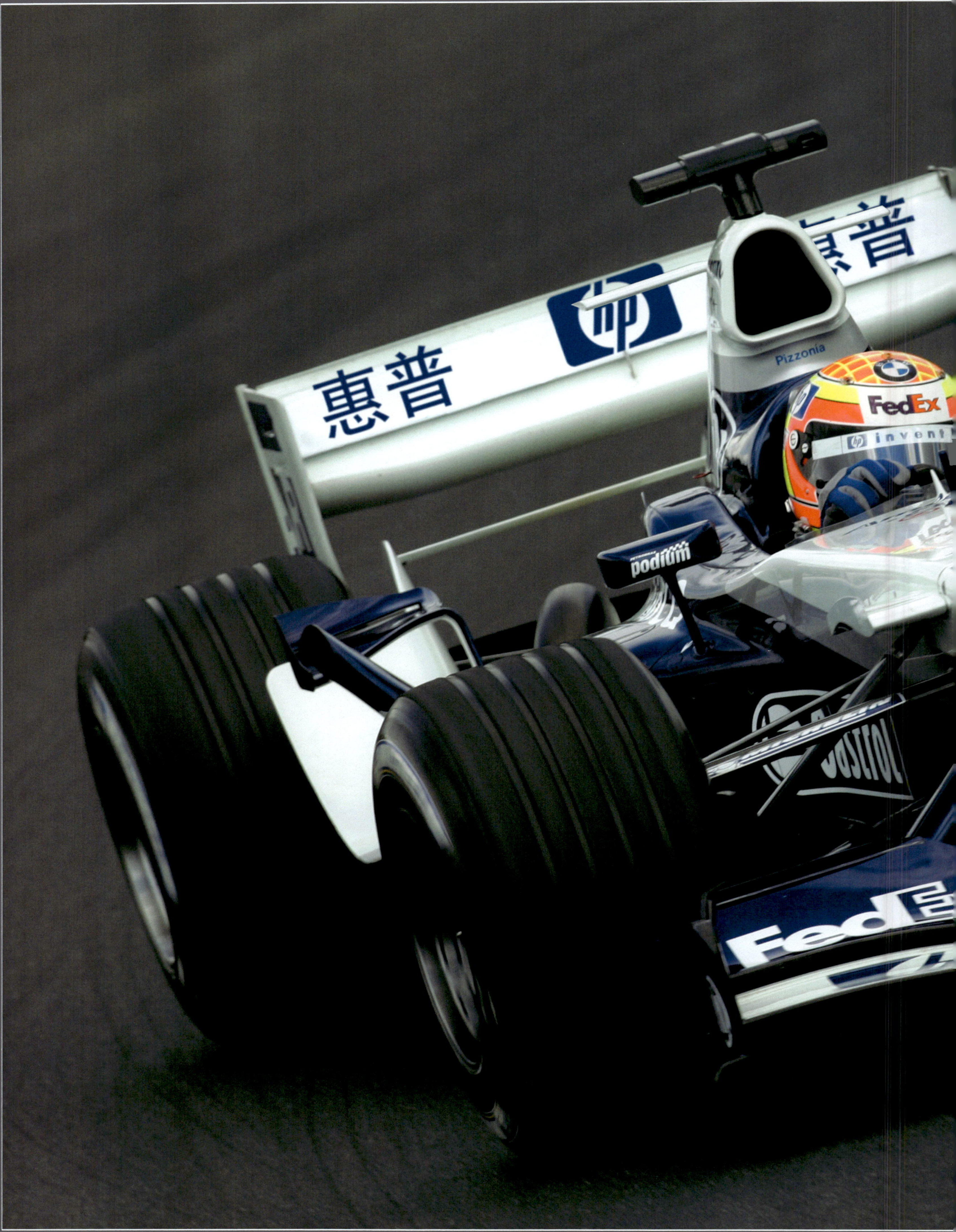
惠普
hp
Pizzonia
FedEx
invent
podium

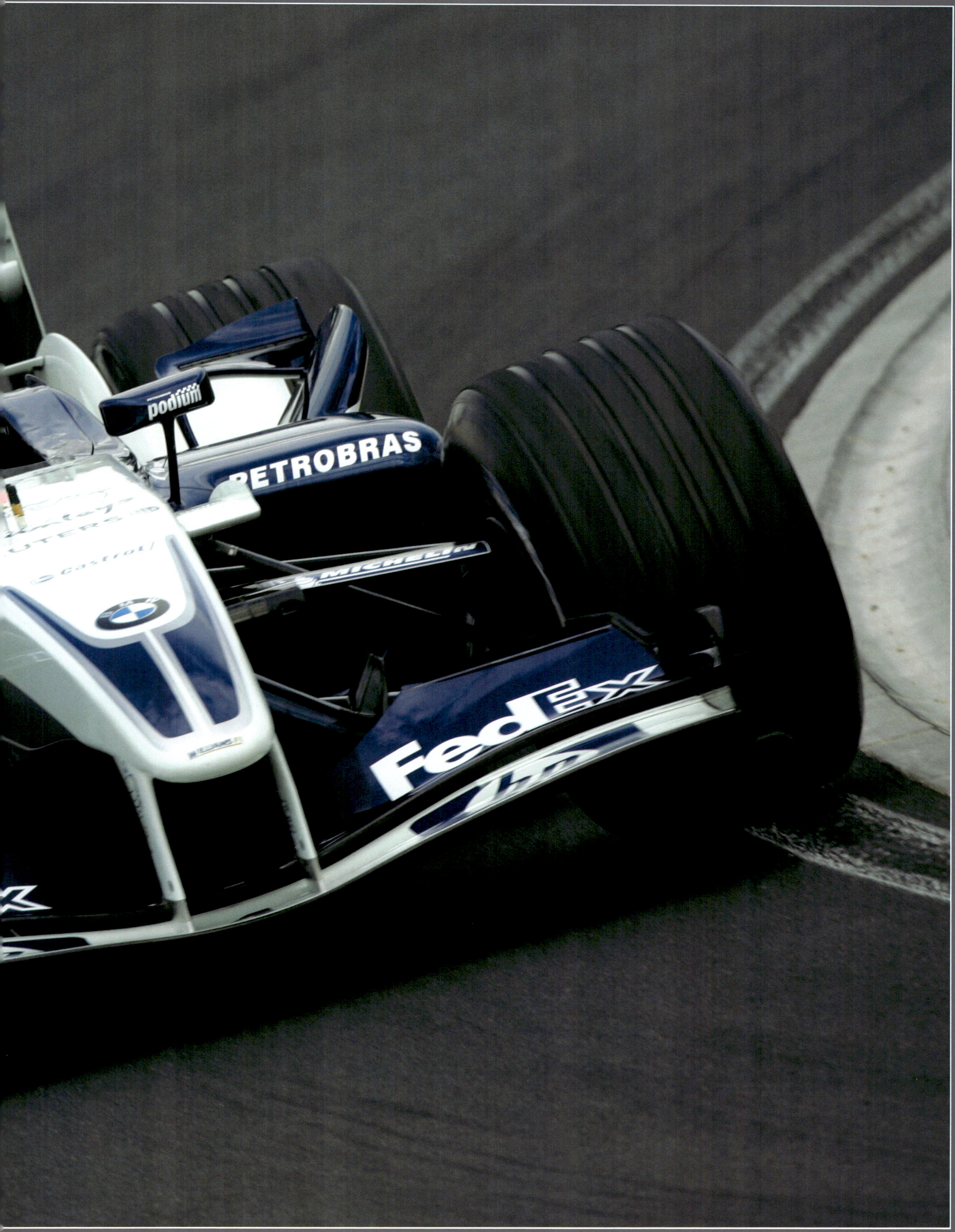
podium
PETROBRAS
MICHELIN
FedEx

86

PETROBRAS
podium
MICHELIN
MICHELIN
FedEx
hp

WILLIAMS
ACK
TC OFF
RAD

88

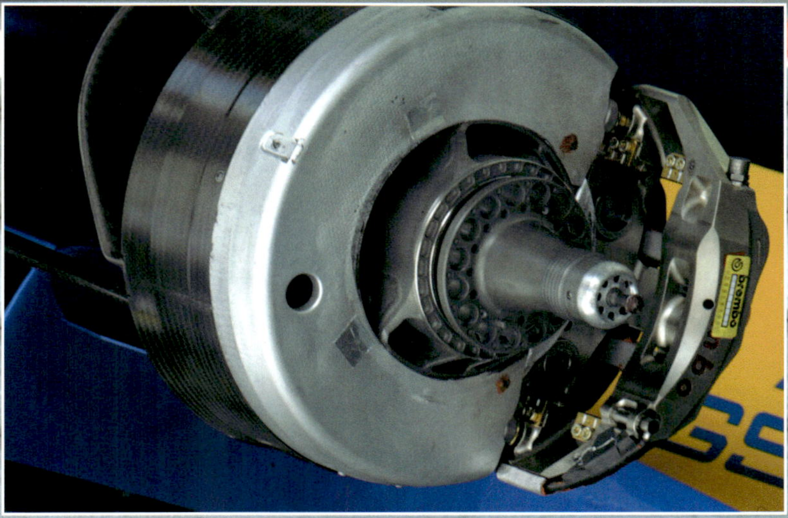
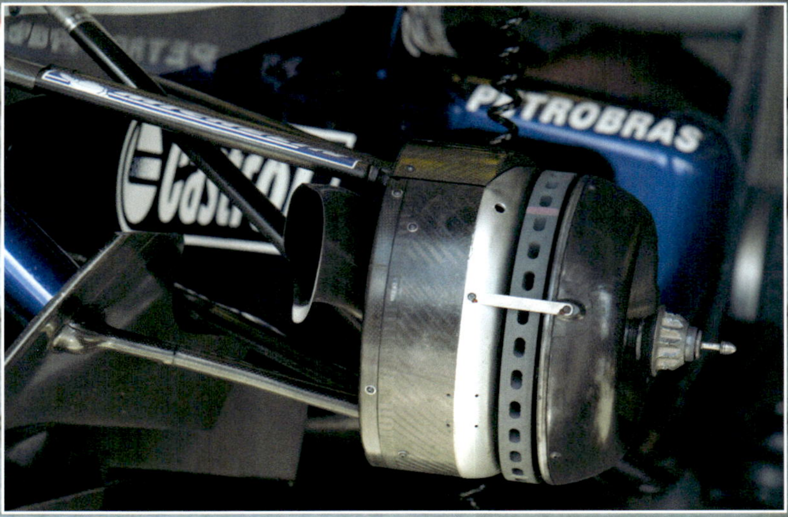
PETROBRAS
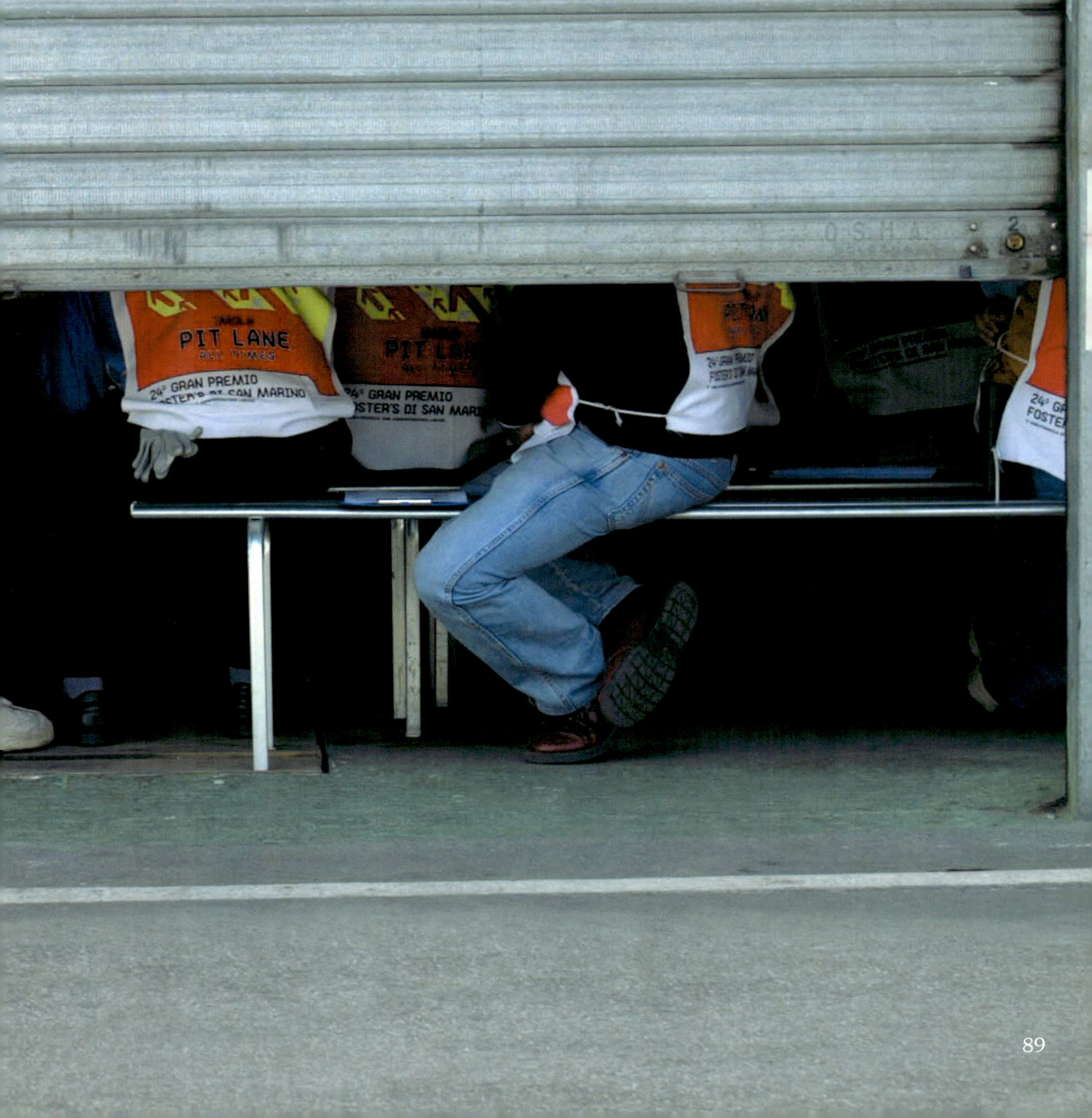
PIT LANE
ALL TIMES
24° GRAN PREMIO

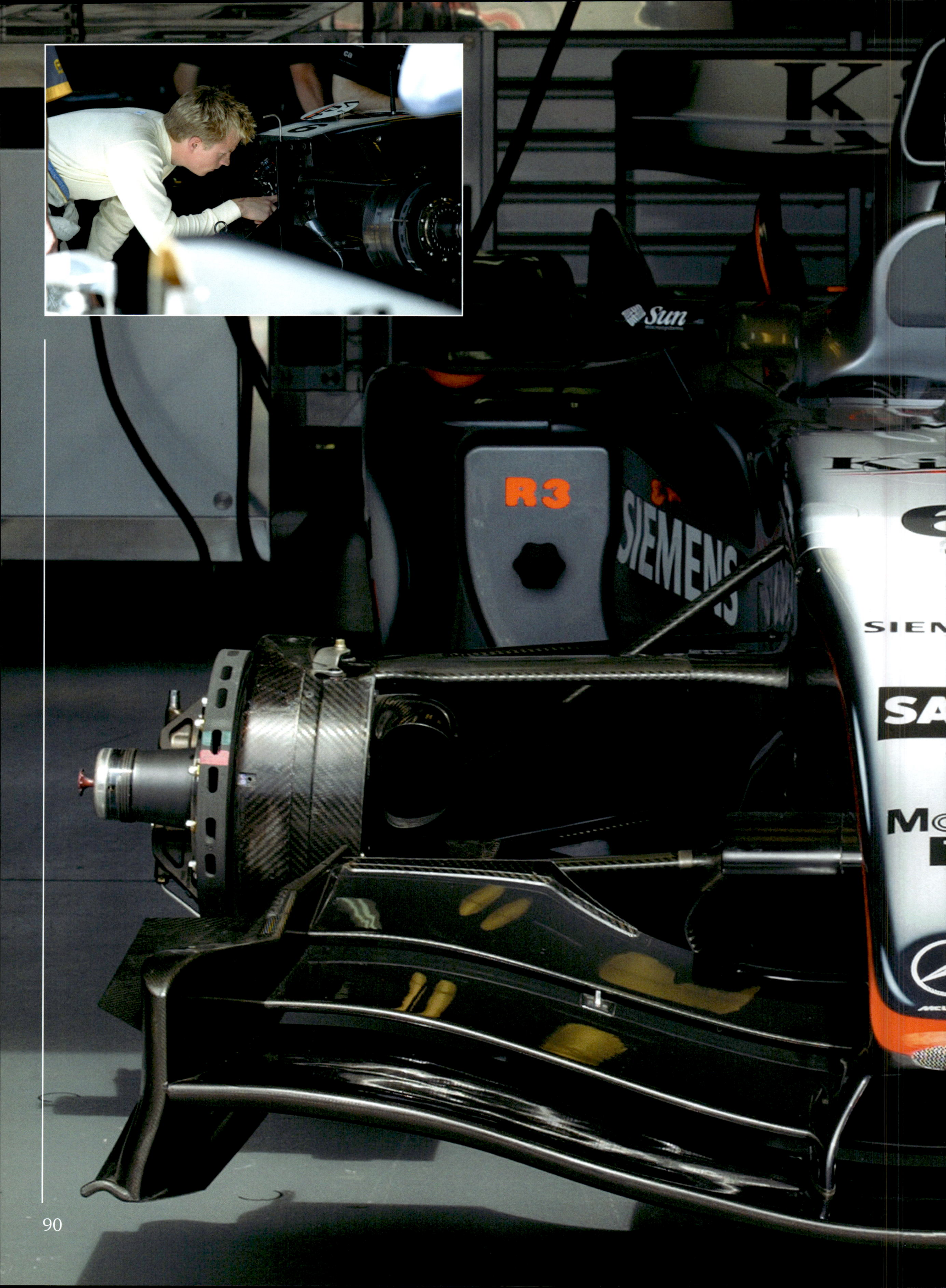
Sun
R3
SIEMENS

91

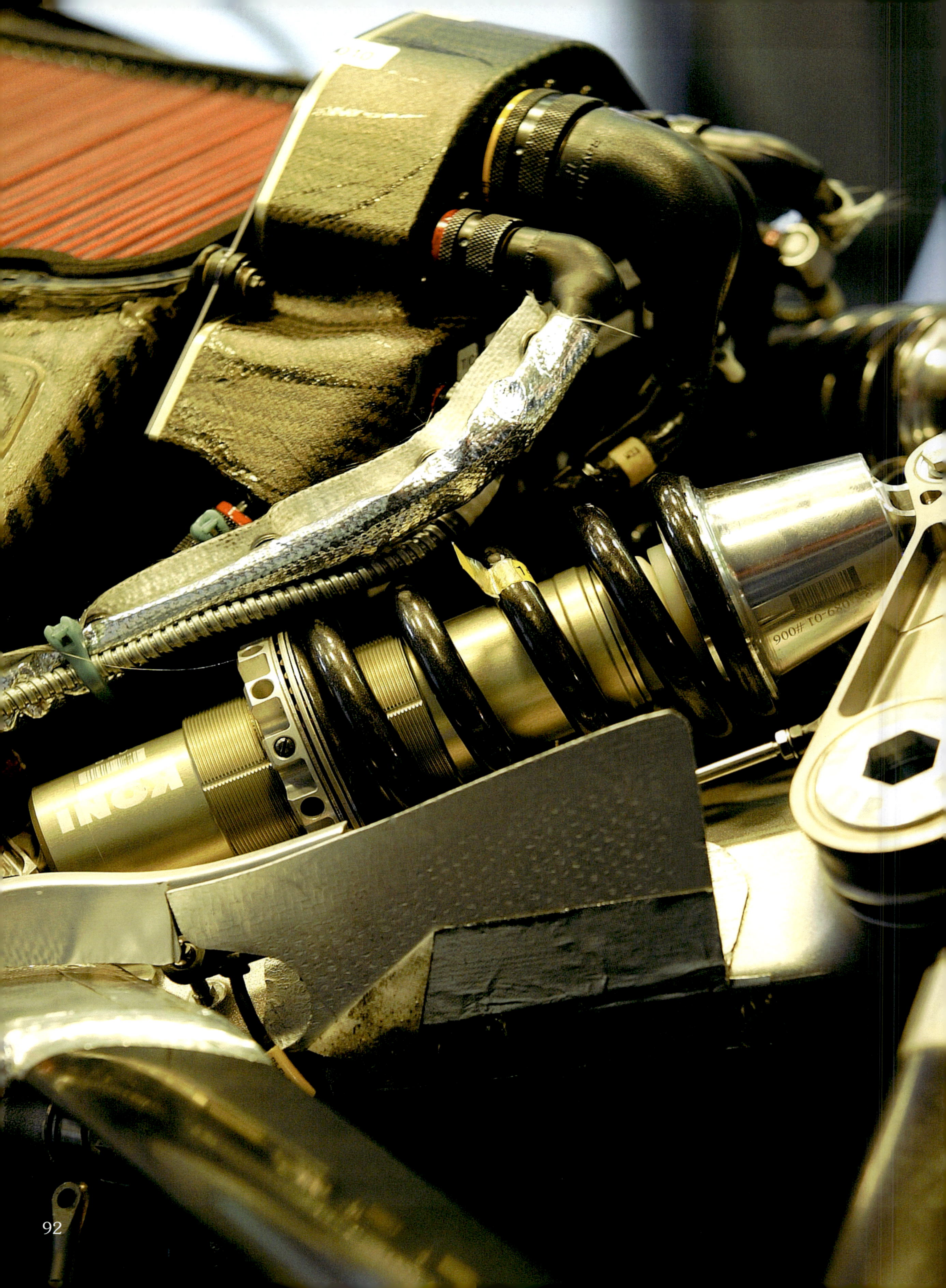

93

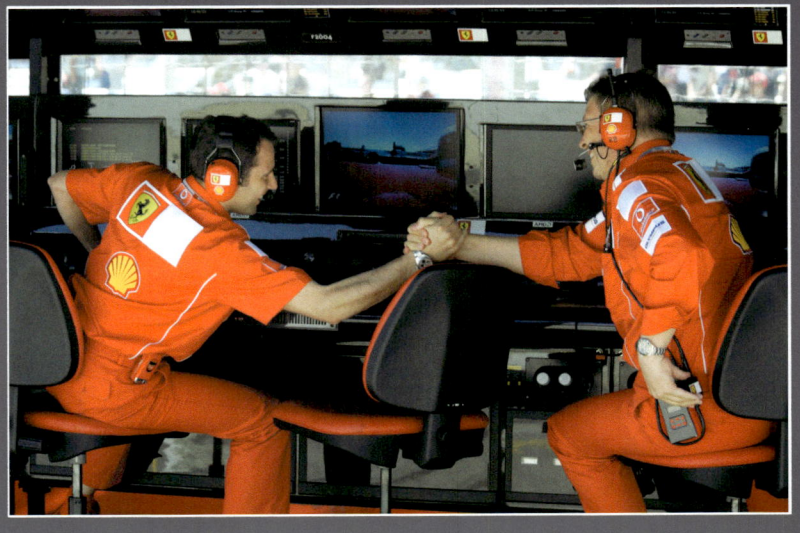

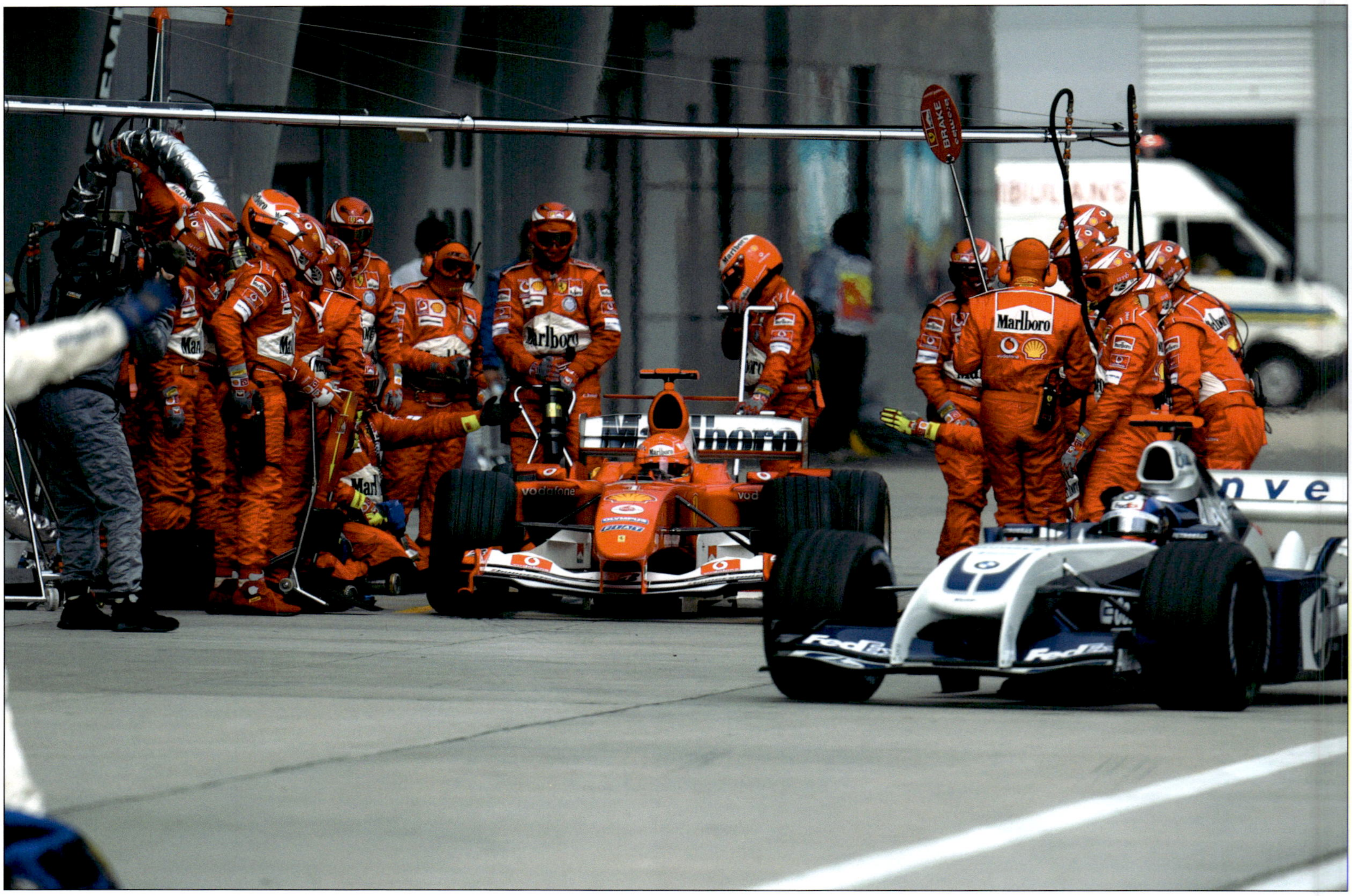

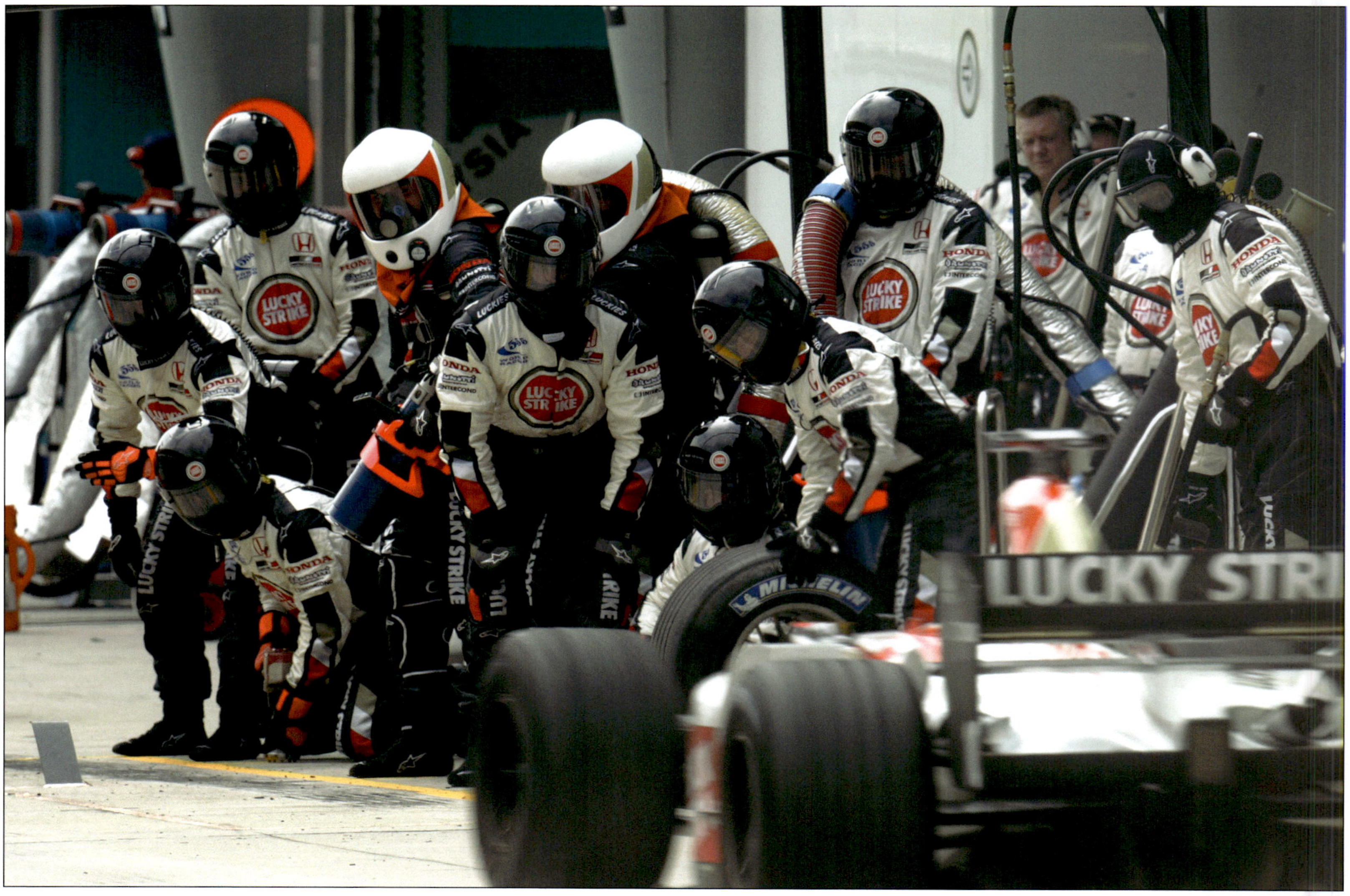

W.WilliamsF1 Team
NiQuitin CQ
BR
FedEx
Castrol

invent
Bud
Castrol
NiQuitin CQ
FedEx
3

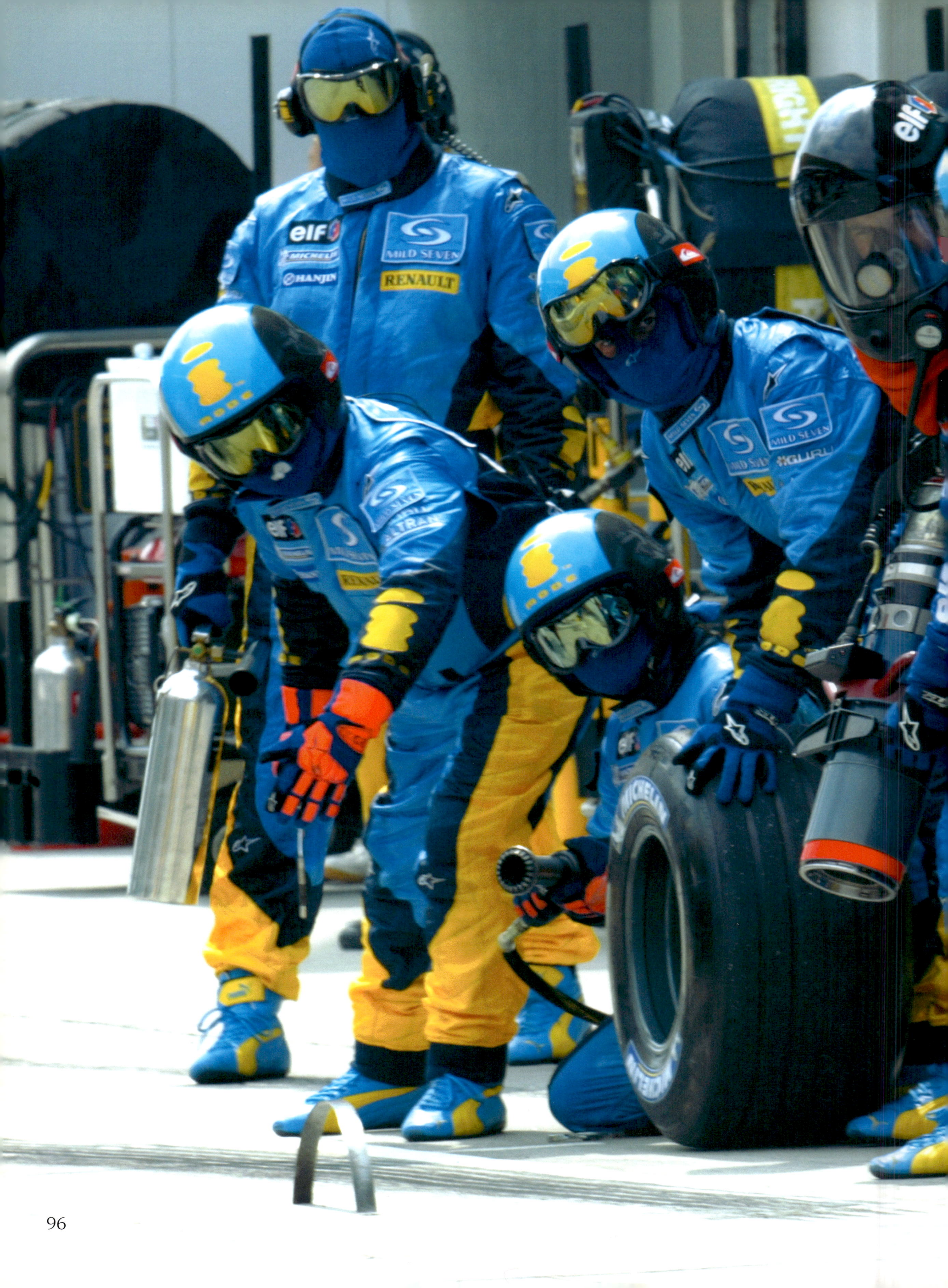
elf
MICHELIN
HANJIN
MILD SEVEN
RENAULT
ALTRAN
GURU

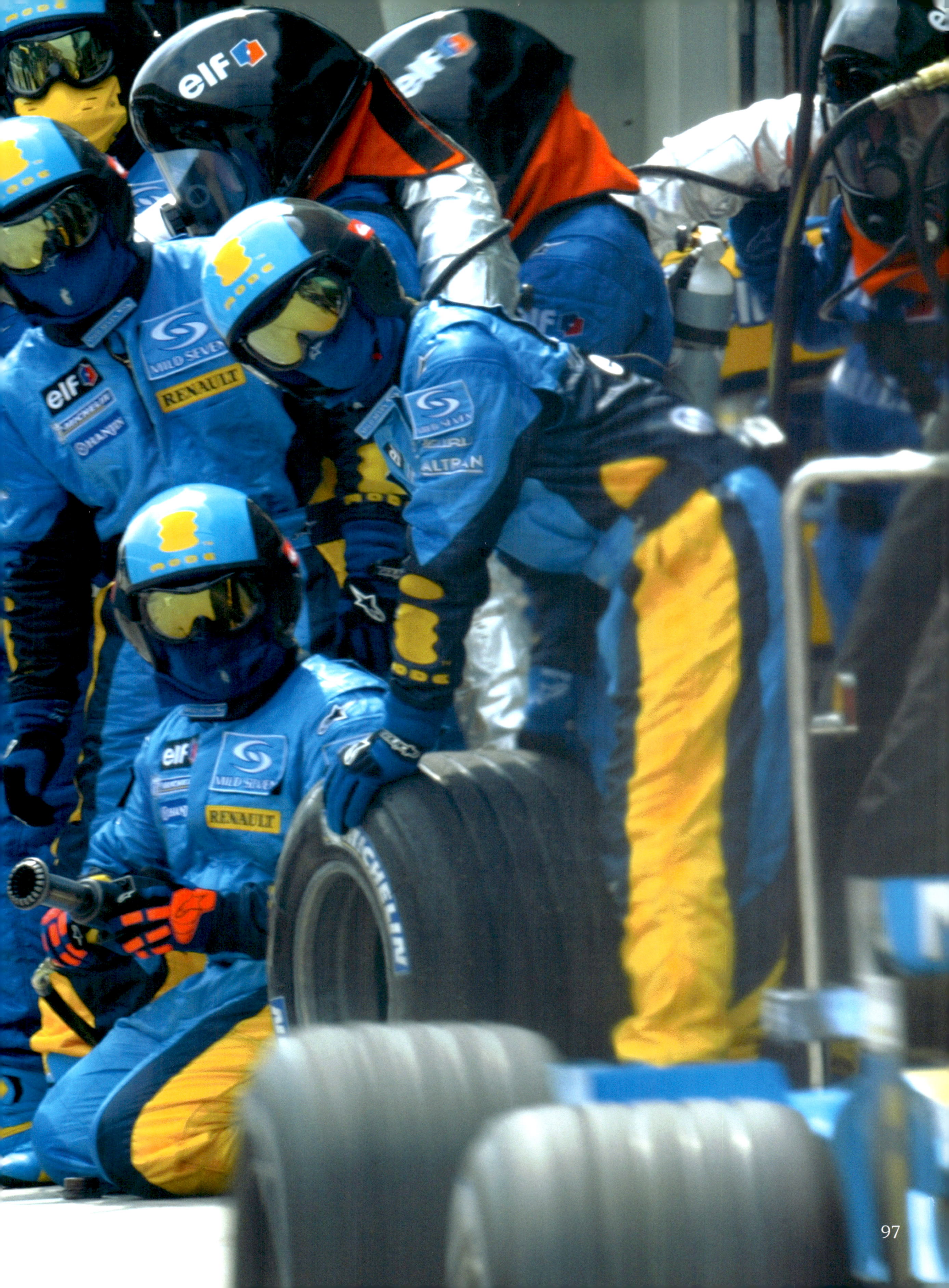
elf
MILD SEVEN
RENAULT
ALTRAN
MICHELIN

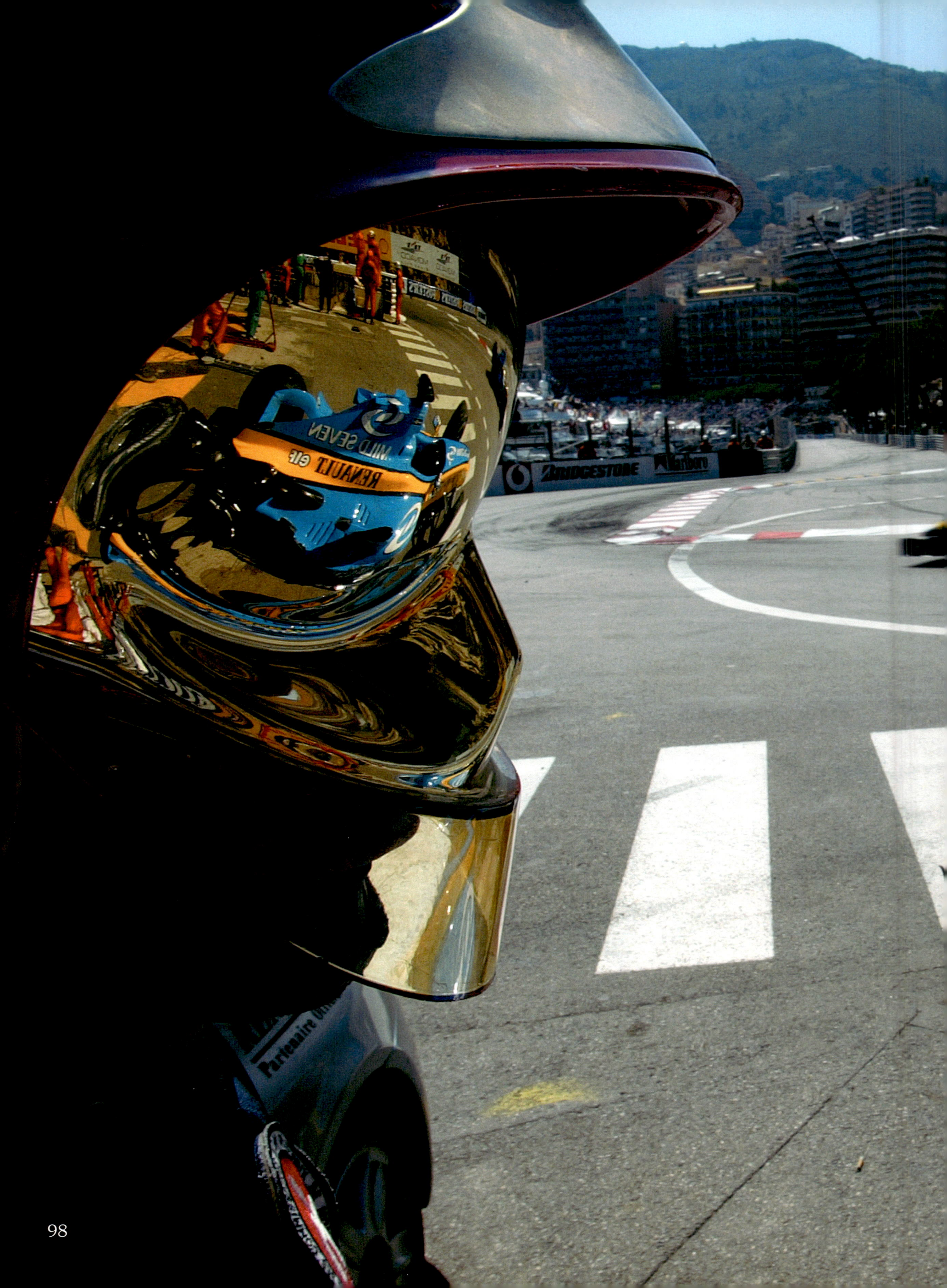
BRIDGESTONE
Marlboro

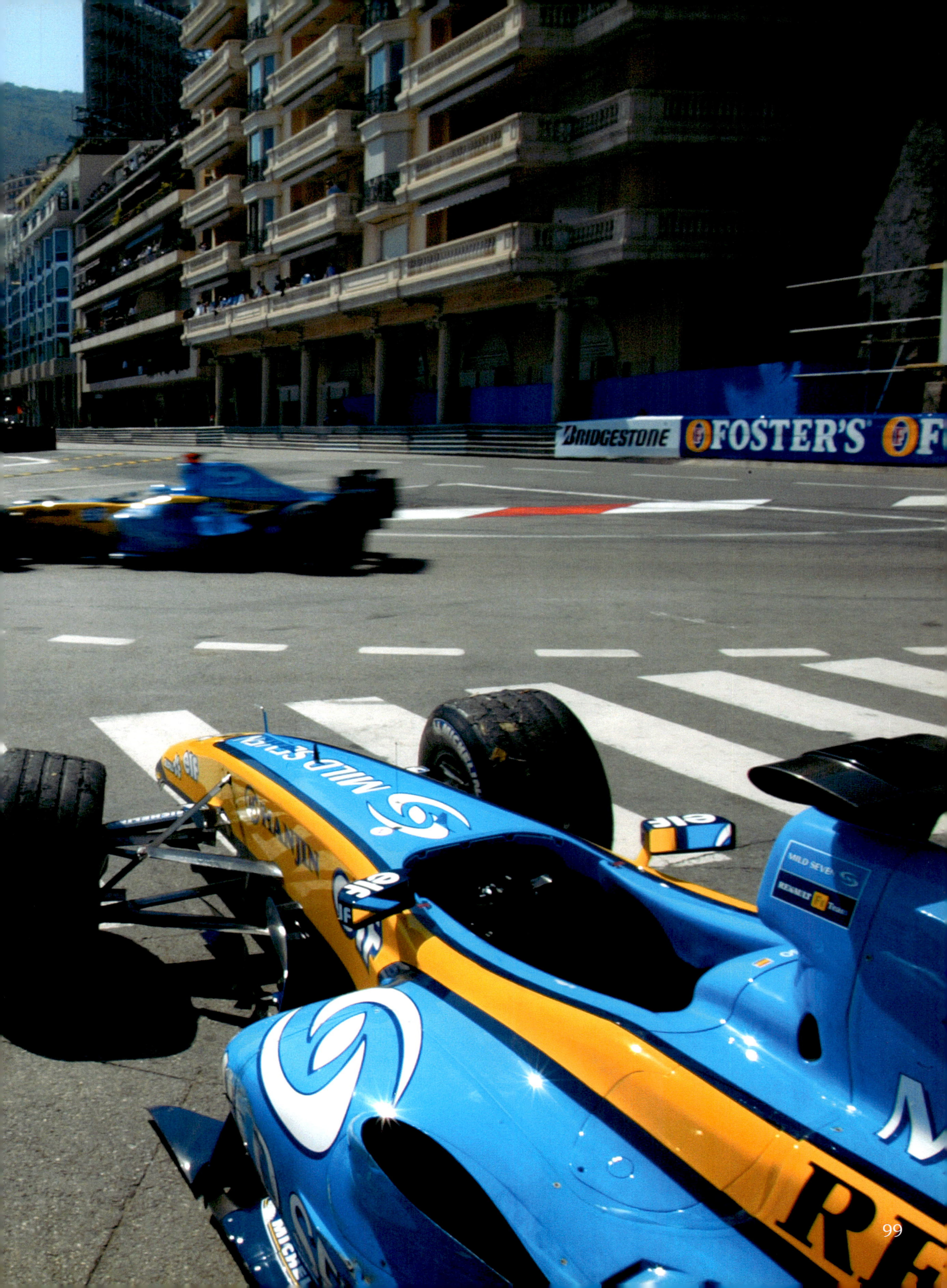
BRIDGESTONE
FOSTER'S

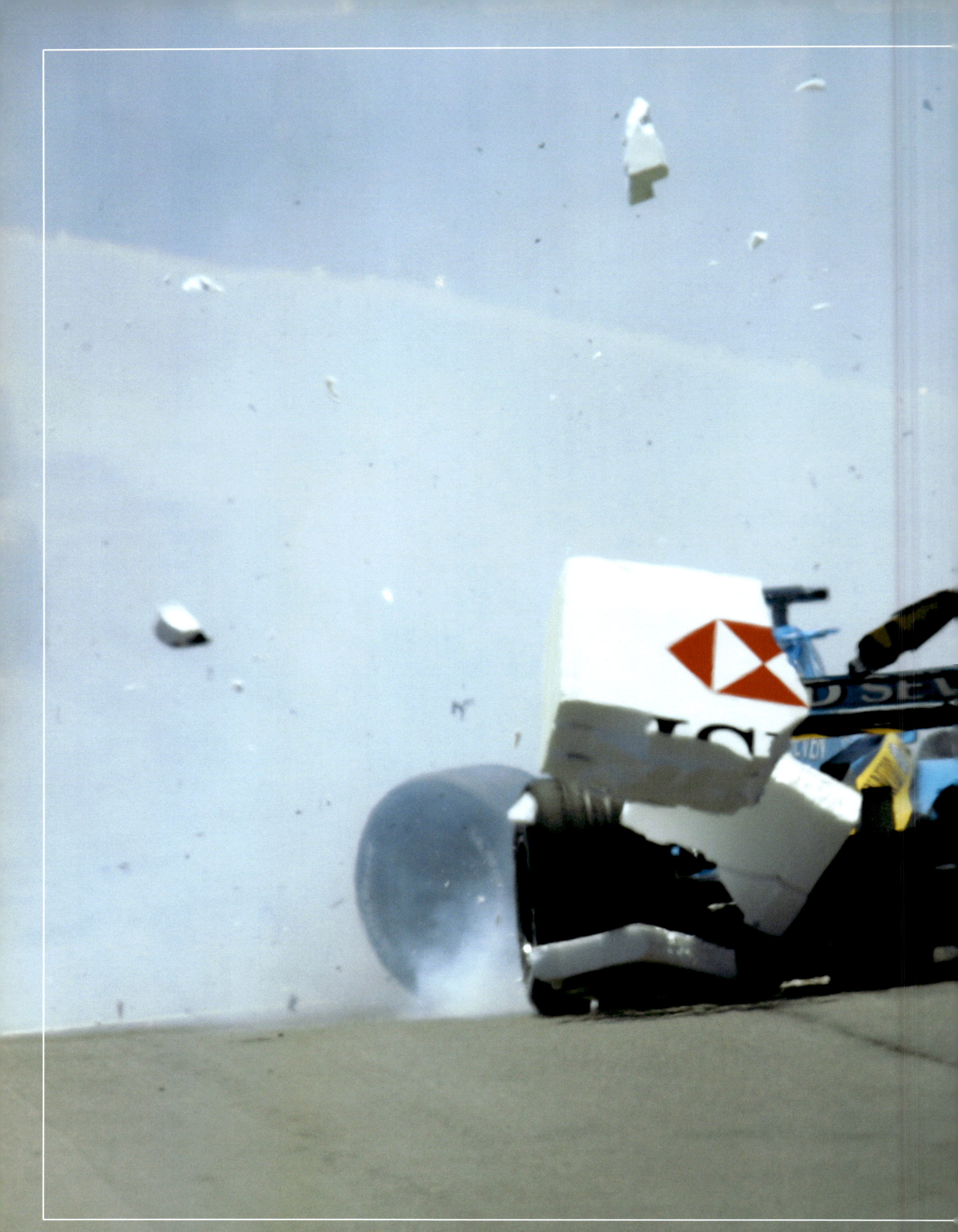

101

102

103

104

FOSTER'S®
Red Bull
MALAYSIA
PETRONAS
PETRONAS
CREDIT SUISSE
SCHÜCO
Henkel
Mobil 1
Mobil
vodafone

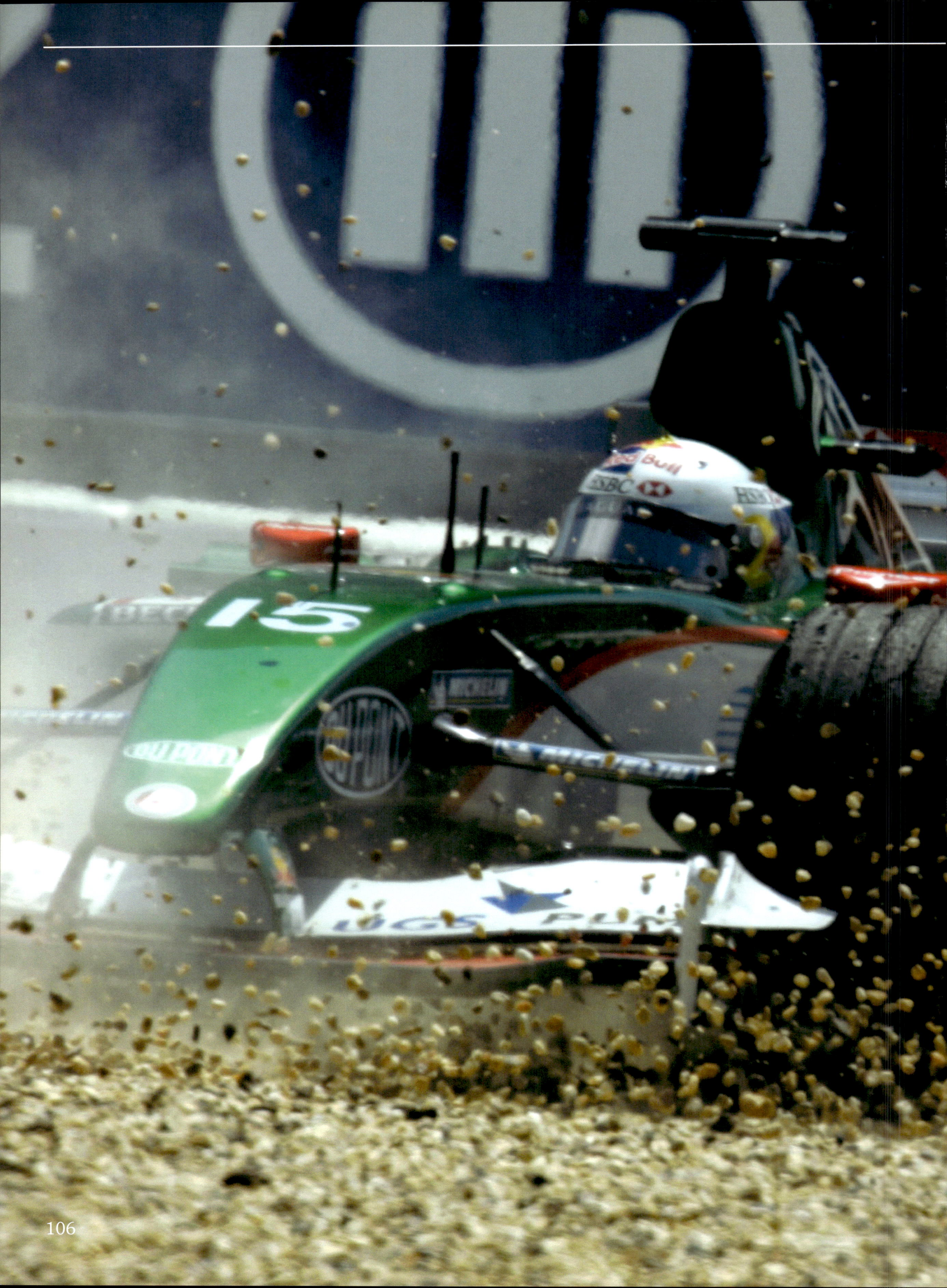
Bull
HSBC
15
MICHELIN
DUPONT

107

108

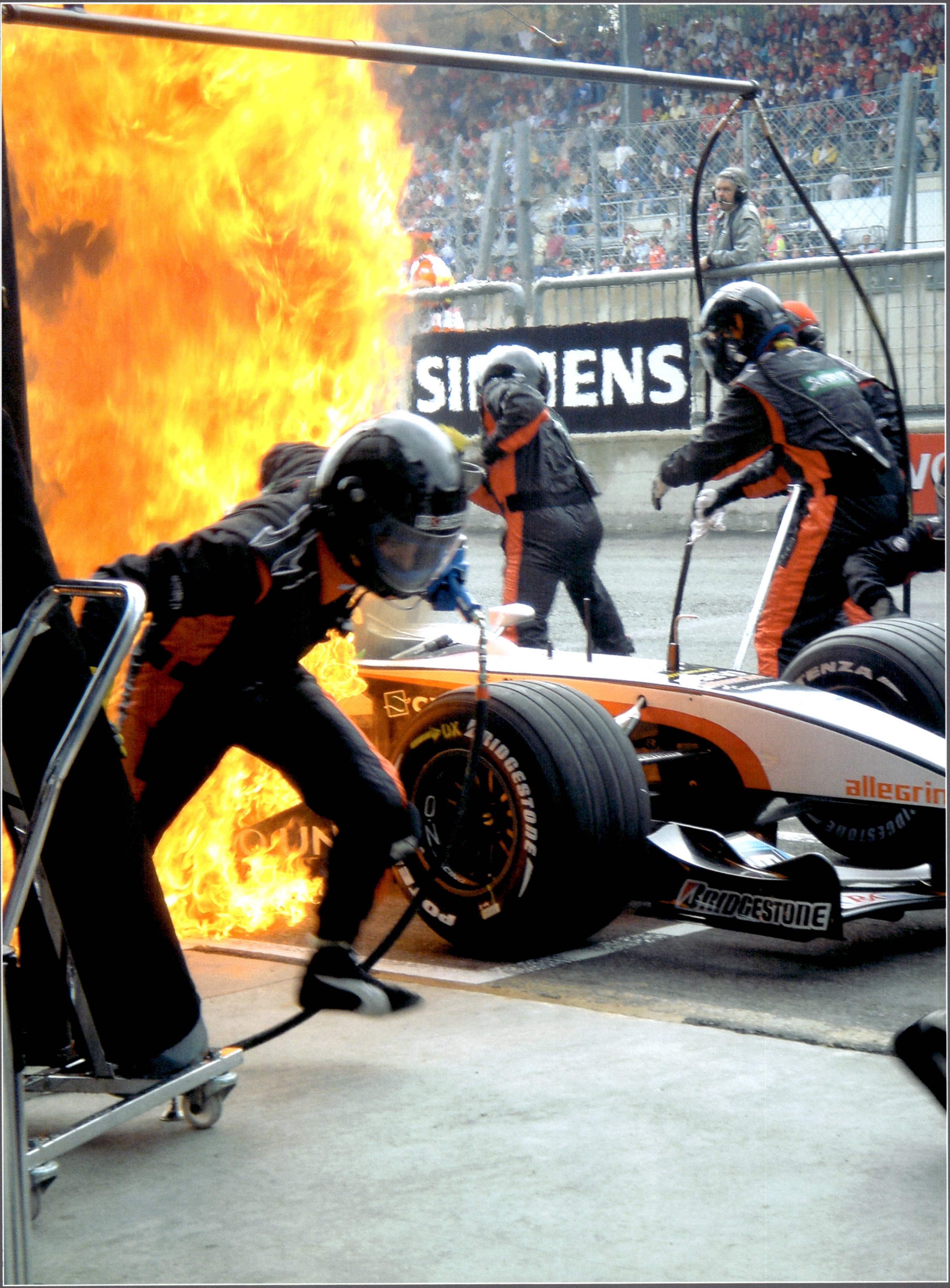
SIEMENS
BRIDGESTONE
allegrin

110

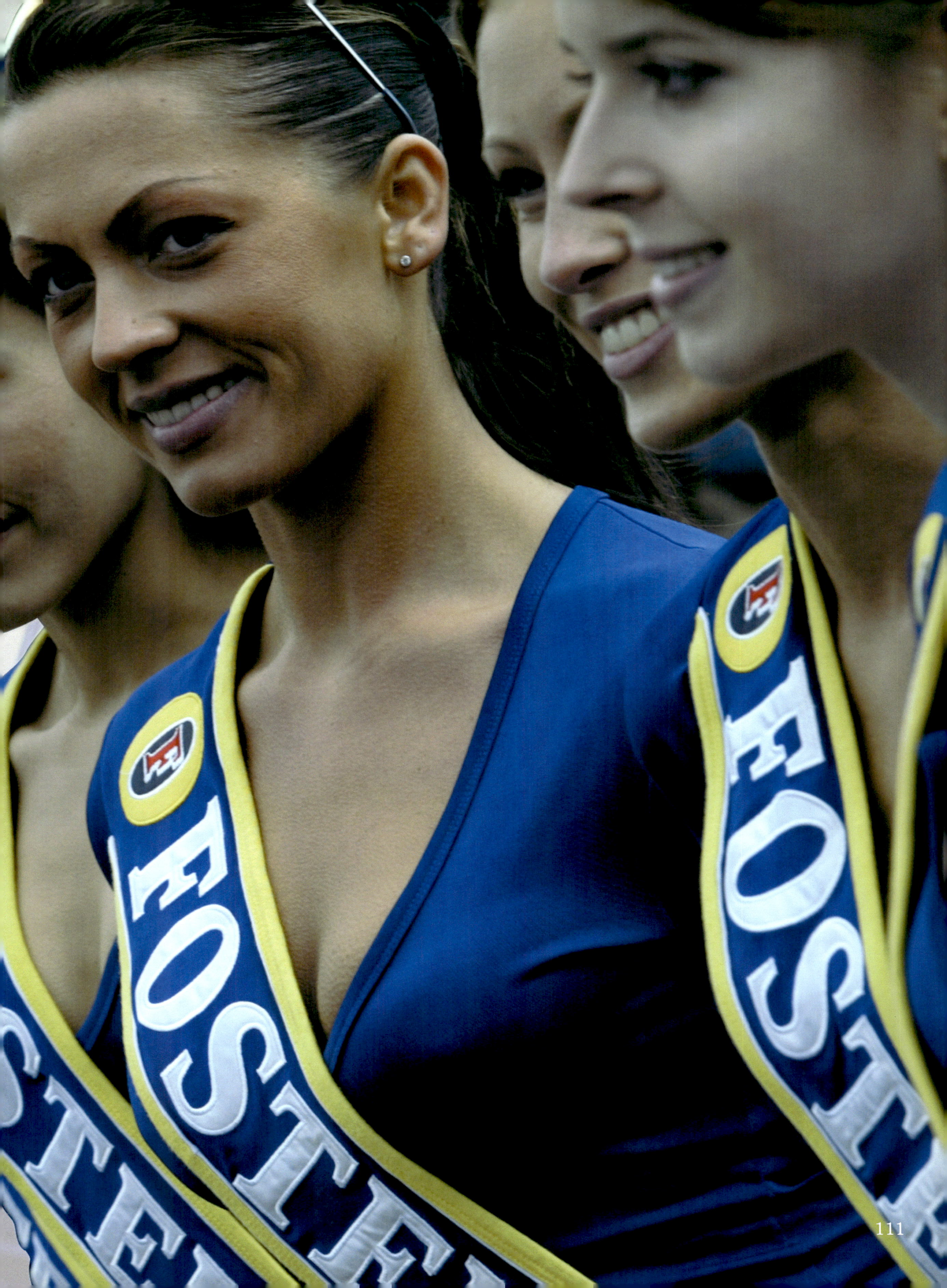

112

FORMULA 1 2004: FERRARI AGAIN!

by Paolo D'ALESSIO

The 2004 season was supposed to have heralded a changing of the guard and a renewed close battle between all the top Formula 1 teams; in short, it was to have brought an end to the Ferrari monopoly that began way back in 1999 when the Italian team won the world constructors' title of its recent successful sequence. The first signs of an inversion in the trend could be seen last year when by the mid-point of the season, Williams, McLaren and above all the Michelin radial tyres, had made a breach in the Ferrari battleship. It seemed that Ferrari was finally coming under serious threat and that an era of domination by the Anglo-German combination of chassis-engine designers (Williams and McLaren, BMW and Mercedes) was about to get underway. One of the top British monthly magazines, in its pre-season presentation, even went so far as to predict that 2004 would see the 'fall of the Gods', with a return to the top for McLaren and its number 1 driver, Kimi Raikkonen and the retirement of Michael Schumacher at the end of the year.

Just a few shakedown laps for the F2004 were all that was required however to get an idea of the potential of Ferrari's latest creation and that it was too early to speak of the end of a cycle. In fact, when testing was over and the racing got underway, pre-season fears soon turned into a nightmare for the opposition. The car that was to have abdicated its throne soon turned into the best Ferrari ever, one that was capable of winning on any circuit, in any circumstances and at any temperature. This car was even better than the legendary F2002 that dominated the 2002 world championship. With the support of clearly superior Bridgestone tyres, Michael Schumacher was in a position to play the role he preferred, at the front, in the lead, and take his record to seven world titles while Ferrari was able to celebrate its sixth successive constructors' crown.

What about the rest? Put quite simply, they were crushed by the Ferrari steamroller, humiliated by the red cars' supremacy and only occasionally got a look-in. Despite massive resources, enormous racing budgets and avant-guard technological facilities, they had to settle for the crumbs and their results were clearly below par. For example McLaren, who after a disastrous start to the year with a series of mechanical breakages and embarrassing performances, were forced to build a third different car in twelve months in an attempt to save face.

A similar situation emerged at Williams-BMW, where the FW26 'walrus' was supposed to be the car that would finally break Maranello's stranglehold on F1. However exactly the opposite happened and the FW26 turned into one of the most uncompetitive cars ever built by Williams. The FW26 never achieved acceptable levels of reliability and was afflicted by numerous aerodynamic and structural problems and this was exacerbated by the relatively poor performance and reliability of the 10 cylinder BMW engine.

Things were different over at BAR, with its Honda V10 engine. The team run by David Richards was the true revelation of 2004, and could become the most serious rival to Ferrari next season. Another leading contender could also be Renault, despite a lack of horsepower and structural problems that conditioned the car's performance on some circuits.

Still showing unfulfilled promise are Sauber, which despite a limited budget, recorded some good performances. This was not only due to the fact that a Ferrari engine powered the car, but also because they succeeded in making progress throughout the year. The same cannot be said of Jaguar and Toyota, the real failures of the 2004 season. The disappointment over the performance of the Detroit giant's arm in the top category was so great that on the eve of the Chinese GP, Ford announced that it was pulling the plus on Jaguar's involvement in F1. It was an obvious decision to make, given the poor results obtained in five seasons of F1, the best being Eddie Irvine's third place in the 2002 Italian GP.

And what about Toyota? On its debut in F1 the largest automobile manufacturer in the world predicted it would win the world championship in four years. After three disappointing seasons however, Toyota has become a squad on the brink of a serious technical crisis rather than a top F1 team, despite a virtually unlimited budget and a technical structure in Cologne that would be the envy of NASA.

If, as is feared, minnows Minardi and Jordan are forced to abandon the F1 scene, they at least have the alibi of not having a factory engine supply, unlimited resources and a massive technical structure to face up to the increasingly costly Formula 1 of the new millennium.

2000: FERRARI F1 2000

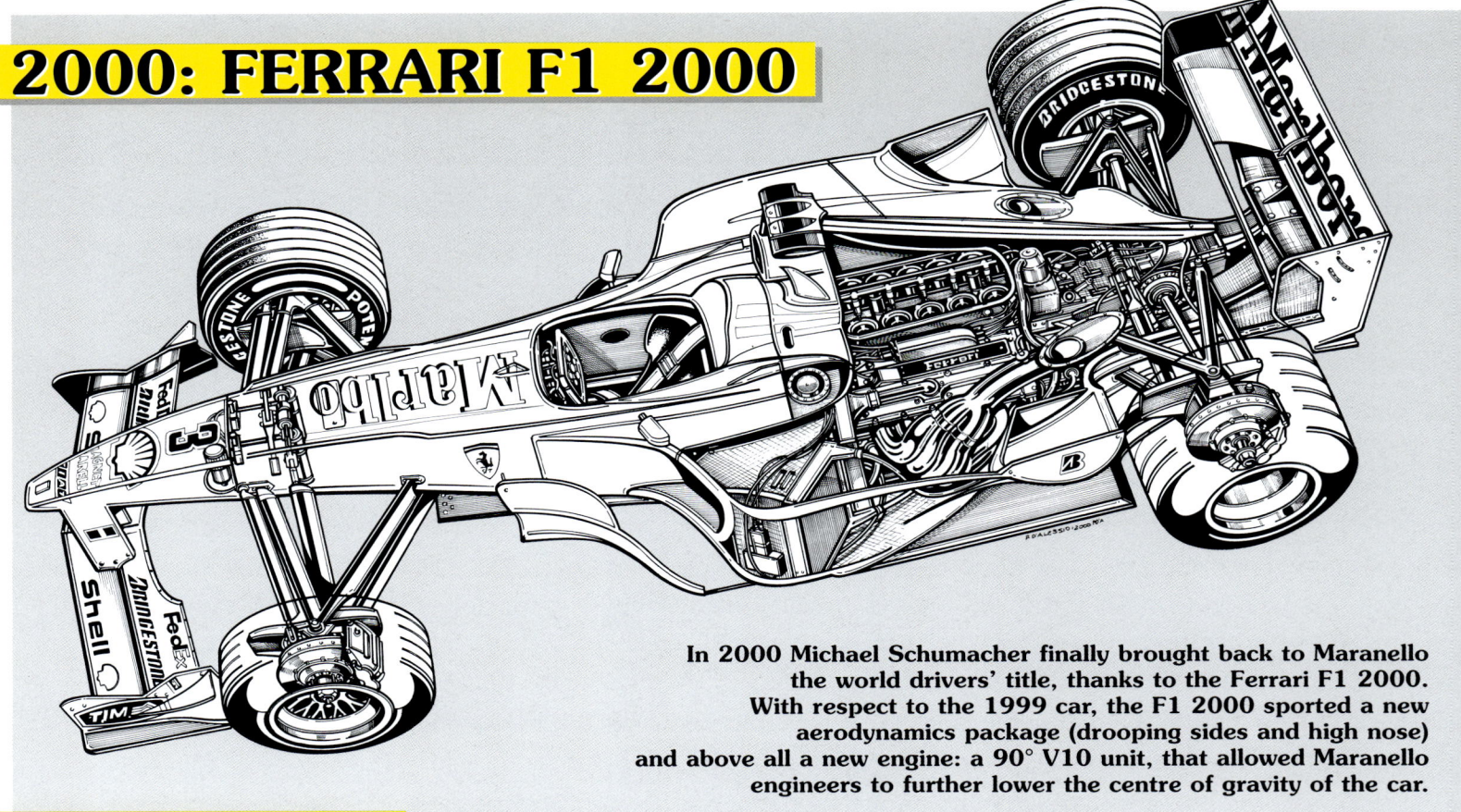

In 2000 Michael Schumacher finally brought back to Maranello the world drivers' title, thanks to the Ferrari F1 2000. With respect to the 1999 car, the F1 2000 sported a new aerodynamics package (drooping sides and high nose) and above all a new engine: a 90° V10 unit, that allowed Maranello engineers to further lower the centre of gravity of the car.

1999: F399

1999: after a sixteen-year gap, Ferrari once again claimed the title of Constructors' champions thanks to the F399, a car that sported a series of important technical innovations. These included a revolutionary 'computer steering wheel' (alongside), and 'contracting' rear suspension (design on the right).

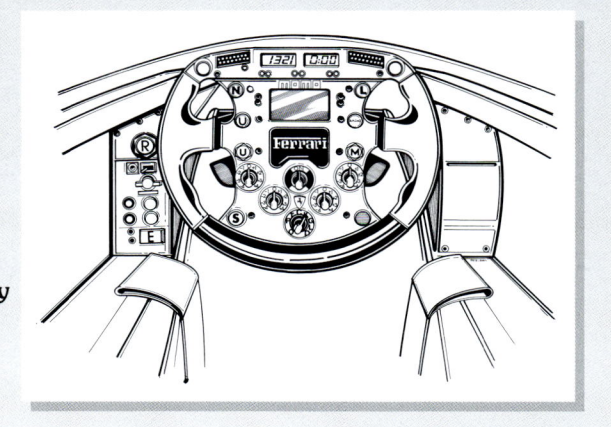

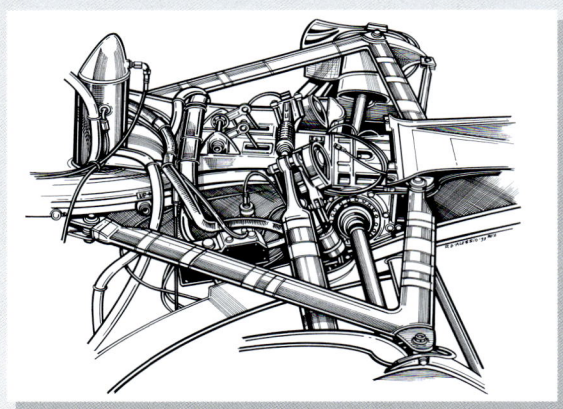

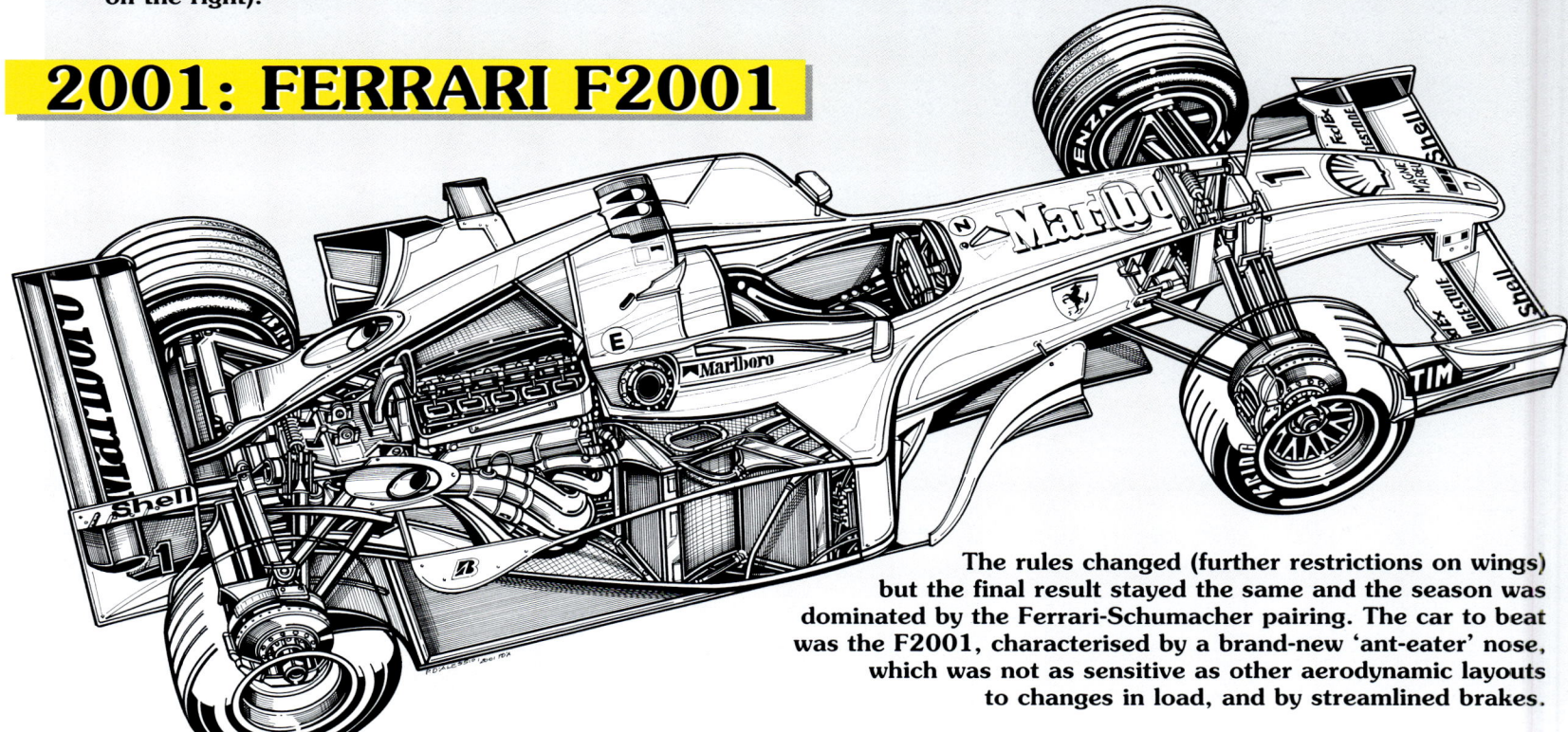

2001: FERRARI F2001

The rules changed (further restrictions on wings) but the final result stayed the same and the season was dominated by the Ferrari-Schumacher pairing. The car to beat was the F2001, characterised by a brand-new 'ant-eater' nose, which was not as sensitive as other aerodynamic layouts to changes in load, and by streamlined brakes.

2002: FERRARI F2002

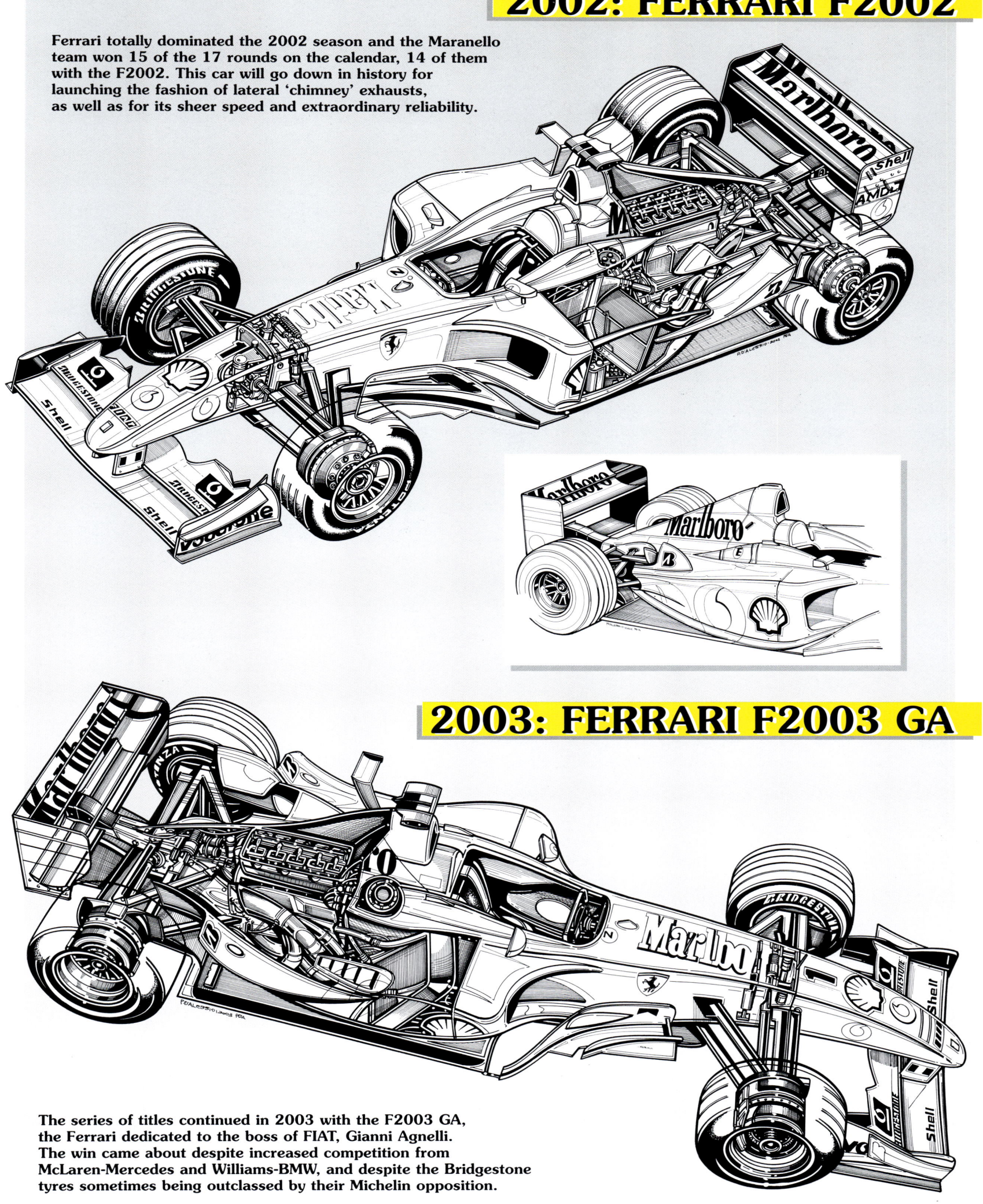

Ferrari totally dominated the 2002 season and the Maranello team won 15 of the 17 rounds on the calendar, 14 of them with the F2002. This car will go down in history for launching the fashion of lateral 'chimney' exhausts, as well as for its sheer speed and extraordinary reliability.

2003: FERRARI F2003 GA

The series of titles continued in 2003 with the F2003 GA, the Ferrari dedicated to the boss of FIAT, Gianni Agnelli. The win came about despite increased competition from McLaren-Mercedes and Williams-BMW, and despite the Bridgestone tyres sometimes being outclassed by their Michelin opposition.

FERRARI F2004

What can one say about a car that dominated what was expected to be one of the most difficult seasons ever faced by Maranello? It dominated from qualifying to the chequered flag, leaving the opposition behind. Faced with this unprecedented supremacy (the F2004 was even more successful that the 2002 Ferrari), media from all over the world started to call the car 'stratospheric' or 'from another planet'. When the F2004 was presented however, few people believed the Prancing Horse engineers when they called it the best Ferrari of all time. Despite the fact that at the time the F2004 didn't look to be that sensational, they were proved to be right. Less exasperated than the McLaren MP4/19, less extreme than the Renault R24 and certainly not as revolutionary as the Williams FW26 'walrus', the F2004 seemed to be a stop-gap car, a pause for reflection on a technical level at the end of a long and victorious cycle. Yet, from its very first shakedown laps it was clear that the project was not a conservative one, and it was the logical evolution of the F2003 GA, which had won the world title the year before. At Maranello however they knew that the GA's potential had been mainly left unfulfilled, due to the regulations and alternating performances from the Bridgestone tyres. In autumn 2003 Ross Brawn, Rory Byrne and Paolo Martinelli decided to persevere on the path undertaken in 2003 and correct the defects of a car that had perhaps been created 12 months too soon. The first significant change to the F2003 GA was a shortening of the wheelbase by around 5 centimetres, and this was made possible thanks to the reduced capacity of the fuel tank. Many apparently insignificant improvements were made to the aerodynamics, which allowed much of the downforce lost following the entry into force of the new regulations to be recov-

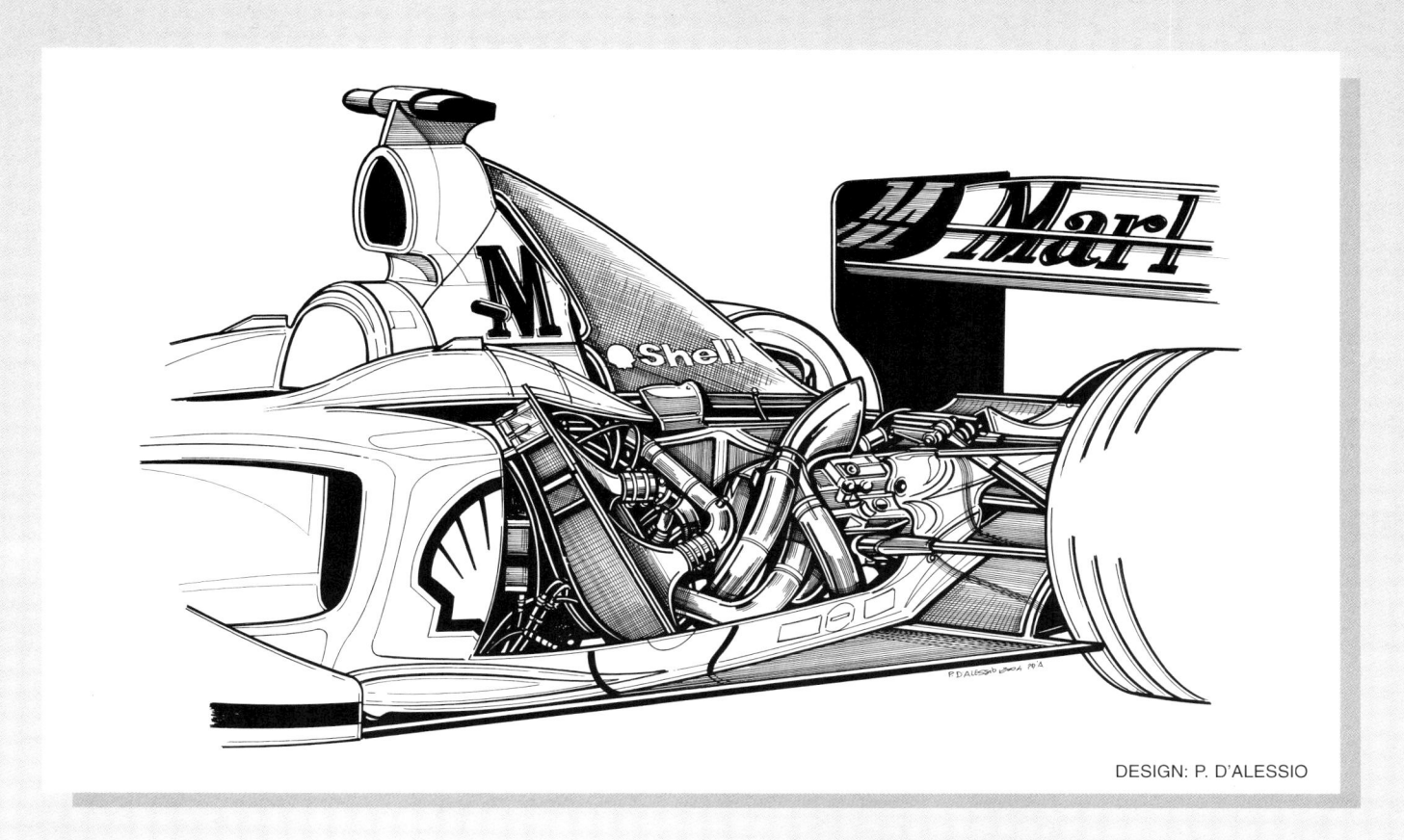

DESIGN: P. D'ALESSIO

ered. With respect to the F2003 GA, at the front the F2004 sported a new wing with a raised external profile, while side deflectors, new periscope exhaust duct fairings and exit slots for the hot air contained in the sidewalls also appeared on the car.

Just as important, although not visible to the naked eye, were the changes made under the bodywork, starting with a renewed fluid dynamics layout. New radiant masses, even smaller than those on the F2003 GA, brought about a better cooling of the mechanical organs and offered less resistance to forward motion, thus improving performance and allowing Schumacher to annihilate the opposition. The real strongpoint of the F2004 however was represented by the new version of the ten-cylinder 053 engine that powered the Maranello car to its many pole positions and victories. The Prancing Horse engineers admitted that in 2004 they had not aimed so much for a reduction in weight but an improvement in performance and duration. A revision of the internal architecture and a reduction of the number of revs to 18,800 rpm (last year the 19,000 rpm barrier was breached) were all that was required to do the job. With over 900 reliable horsepower on tap, and with an incredibly smooth progression available, the 053 unit was once again the best engine in F1, even better than the acclaimed German, French and Japanese V10s. Above all it proved to be superbly reliable while the title ambitions of its rivals were ruined by traces of white smoke, the unmistakeable sign of engine failure. Last but not least, the tyre situation; Bridgestone made a major effort after last year and outclassed Michelin in every condition and at every temperature.

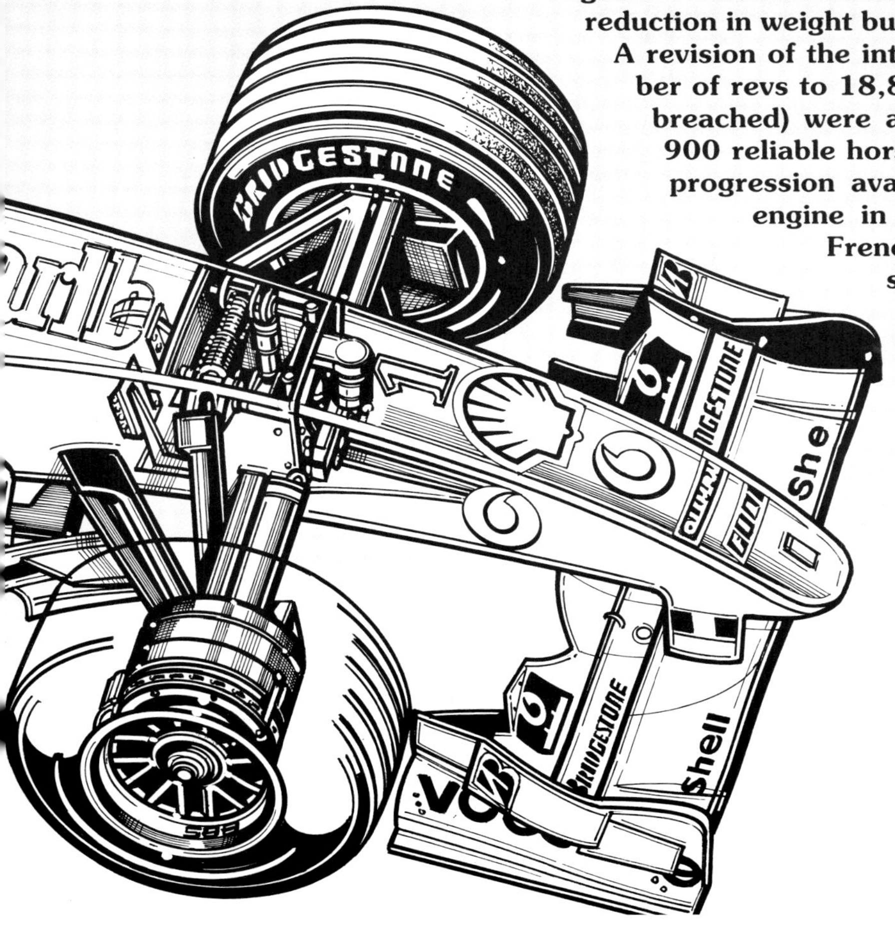

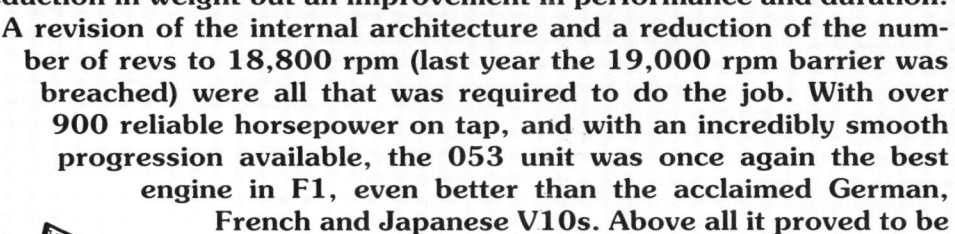

FERRARI F2004

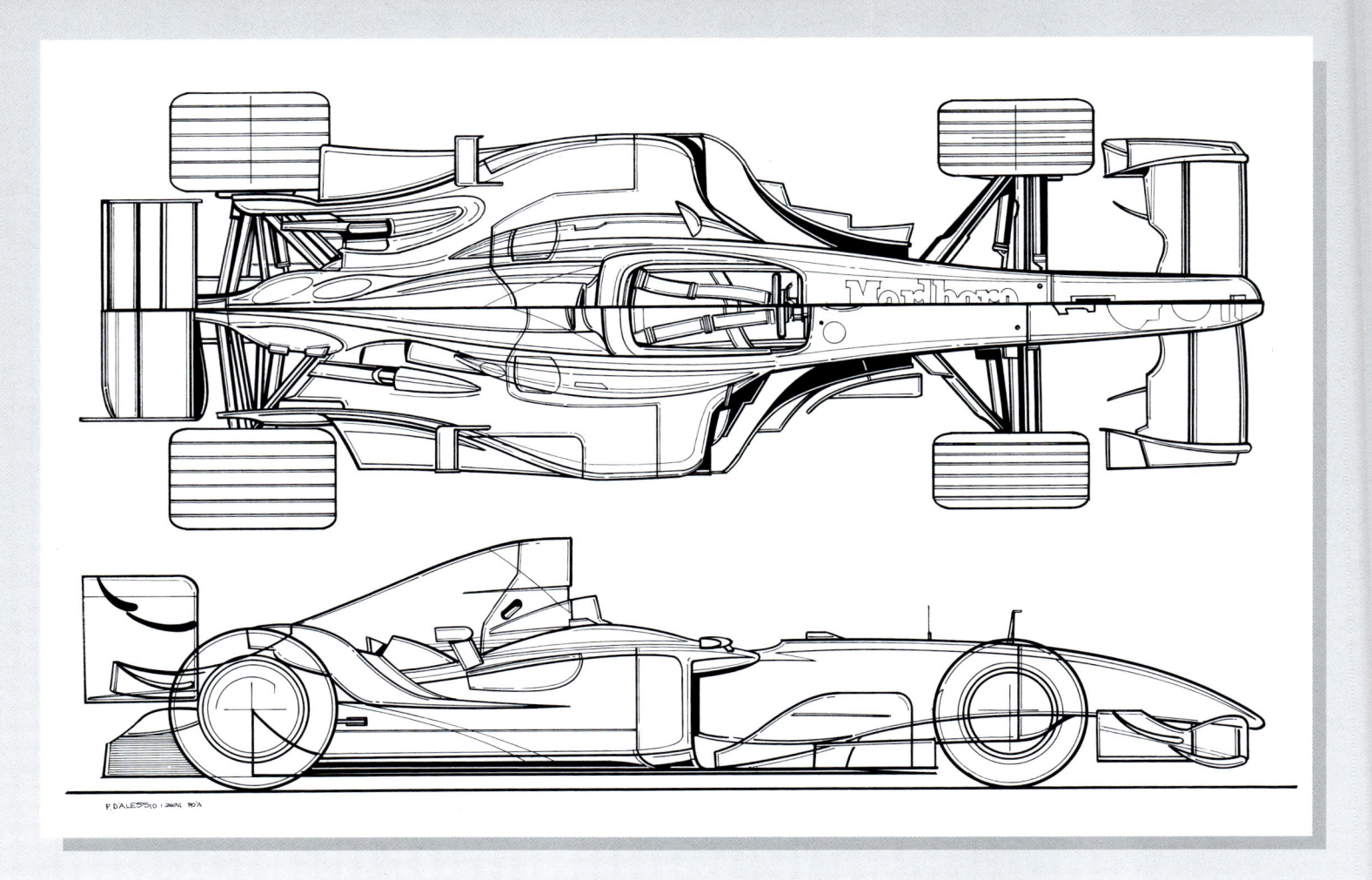

The comparison from the side and above view of last year's F2003 GA and the F2004 clearly shows the similarity between the two versions. The 2004 car differs in the shape of the nose, which is lower and more curved; in the front wing, which has a marked external curved profile, and in the shape of the barge-boards. The shape of the sides, the aerodynamic devices in the centre of the sidepods and the rear wing, with two flaps as per the 2004 regulations, were also different.

The sides of the F2004 are characterised by having a pronounced dip in their lower part and by the presence of a smaller duct. Another characteristic of the F2004 is the rear tapering, which was taken to record levels thanks also to the miniaturization of the new transmission.

DESIGN: P. D'ALESSIO

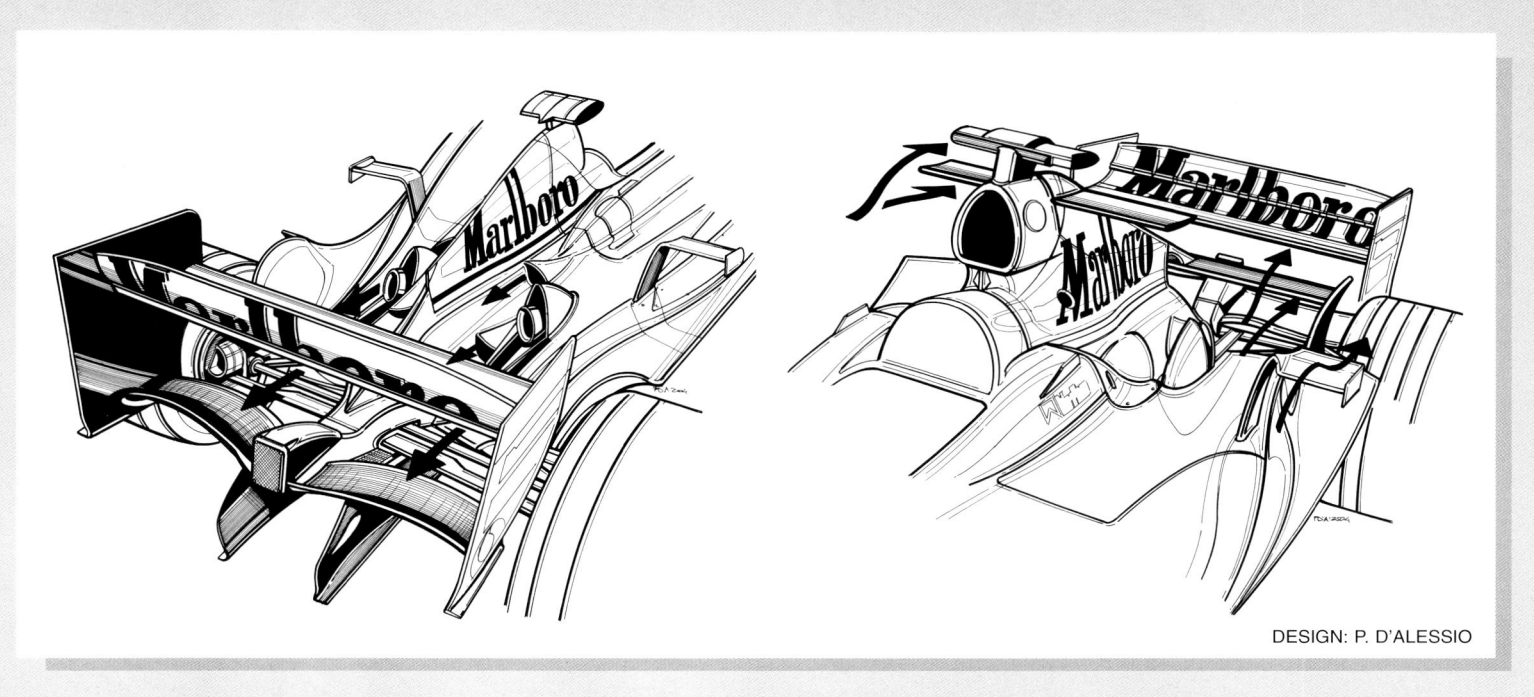

The aerodynamic devices on modern-day Formula 1 cars are there for two purposes: to generate downforce and to turn the car, on which open wheels offer considerable resistance to air flow, into a sort of prototype. The front wing, with its deflectors, and the rear flaps are used to 'protect' the tyres and create a sort of 'air bodywork'. To improve the flow of air along the sides and radiator cooling, a lot of work needs to be done on sidepod design. The F2004's were characterised by a pronounced indentation in the lower part and the presence of a smaller intake. Again to improve downforce, engineers on the F2004 exasperated the design of the winglets, mounted half-way up the sides, and added two small spoilers on the side of the engine air intake.

In the last few years Ferrari has led the way in Formula 1, but it has sometimes copied solutions introduced by its rivals. The small winglets on the side of the engine air intakes are influenced by the 2001 Jordan while the lateral 'chimneys', which evacuate the hot air upstream from the aerodynamic devices on the sides, were copied from Renault.

The F2004 has a different front wing from last year. The shape is different, more twisted and raised at both ends, and it has different side plates. Changes have also been made to the engine air intake and the rear wing, which has a more indented shape.

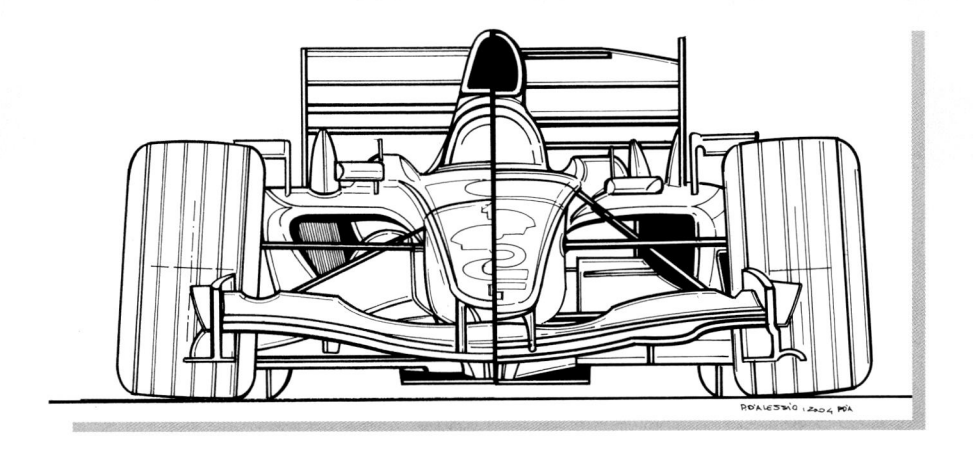

BAR HONDA 006

Unlike the other Formula 1 front-runners, the BAR 006 does not use the conventional lateral 'chimney' exhausts for getting rid of hot air from the engine bay, but instead it is evacuated through a series of slots at the base of the side deflectors. Below, the bodywork for slow tracks, where a high amount of downforce is required.

David Richards and BAR had a great year and those who thought that their pre-season testing had been a bluff had to mince their words. Behind Ferrari, BAR was the real surprise of the season: all credit must go to engine suppliers Honda, who over the winter made major improvements to the Japanese V10 engine, but also and above all to Geoff Willis, the former Williams designer, who moved to BAR a couple of years ago.

Fully in line with the British way of thinking, the pragmatic Willis did not waste time in pointlessly revolutionising the car, like his colleagues in McLaren and Williams. On the contrary, he preferred to work on the 'package' inherited from his predecessors by exasperating its development. Special attention was given to aerodynamics, a sector in which BAR introduced several interesting innovations to the design of the sides and lateral deflectors. The exuberant Willis went even further in the use of composite materials, exploiting their deformability, to offer less resistance. As always in these cases, the opposition protested and the Federation demanded an explanation, but in the end nothing happened because in Formula 1 'the innocents are always the ones who throw the first stones'. The FIA instead soon put a stop to the idea of a revolutionary rear wing, which was never used in testing by BAR but which the usual 'insiders' described as a twin rear wing profile capable of considerably increasing downforce.

Something else that the opposition never got a look at was BAR's innovative transmission, which was entirely made of composite materials. The gearbox and its stiffness together with the new RA0004E Honda power-unit were the main reasons behind the car's brilliant performances and they turned the BAR-Honda combination into not only the revelation of 2004 but also possibly the most feared rival for Ferrari in the future. Once the reliability problems of the Japanese engine have been sorted out, and the car's handling on certain tracks has been improved, David Richards's squad aims to be a title contender, even more so than a down-on-power Renault or Williams and McLaren, two teams that need a real shake-up.

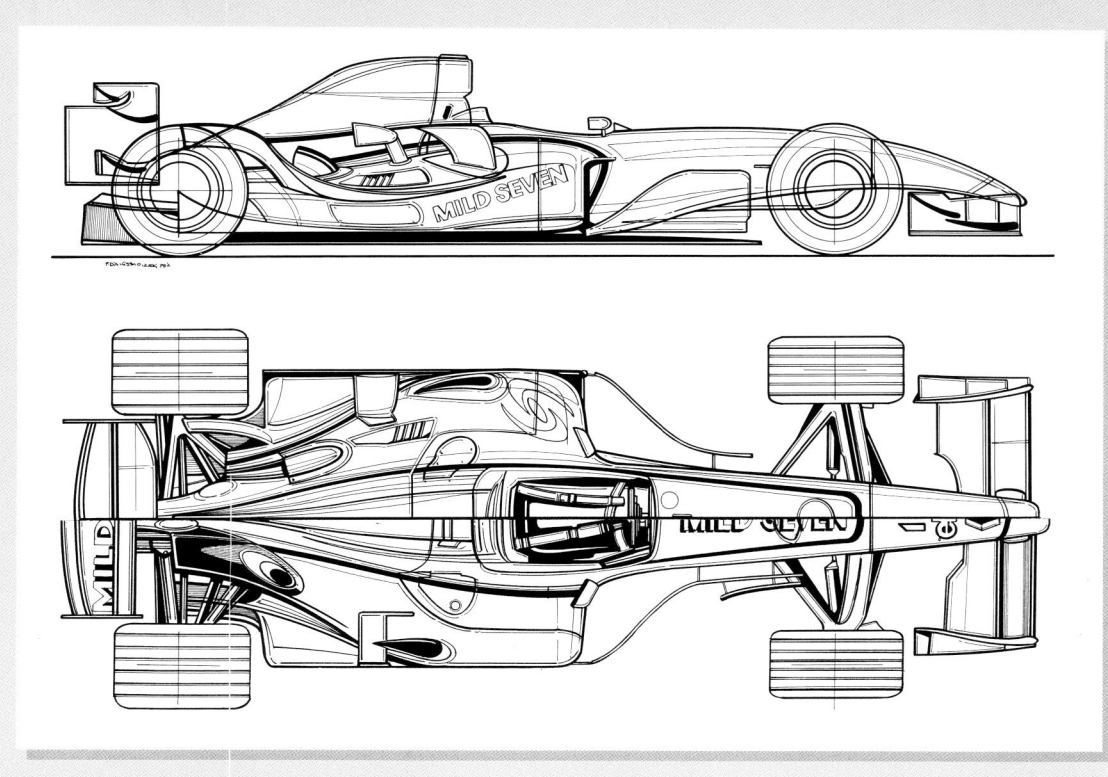

As can be seen in the side view of the R24 and the comparison from above between the 2004 car and the R23, this year's Renault went on a drastic diet to reduce the size of the sides and improve air flow towards the rear, where the tapering was extremely pronounced.

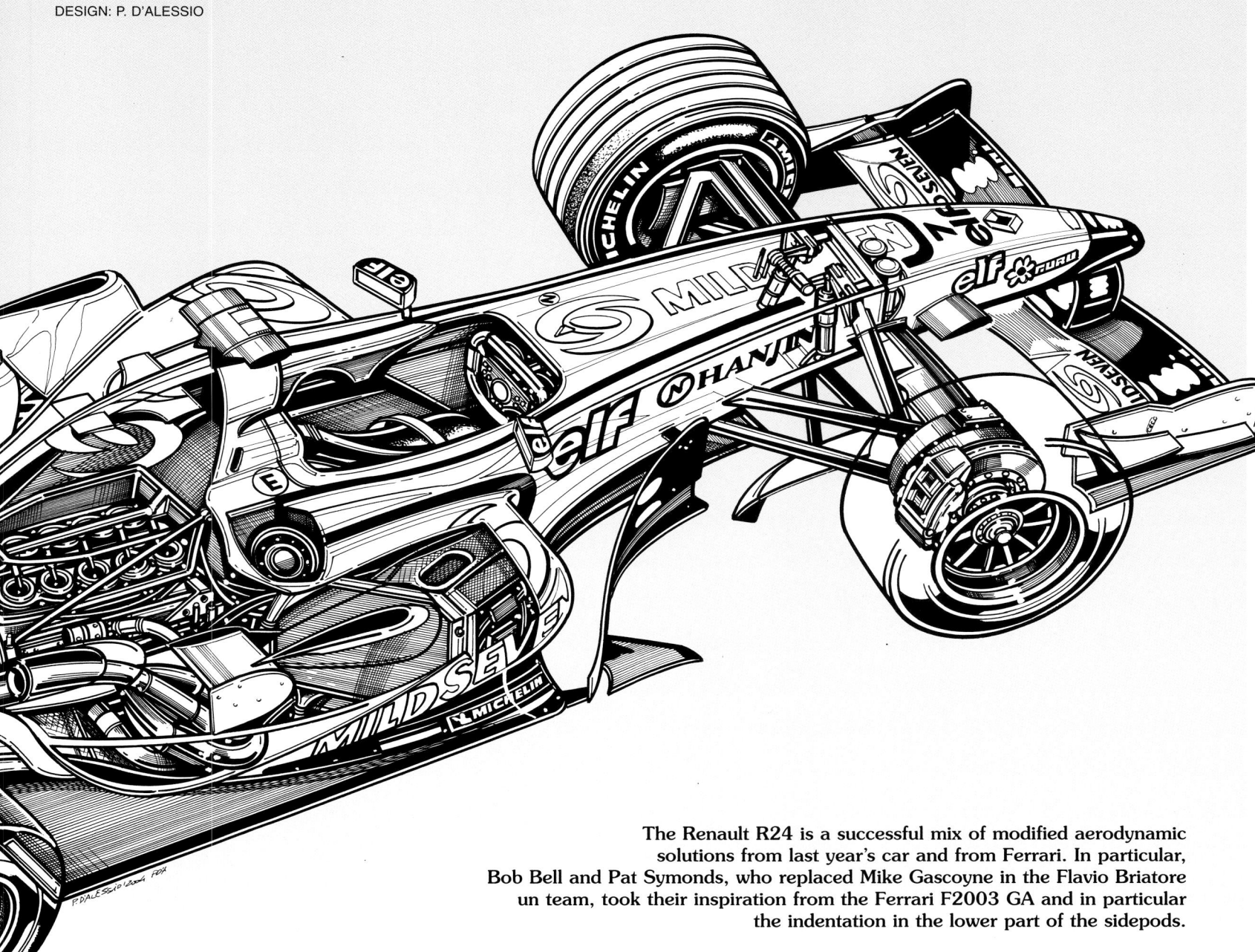

DESIGN: P. D'ALESSIO

The Renault R24 is a successful mix of modified aerodynamic solutions from last year's car and from Ferrari. In particular, Bob Bell and Pat Symonds, who replaced Mike Gascoyne in the Flavio Briatore un team, took their inspiration from the Ferrari F2003 GA and in particular the indentation in the lower part of the sidepods.

123

McLAREN MERCEDES MP4-19

McLaren seemed to be like Ferrari in its worst years. Ron Dennis's team had to build three different cars in twelve months in a desperate attempt to remain on the same competitive level as the other top teams. After the failure of the MP4/18, the Anglo-German team introduced the MP4/19 (above), and then switched to the MP4/19B (alongside and in cross-section below), which won in Belgium.

DESIGN: P. D'ALESSIO

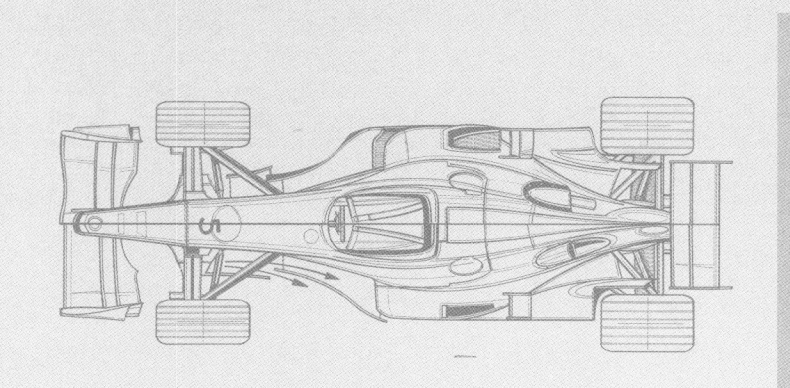

Ron Dennis's team had started the season as one of the favourites, convinced that it could oust its Italian rivals from the top, but the start of the season was embarrassing on the performance and reliability front to say the least, and a third car in the space of twelve months had to hurriedly be prepared to restore the smiles to the faces of Silver Arrows team members. Early pointers to a disastrous start to the season had emerged back in the summer of 2003 after the Monaco GP, when in top secret McLaren debuted the MP4/18. It might have been one of the best-looking cars around but it suffered from chronic unreliability. The MP4/18 was quick over one lap, but was totally unreliable and gave up the ghost after just a few laps. As if that wasn't enough, moving the exhausts to the base of the rear diffuser made the car undriveable coming out of corners. Last but not least, the small matter of the crash-test: the car never managed to pass the test and after several attempts was turned into a 'hack' car, to be used for the development of the 2004 version. To shore up the disastrous image created by the failure of the MP4/18 project (which cost McLaren and Mercedes approximately 50 million Euro) and prove to the entire world that it was just an uncharacteristic 'blip' on the radar, McLaren and Mercedes decided to transform the unsuccessful MP4/18 into the MP4/19. The similarity between the two cars was remarkable, but team bosses spoke about it as being a completely new car, one that was capable of aiming for the world title. However neither did this machine deliver the goods. The new car was thrown into the fray at the first tests last December and immediately set records, but as the months went by the first doubts about the potential of the new car and its reliability began to emerge. On the eve of the Melbourne race Kimi Raikkonen, not normally a man of many words, even declared that he doubted whether he could finish the race and score some points. And so it proved …

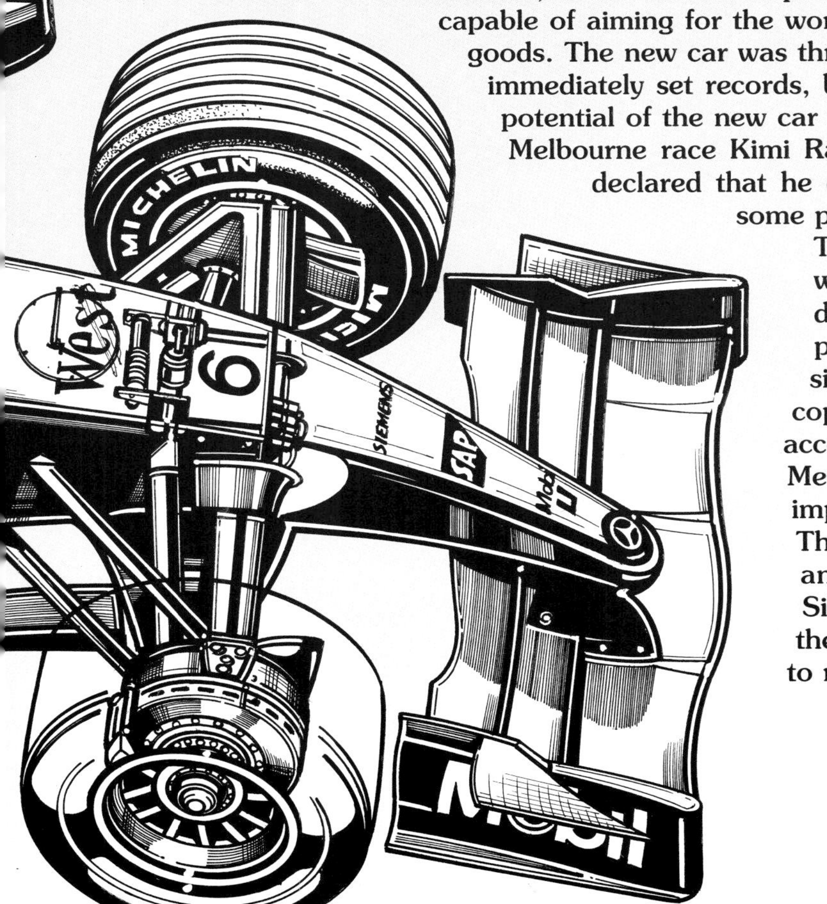

The situation remained the same until the French GP, when the Adrian Newey-revised MP4/19B made its debut. The car maintained the nose shape of the previous model, but it was radically new from the sidepods onwards. Just to be on the safe side Newey copied the lower indented sidepods of Ferrari and accentuated the rear tapering, while his colleagues at Mercedes lowered the V10 engine by a few millimetres to improve lubrication and resolve the reliability problems. The result was that the McLaren was competitive again and after Raikkonen's brilliant second place at Silverstone, in Belgium the Finn took McLaren back to the winners' circle. But there was still a long way to go to rival Ferrari…

WILLIAMS BMW FW 26

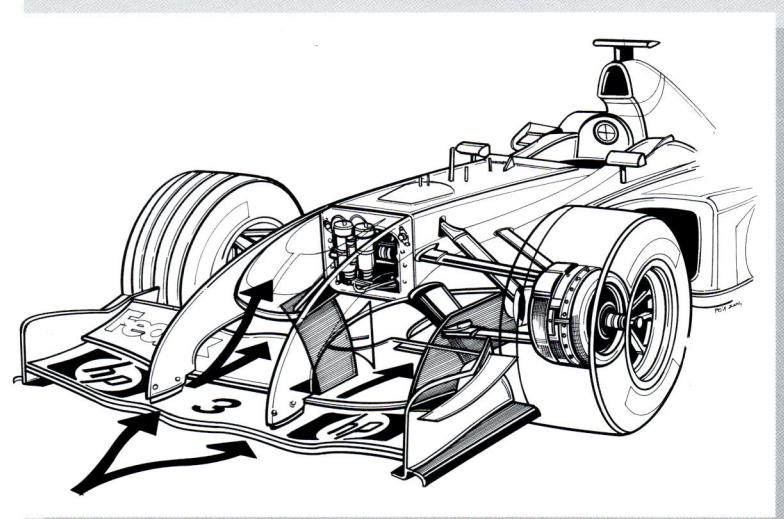

The Williams-BMW FW26 was possibly the biggest disappointment of the 2004 season. After excellent performances last year (at the season mid-point, thanks to Michelin radials, the Anglo-German team had overtaken Ferrari), Williams, together with McLaren, was considered to be the number 1 favourites for the title. Their credentials were boosted even more after the international media presentation of the FW26, with its 'walrus' nose. The most innovative car on the grid, extremely ungraceful but very aggressive, appeared to have all the charisma and technical characteristics required to break Ferrari's stranglehold on F1. Instead the first glimpse of the Williams in action in Australia, at the opening round of the season, soon revealed that the FW26 project was full of holes. The car appeared to reach a 'cut-off' point, beyond which it was incapable of being competitive. Relatively slow on the straight, unstable in curves, where the 'walrus' nose design caused mishandling problems, the FW26 was proof that wind tunnel results do not always produce a competitive machine. This was a similar situation to that of Ferrari in 1992 with the twin-bottomed F92A, when they were convinced they had discovered a new construction technique but instead found themselves with one of the worst cars in their history. But back to the unsuccessful FW26; as always on these occasions, faced with the possibility of poor results and Ferrari domination, the accusations started to fly between the German engine designers, who were convinced they had produced another superb engine, and the chassis designers for the

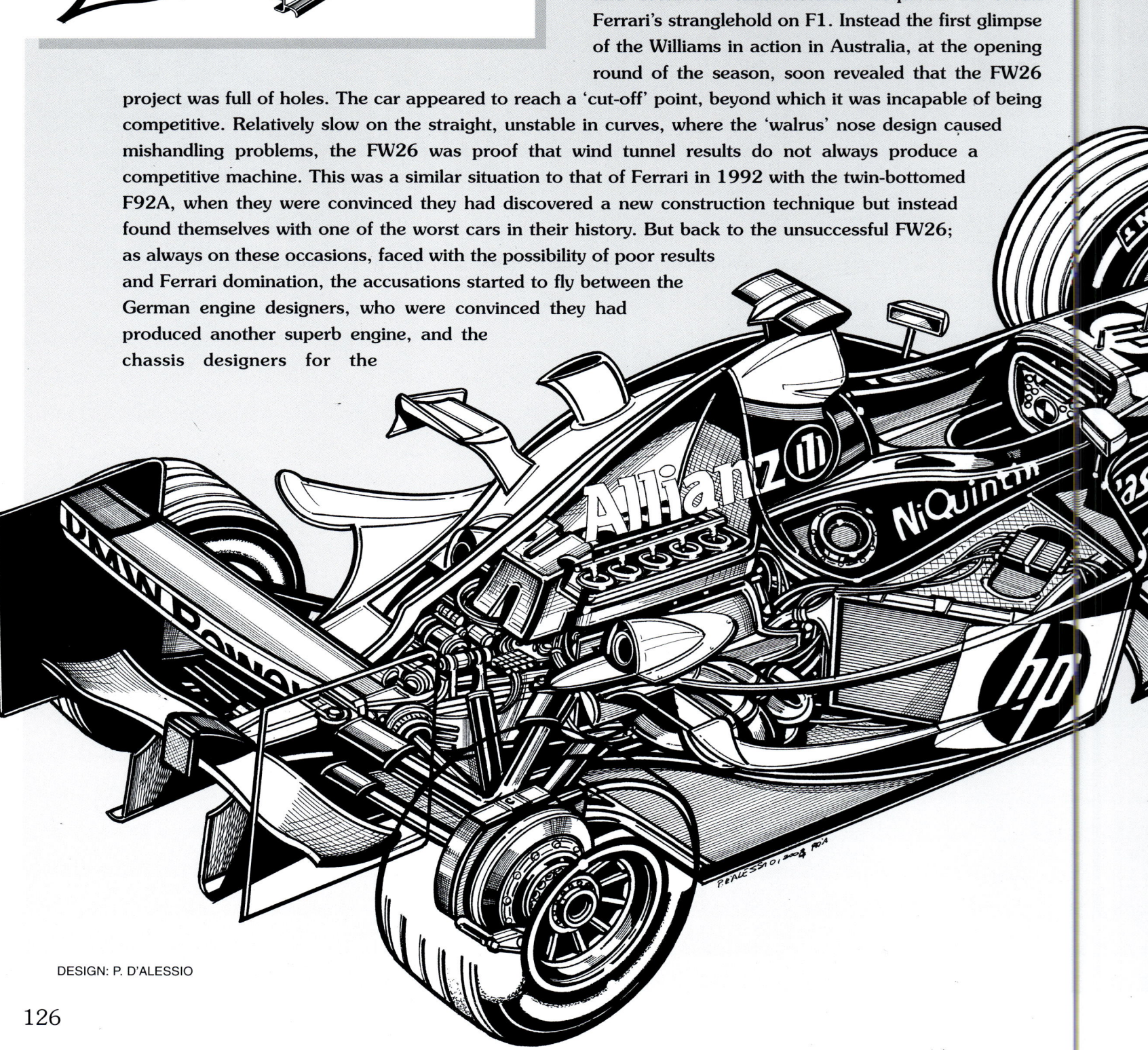

DESIGN: P. D'ALESSIO

Apart from its 'walrus' nose design, under the skin the FW26 was a conventional F1 car. The area between the sidepods and the rear was just an evolution of the FW25 model from last year, with a few minor changes here and there. From the Hungarian GP onwards the 'walrus' nose (left) was repudiated and the car returned to a more conventional front-end design (below).

British team. The main culprit was thought to be the 'walrus' nose profile, but Williams engineers also realised that the FW26 was one of the most conventional cars on the grid. All the space between the sidepod mounting point and the rear tapering had not undergone any changes over last year's design, while teams such as Ferrari, BAR and Renault had been much more adventurous in their aerodynamic development. In short, the FW26 was too conservative a car to aim for the title. The person who paid the price for this was Patrick Head, Frank Williams's partner and team technical director since time immemorial, who was replaced by Sam Michael half-way through the season. A new 'B' version of the FW26 was readied in no time at all and it made its debut in the French GP. The car appeared to be an improvement, but things changed when it came to the race. Excessive tyre wear and unpredictable front-end handling soon put a halt to the title ambitions of the Williams drivers, while BMW top brass admitted openly that the Ferraris were on another plant......

The final chapter of the Williams story in 2004 came in Hungary, when the 'walrus' was repudiated and replaced with a nose that was similar, if not identical, to that of last year. The situation failed to change much however and, even though Montoya declared that the car's handling had improved, the gap to Ferrari, Bar, Renault and McLaren was too wide to hope for an immediate resurrection ...

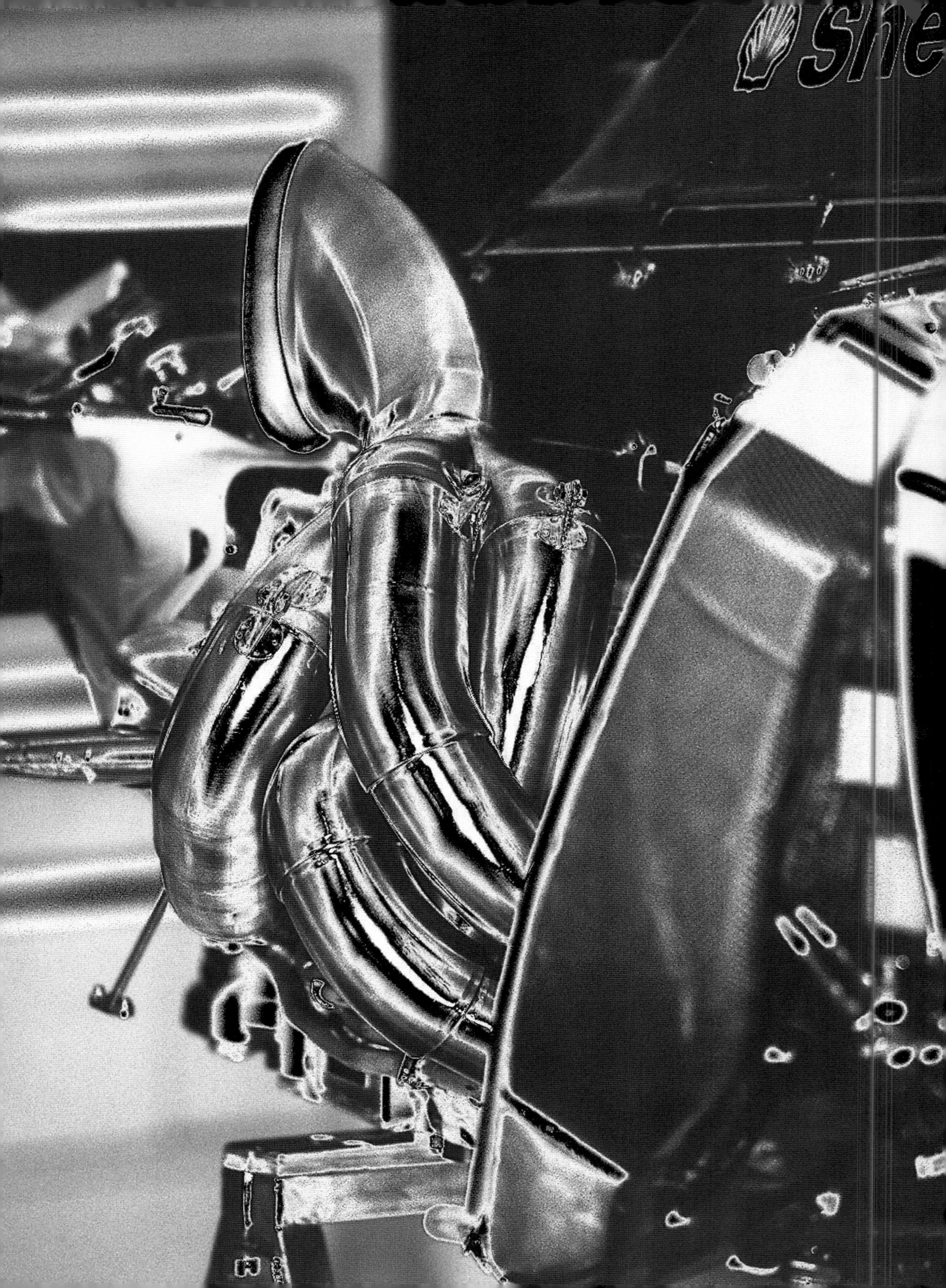

PHOTOCOLOR: P. D'ALESSIO

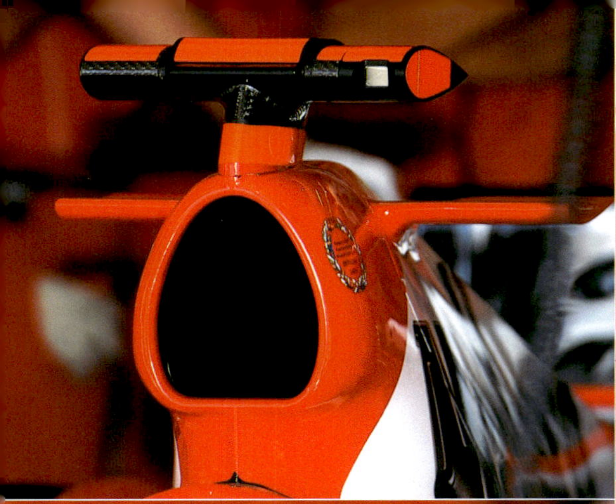

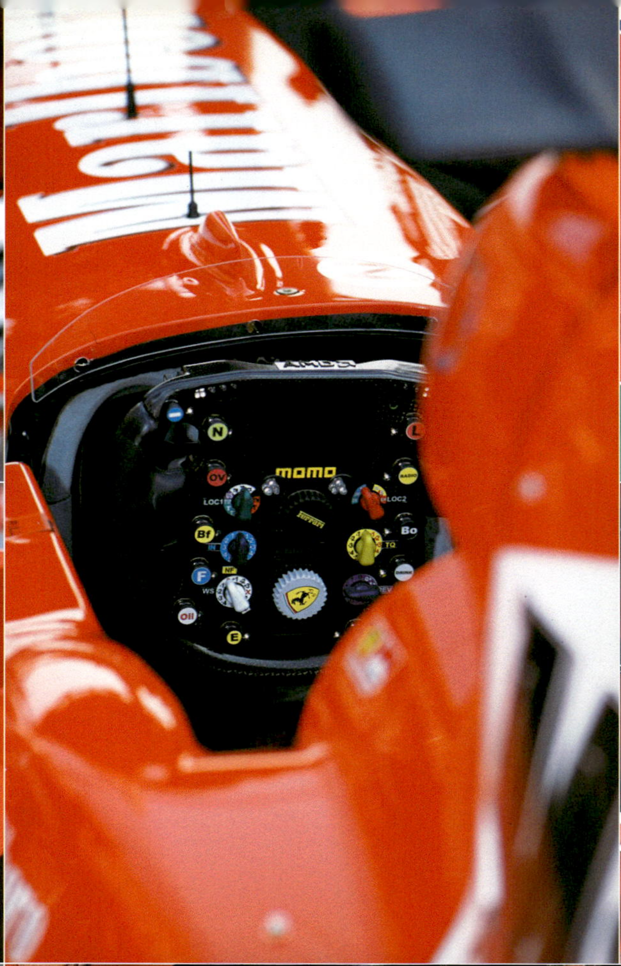
momo

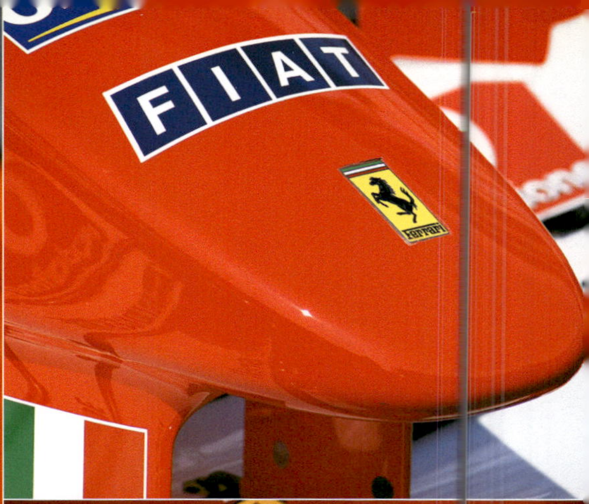
FIAT

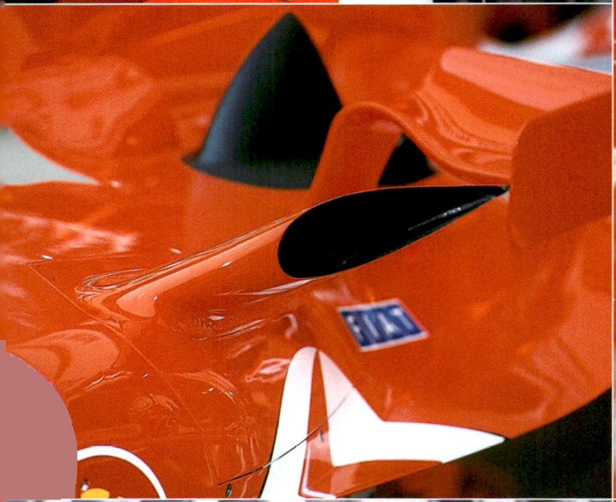

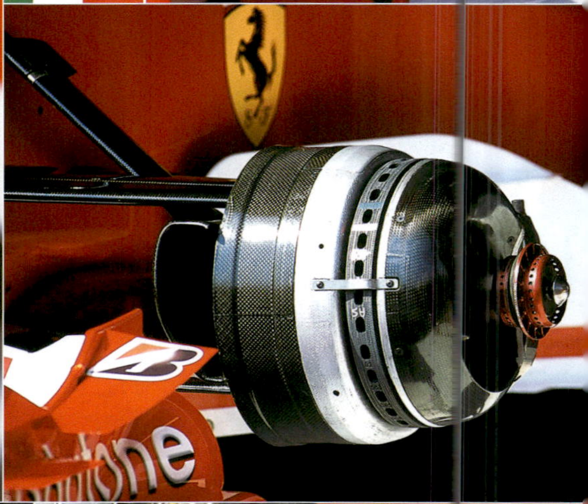

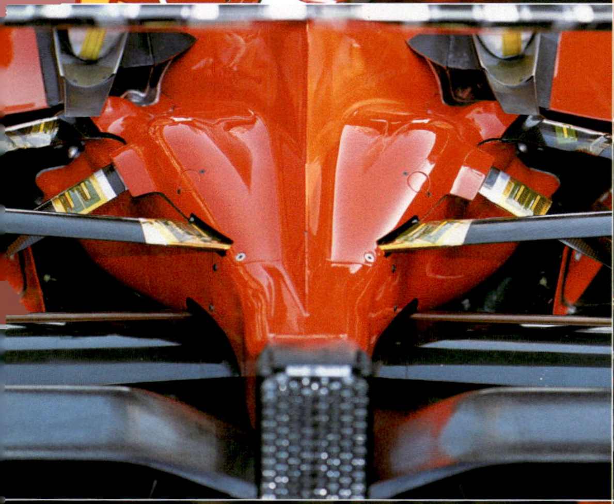

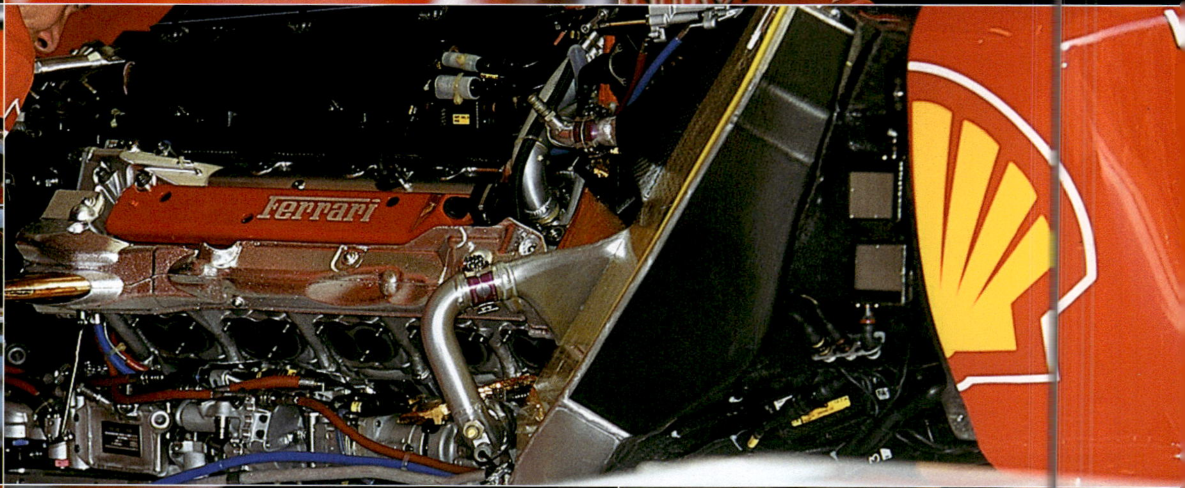
Ferrari

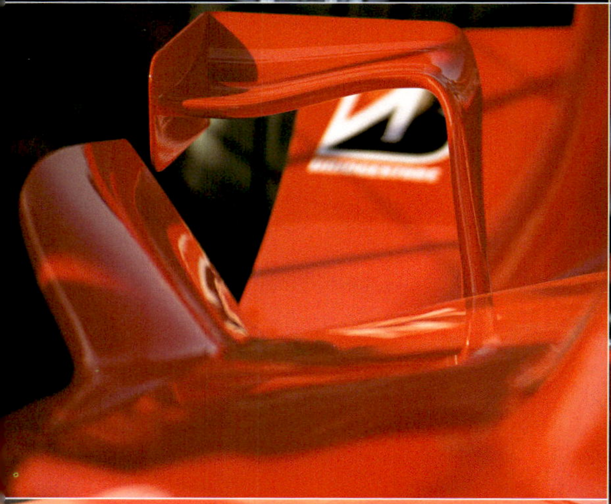

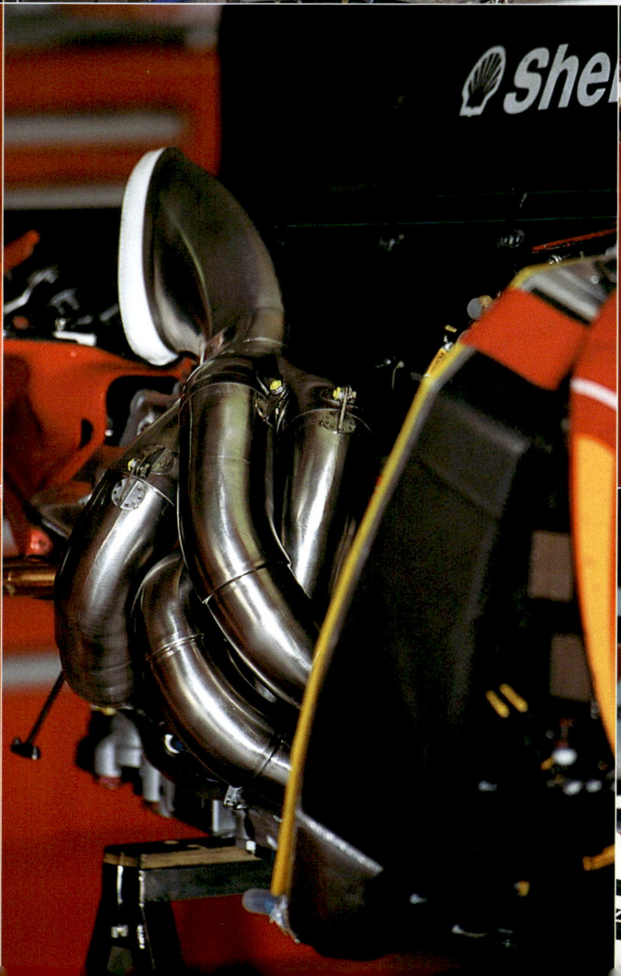

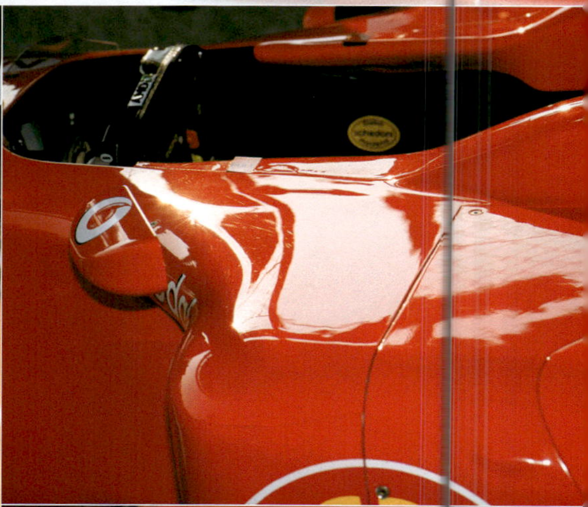

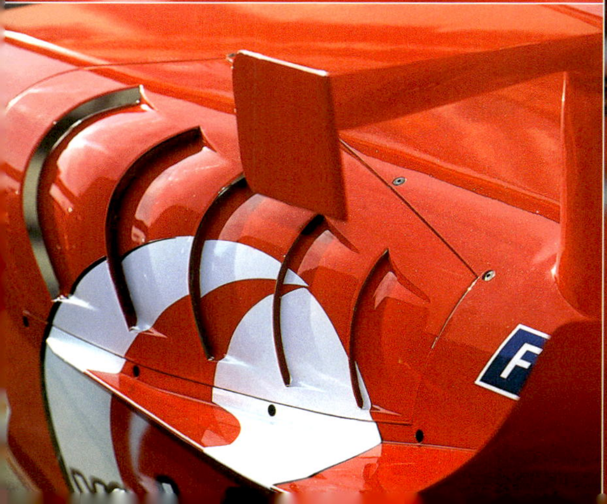

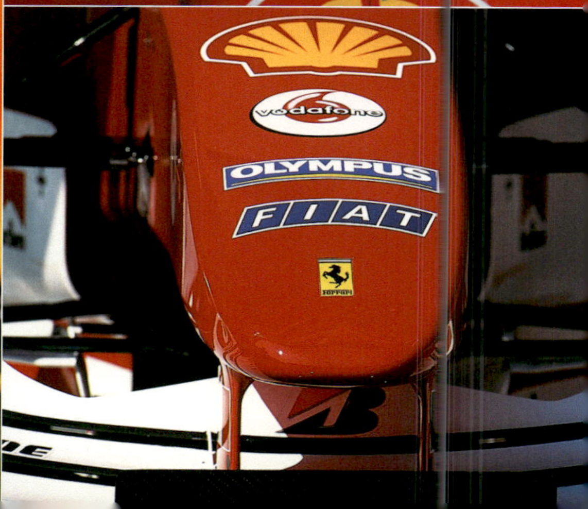
OLYMPUS
FIAT

PHOTOCOLORS: P. D'ALESSIO

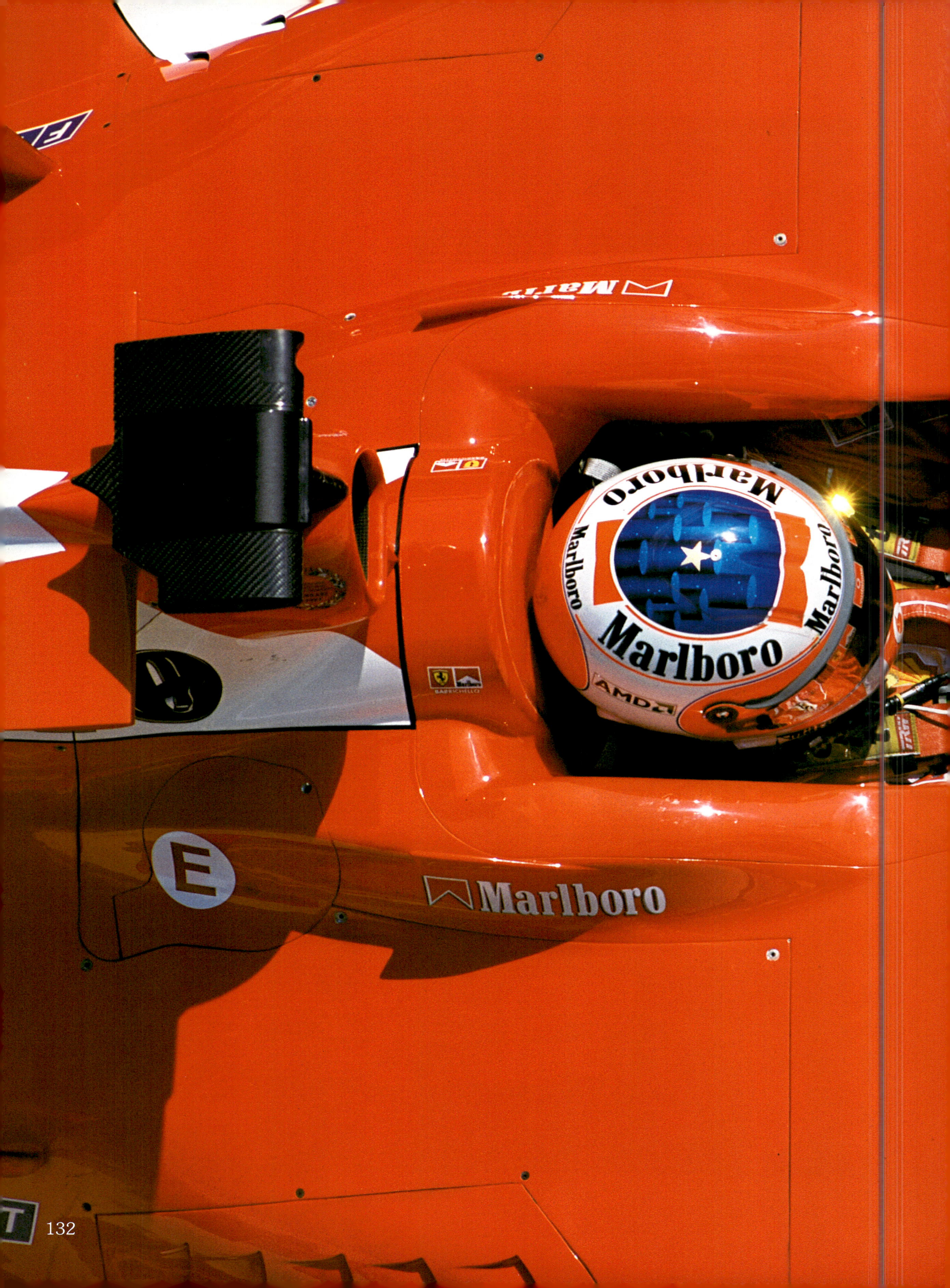
Marlboro
Marlboro
AMD

PHOTOCOLOR: P. D'ALESSIO

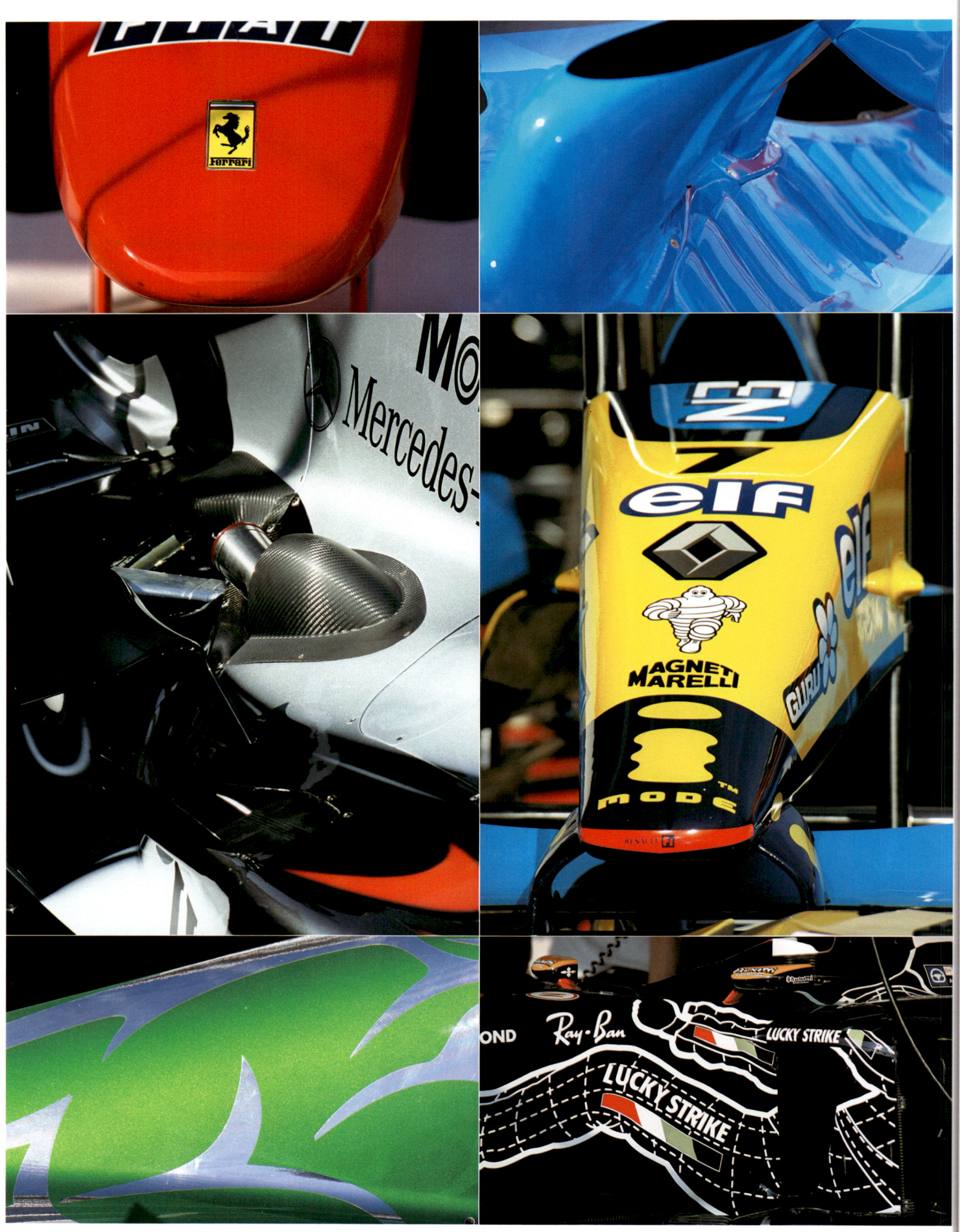

PHOTOCOLORS: P. D'ALESSIO

135

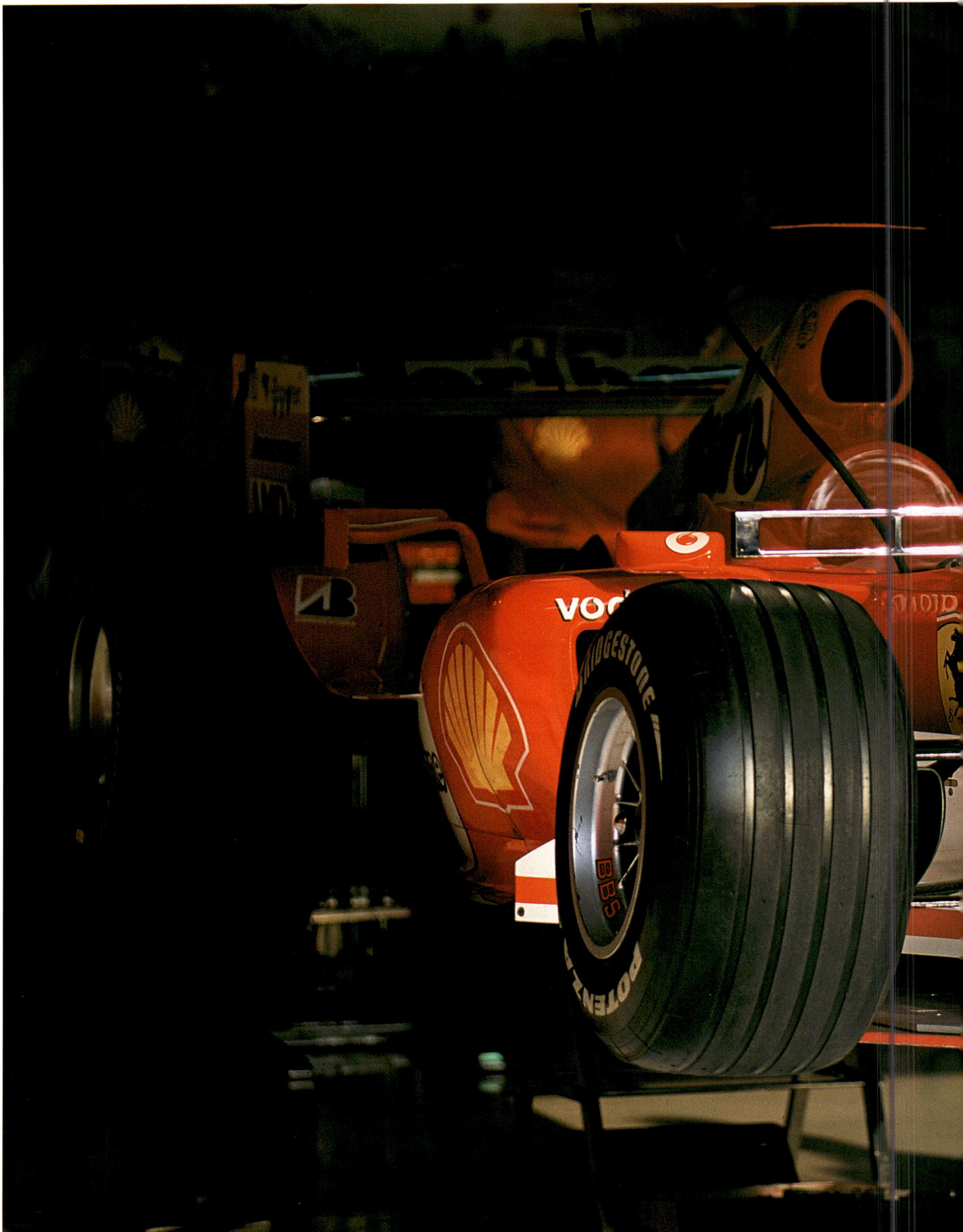

PHOTOCOLOR: P. D'ALESSIO

PHOTOCOLORS - P. D'ALESSIO

avex
group

FUTURE OF INVESTING
www.superfund.com
COSWORTH

RENAULT

RENAULT
MICHELIN
TM
MODE
3511538

PHOTOCOLORS: P. D'ALESSIO

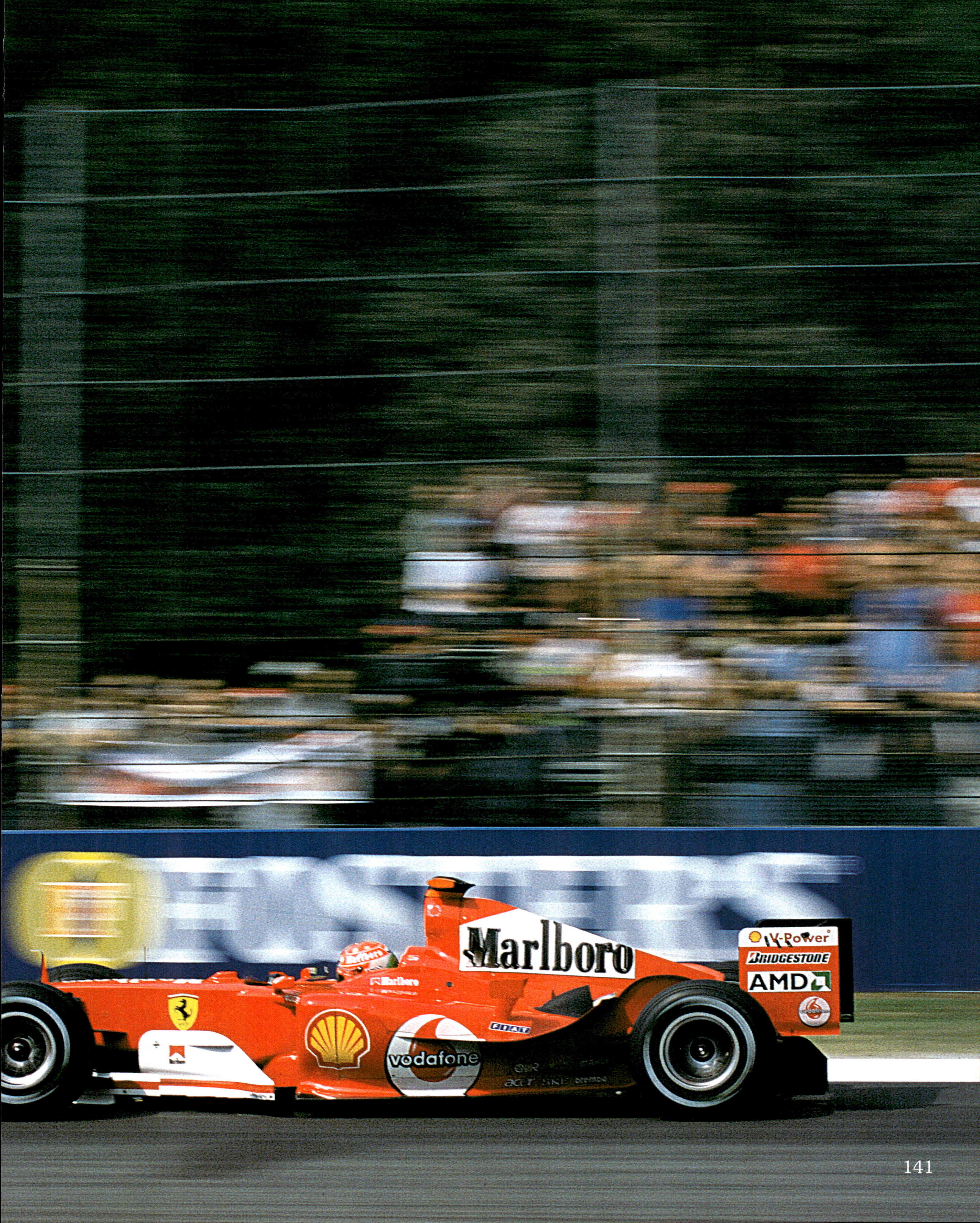
Marlboro
V-Power
BRIDGESTONE
AMD
vodafone
FIAT

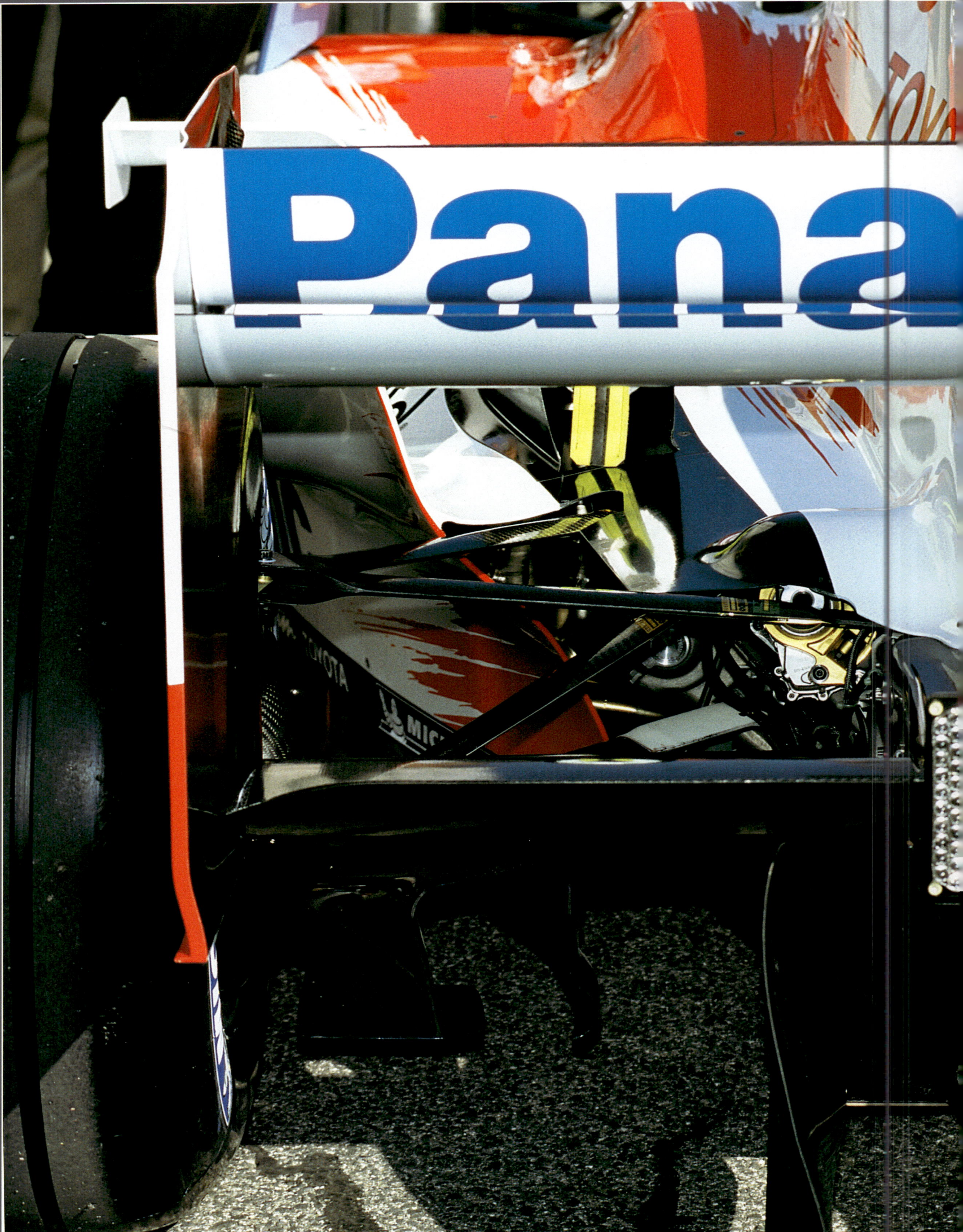
Pana
TOYOTA

PHOTOCOLOR: P. D'ALESSIO

PHOTOCOLORS: P. D'ALESSIO

FORMULA 1 FOOTBALLERS FOR CHARITY

Michael Schumacher has been the captain of an All-Star drivers' team on football grounds throughout Europe for the last few years in aid of charity. It is thanks to the German, as well as to Riccardo Patrese (the Italian F1 driver of the 1980s who holds the record for the highest number of GP starts - 256), to their friend Mario Di Natale, and to their passion that the Footballers' national side manages to attract some of the great names of motorsport to within its ranks.

In 2004 alone, Fernando Alonso, Giancarlo Fisichella, Felipe Massa, Jarno Trulli, Giorgio Pantano, Gianmaria Bruni, but also Max Biaggi, Andrea Dovizioso and Fabrizio Lai played a dozen or so matches, not only in Italy but also in Belgium and Monte Carlo.

The national side also includes Matteo Montezemolo, the son of the president of Ferrari and a keen participant in the matches. At Imola, on the Wednesday before the San Marino GP, they played against the Brazilian World Cup winners, which included Dunga, Bebeto and Jorginho. At Monte Carlo, they went up against a Prince Albert of Monaco side, which was made up of champions from all sports: runners Cova and Panatta, skiers Ghedina and Runggaldier and Didier Dechamps from the world of football.

In September, the traditional match against the actors' national side was held before the Italian GP at Monza and was repeated at Spa-Francorchamps, in Rome, Naples and Padova. It is a real tour de force for the drivers, but all of them are keen footballers and they know that every year their efforts help to accumulate hundreds of thousands of dollars for charity.

146 - Fotografie Agenzia Liverani.

Fotografie Villa.

147

Marlboro
vodafone
BRIDGESTONE
Marlboro
vodafone
Marlboro
SKF brembo
MAHLE

149

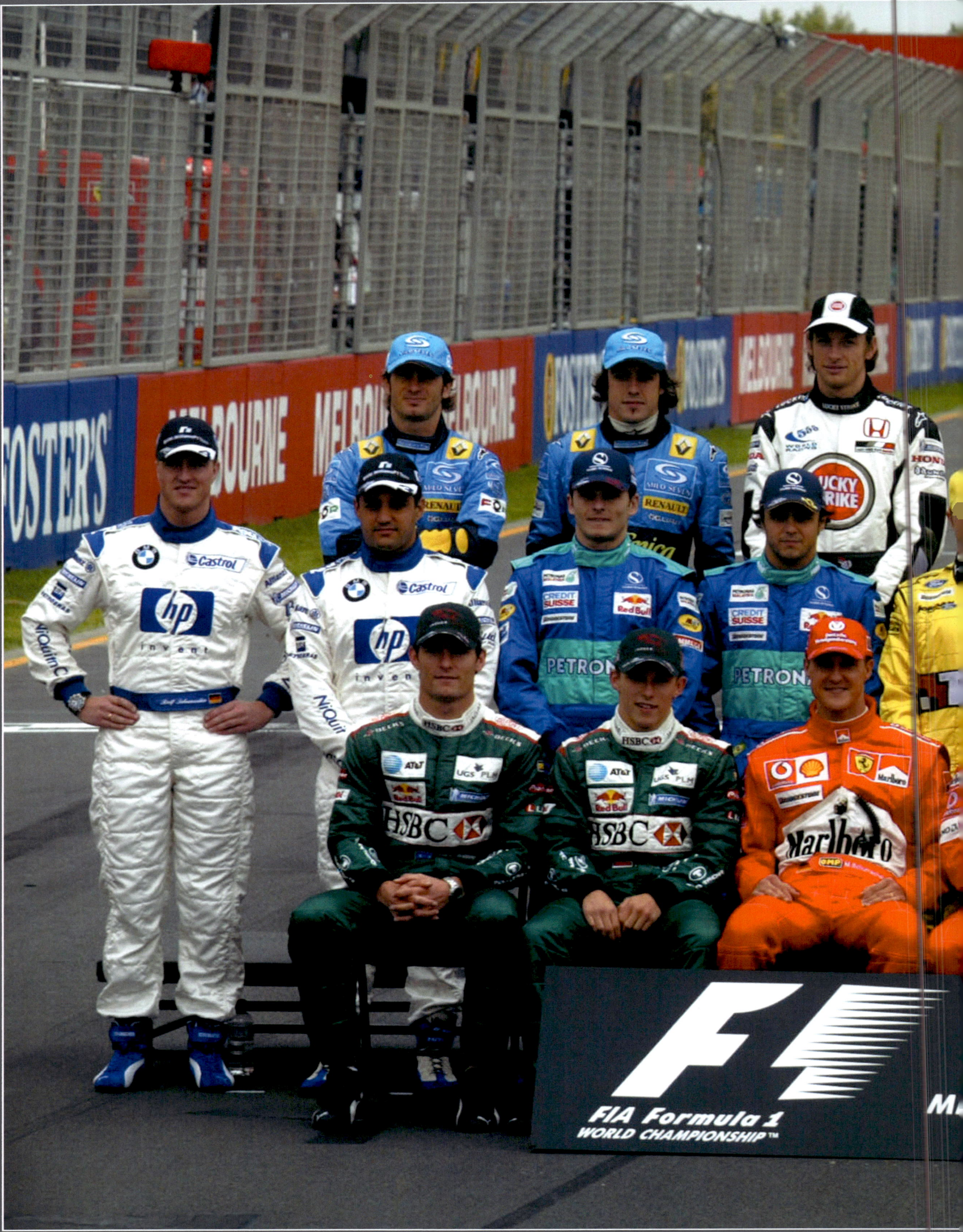
FOSTER'S
MELBOURNE
FIA Formula 1
WORLD CHAMPIONSHIP™

FOSTER'S AUSTRALIAN GRAND PRIX MELBOURNE 2004

MELBOURNE - 7 MARCH 2004

POLE POSITION

- '90 A. Senna
- '91 A. Senna
- '92 N. Mansell
- '93 A. Senna
- '94 N. Mansell
- '95 D. Hill
- '96 J. Villeneuve
- '97 J. Villeneuve
- '98 M. Hakkinen
- '99 M. Hakkinen
- '00 M. Hakkinen
- '01 M.Schumacher
- '02 R.Barrichello
- '03 M.Schumacher

2004 MICHAEL SCHUMACHER

STARTING GRID

1 
- Michael Schumacher — Ferrari — 1'24"408
- Rubens Barrichello — Ferrari — 1'24"482 

2 
- Juan-Pablo Montoya — Williams — 1'24"998
- Jenson Button — BAR — 1'24"998 

3 
- Fernando Alonso — Renault — 1'25"699
- Mark Webber — Jaguar — 1'25"805 

4 
- Takuma Sato — BAR — 1'25"851
- Ralf Schumacher — Williams — 1'25"925 

5 
- Jarno Trulli — Renault — 1'26"290
- Kimi Raikkonen — McLaren — 1'26"297 

6 
- Felipe Massa — Sauber — 1'27"065
- David Coulthard — McLaren — 1'27"294 

7 
- Cristiano Da Matta — Toyota — 1'27"823
- Giancarlo Fisichella — Sauber — 1'27"845 

8 
- Nick Heidfeld — Jordan — 1'28"178
- Giorgio Pantano — Jordan — 1'30"140 

9 
- Zsolt Baumgartner — Minardi — 1'30"681
- Olivier Panis — Toyota — No Time 

10 
- Christian Klien — Jaguar — No Time
- Gianmaria Bruni — Minardi — No Time 

FOSTER'S AUSTRALIAN GRAND PRIX MELBOURNE 2004

	1°	2°	3°
'90	N. Piquet	N. Mansell	A. Prost
'91	A. Senna	N. Mansell	G. Berger
'92	G. Berger	M. Schumacher	M. Brundle
'93	A. Senna	A. Prost	D. Hill
'94	N. Mansell	G. Berger	M. Brundle
'95	D. Hill	O. Panis	G. Morbidelli
'96	D. Hill	J. Villeneuve	E. Irvine
'97	D. Coulthard	M. Schumacher	M. Hakkinen
'98	M. Hakkinen	D. Coulthard	H.H. Frentzen
'99	E. Irvine	H.H. Frentzen	R. Schumacher
'00	M. Schumacher	R. Barrichello	R. Schumacher
'01	M. Schumacher	D. Coulthard	R. Barrichello
'02	M.Schumacher	J.P. Montoya	K. Raikkonen
'03	D. Coulthard	J.P. Montoya	K. Raikkonen

RESULTS

	DRIVER	CAR	KPH	GAP
1	M. Schumacher	Ferrari	219,010	-
2	R. Barrichello	Ferrari	218,423	13"605
3	F. Alonso	Renault	217,519	34"673
4	R. Schumacher	Williams	216,424	1'00"423
5	J.P. Montoya	Williams	216,081	1'08"536
6	J. Button	BAR	215,994	1'10"598
7	J. Trulli	Renault	215,191	1 lap
8	D. Coulthard	McLaren	215,004	1 lap
9	T. Sato	BAR	213,998	1 lap
10	G. Fisichella	Sauber	212,448	1 lap
11	C. Klien	Jaguar	210,693	2 laps
12	C. Da Matta	Toyota	210,376	2 laps
13	O. Panis	Toyota	208,686	2 laps
14	G. Pantano	Jordan	207,645	3 laps

RETIREMENTS

F. Massa	Sauber	44	Engine
N. Heidfeld	Jordan	43	Clutch
G. Bruni	Minardi	43	not qualified
M. Webber	Jaguar	29	Gearbox
Z. Baumgartner	Minardi	13	Engine
K. Raikkonen	McLaren	9	Engine

THE RACE

DRIVER	CAR	LAP	FASTEST LAP	TOP SPEED
M. Schumacher	Ferrari	29	1'24"125	323,4
R. Barrichello	Ferrari	8	1'24"179	323,9
F. Alonso	Renault	10	1'25"088	312,3
J.P. Montoya	Williams	42	1'25"286	320,1
R. Schumacher	Williams	11	1'25"824	321,8
M. Webber	Jaguar	15	1'25"952	319,9
J. Button	BAR	24	1'25"982	319,3
T. Sato	BAR	43	1'26"077	318,8
J. Trulli	Renault	9	1'26"275	311,6
G. Fisichella	Sauber	39	1'26"282	323,0
D. Coulthard	McLaren	13	1'26"328	318,2
F. Massa	Sauber	11	1'26"846	323,9
N. Heidfeld	Jordan	27	1'27"503	311,5
O. Panis	Toyota	35	1'27"807	313,1
C. Da Matta	Toyota	41	1'27"820	315,4
C. Klien	Jaguar	6	1'27"840	318,9
K. Raikkonen	McLaren	7	1'27"936	318,7
G. Pantano	Jordan	15	1'28"523	310,4
G. Bruni	Minardi	10	1'30"161	311,2
Z. Baumgartner	Minardi	8	1'30"621	312,4

AUSTRALIAN GP

FERRARI KICKS OFF THE 2004 SEASON WITH ANOTHER 1-2

Ferrari kicked off the season in grand style with the quickest times in qualifying and a 1-2 finish for Schumacher and Barrichello at the chequered flag. The opposition could be forgiven for feeling despondent, with Ferrari showing perfect reliability and potential, its two drivers on the top of their form and the team running faultlessly throughout the weekend.

Things were totally different over at McLaren. The Anglo-German cars went badly in qualifying and then in the race Raikkonen's engine gave up on lap 9 while Coulthard took the final point for eighth place after a two-stop strategy. The performance of the Williams team was slightly better but not much. Ralf Schumacher came in fourth followed by Montoya, who was penalised by three slow pit-stops, which meant he had to push harder out on the track to make up time.

Fernando Alonso finished a strong third for Renault after a lightning start when he muscled his way past Montoya at the first corner. The rest of the race saw Alonso demonstrate both his and the Renault's potential and the popular Spaniard took a well-deserved third on the podium with the two Ferrari drivers. Finally a mention for Button and his BAR. The Melbourne race confirmed that the excellent times set during winter testing were not merely for the benefit of the sponsors. The car is competitive and Jenson looks to be returning to the superb form he showed during his debut year, when he was considered to be F1's rising star. Fourth in qualifying and sixth at the flag are results that bode well for the rest of the season.

What about the 2004 rookies? Gianmaria Bruni (Minardi) managed to finish the race, albeit 15 laps down on the winner. The Italian was not classified after problems with his electronics and a never-ending pit-stop and he returned to the track solely to gain some more experience.

The young Austrian Christian Klien (Jaguar) finished in eleventh place just two laps down on the winner. Klien put in a good race considering his limited experience and lack of knowledge of the circuit.

The final place, three laps behind Schumacher, went to Giorgio Pantano. Despite the fact that an ill-fitting seat caused him much agony throughout the 57-lap race, the Italian made no mistakes in a Jordan that was only completed in a last minute rush.

MELBOURNE
Length: **5,303 km**
Laps: **58** - Distance: **307,574 kms**

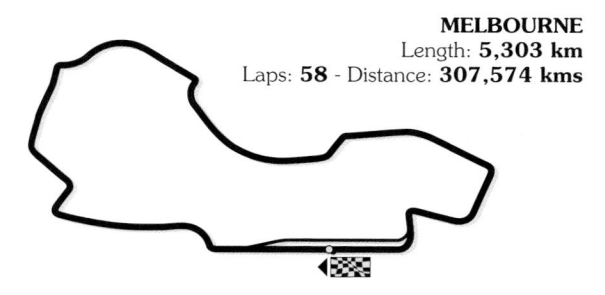

The first Australian GP dates back to 1928 but it was only in 1985 that the event officially became one of the rounds of the Formula 1 World Championship; first Adelaide, then Melbourne, the venue for the current race which uses the normal roads surrounding the lake in Albert Park.

HIGHLIGHTS

BAR brought both of its cars to the chequered flag, Button finishing sixth and Sato ninth despite technical problems in the final part of the race. This was an important result for David Richards, who is having to deal with a difficult situation within the team because of the departure of Villeneuve, the drastic restructuring and a powerful but fragile Honda engine. For his part however Richards had said at the start of the season that Button stood a good chance of getting onto the podium.

PHOTO PORTFOLIO
FOLLOWING PAGES

Valentino Rossi was present in the Melbourne pits to watch Ferrari's triumph. The MotoGP star spoke to Schumacher and then to Bernie Ecclestone, who needs someone like Valentino to liven up the Formula 1 scene. Photo above, the start of the GP with Alonso (Renault), on the right, getting off the line the quickest.

CHAMPIONSHIPS POINTS	AUSTRALIAN GP	MALAYSIAN GP	BAHRAIN GP	SAN MARINO GP	SPANISH GP	MONACO GP	EUROPEAN GP	CANADIAN GP	UNITED STATES GP	FRENCH GP	BRITISH GP	GERMAN GP	HUNGARIAN GP	BELGIUM GP	ITALIAN GP	CHINA GP	JAPANESE GP	BRAZILIAN GP	TOTAL POINT
1 M. Schumacher	10																		10
2 R. Barrichello	8																		8
3 F. Alonso	6																		6
4 R. Schumacher	5																		5
5 J.P. Montoya	4																		4
6 J. Button	3																		3
7 J. Trulli	2																		2
8 D. Coulthard	1																		1
9 T. Sato	-																		-
10 G. Fisichella	-																		-
11 C. Klien	-																		-
12 C. Da Matta	-																		-
13 O. Panis	-																		-
14 G. Pantano	-																		-
15 K. Raikkonen	-																		-
16 F. Massa	-																		-
17 M. Webber	-																		-
18 N. Heidfeld	-																		-
19 G. Bruni	-																		-
20 Z. Baumgartner	-																		-

154

Melbourne

SEPANG - 21 MARCH 2004

POLE POSITION

2004 Michael Schumacher

'90 -	'97 -
'91 -	'98 -
'92 -	'99 M. Schumacher
'93 -	'00 M. Schumacher
'94 -	'01 M. Schumacher
'95 -	'02 M. Schumacher
'96 -	'03 F. Alonso

	1°	2°	3°
'90	-	-	-
'91	-	-	-
'92	-	-	-
'93	-	-	-
'94	-	-	-
'95	-	-	-
'96	-	-	-
'97	-	-	-
'98	-	-	-
'99	M. Hakkinen	M. Schumacher	E. Irvine
'00	M. Schumacher	D. Coulthard	R. Barrichello
'01	M. Schumacher	R. Barrichello	D. Coulthard
'02	R. Schumacher	J.P. Montoya	M. Schumacher
'03	K. Raikkonen	R. Barrichello	F. Alonso

STARTING GRID

1. Michael Schumacher – Ferrari – 1'33"074
Mark Webber – Jaguar – 1'33"715 

2. Rubens Barrichello – Ferrari – 1'33"756
Juan-Pablo Montoya – Williams – 1'34"054 

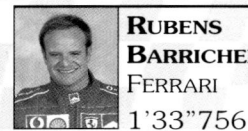

3. Kimi Raikkonen – McLaren – 1'34"164
Jenson Button – BAR – 1'34"221 

4. Ralf Schumacher – Williams – 1'34"235
Jarno Trulli – Renault – 1'34"413 

5. David Coulthard – McLaren – 1'34"602
Cristiano Da Matta – Toyota – 1'34"917 

6. Felipe Massa – Sauber – 1'35"039
Giancarlo Fisichella – Sauber – 1'35"061 

7. Christian Klien – Jaguar – 1'35"158
Olivier Panis – Toyota – 1'35"617 

8. Nick Heidfeld – Jordan – 1'36"569
Gianmaria Bruni – Minardi – 1'38"577 

9. Zsolt Baumgartner – Minardi – 1'39"272
Giorgio Pantano – Jordan – 1'39"902 

10. Fernando Alonso – Renault – No Time
Takuma Sato – BAR – No Time 

RESULTS

	DRIVER	CAR	KPH	GAP
1	M. Schumacher	Ferrari	204,384	-
2	J.P. Montoya	Williams	204,196	5"022
3	J. Button	BAR	203,952	11"568
4	R. Barrichello	Ferrari	203,876	13"616
5	J. Trulli	Renault	202,997	37"360
6	D. Coulthard	McLaren	202,418	53"098
7	F. Alonso	Renault	201,877	1'07"877
8	F. Massa	Sauber	200,013	1 lap
9	C. Da Matta	Toyota	199,780	1 lap
10	C. Klien	Jaguar	198,572	1 lap
11	G. Fisichella	Sauber	197,941	1 lap
12	O. Panis	Toyota	197,464	1 lap
13	G. Pantano	Jordan	194,395	2 laps
14	G. Bruni	Minardi	192,656	3 laps
15	Z. Baumgartner	Minardi	189,658	4 laps

RETIREMENTS

T. Sato	BAR	52	Engine
K. Raikkonen	McLaren	40	Transmission
N. Heidfeld	Jordan	34	Gearbox
R. Schumacher	Williams	27	Engine
M. Webber	Jaguar	23	Spin

THE RACE

DRIVER	CAR	LAP	FASTEST LAP	TOP SPEED
J.P. Montoya	Williams	28	1'34"223	319,1
M. Schumacher	Ferrari	6	1'34"819	315,7
J. Button	BAR	28	1'34"967	312,6
J. Trulli	Renault	12	1'35"039	309,9
K. Raikkonen	McLaren	12	1'35"156	313,4
R. Barrichello	Ferrari	7	1'35"350	317,8
R. Schumacher	Williams	10	1'35"607	320,9
T. Sato	BAR	13	1'35"679	314,3
D. Coulthard	McLaren	26	1'35"852	312,5
F. Alonso	Renault	7	1'35"888	309,7
O. Panis	Toyota	23	1'35"951	314,4
C. Da Matta	Toyota	22	1'36"544	313,7
F. Massa	Sauber	7	1'36"570	317,3
G. Fisichella	Sauber	54	1'36"675	315,4
M. Webber	Jaguar	9	1'36"922	314,5
C. Klien	Jaguar	12	1'37"031	312,2
N. Heidfeld	Jordan	15	1'37"433	309,3
G. Pantano	Jordan	41	1'39"527	308,0
G. Bruni	Minardi	11	1'39"911	307,2
Z. Baumgartner	Minardi	12	1'40"123	307,6

MALAYSIAN GP

JENSON BUTTON'S FIRST PODIUM

Several observers declared after Melbourne that Ferrari's win had been helped by the cool temperatures that favoured the Bridgestone tyres. But at Sepang, with an air/track temperature of over 35°/40°C, the result was still the same: pole position and victory for Schuey.

In qualifying Webber did a fantastic job with the Jaguar to get onto the front row alongside the German's Ferrari but he ruined everything in the race, first with a slow start and then when he was hit by Ralf Schumacher, causing him to pit with a punctured rear tyre. The Australian came in on his rim but was penalised for exceeding the 100 km/h pit-lane speed limit. Having pitted for new tyres, he then spun off on lap 23. Despite a poor start, Webber demonstrated the car's potential in the early stages as he twice overtook the Williams of Ralf Schumacher.

Instead Jenson Button drove like a true champion. Starting from row 3 on the grid, the young Brit battled with Trulli right from the start, even involving some wheel-banging, and their duel continued for a number of laps with some superb overtaking moves.

When the Italian's Renault started to lose the pace, the BAR driver powered ahead to finish third and score the first podium finish in his career. Second place went to Montoya, who drove a gutsy race, while Ralf Schumacher stopped with engine failure half-way through. Barrichello finished fourth followed by Trulli, Coulthard, Alonso and Massa. This time all three rookies made it to the chequered flag despite a series of problems. Klien, tenth at the finish, lost precious time during a pit-stop when his refuelling flap failed to open. Pantano finished the race exhausted because of the heat and humidity and due to the fact that his drinks bottle had failed to work.

Finally Bruni finished in fourteenth position three laps down on the winner after driving for half the race without power-steering, no mean feat in a exhausting race like the Malaysian GP.

SEPANG
Length: **5,543 km**
Laps: **56** - Distance: **310,408 kms**

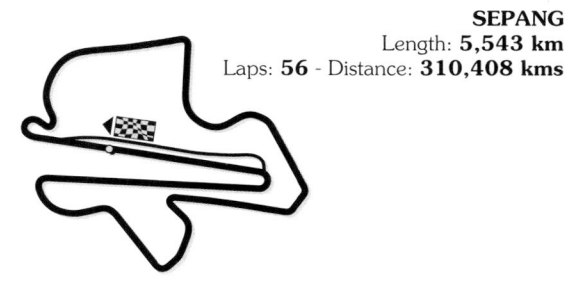

Inaugurated in 1998, the Malaysian circuit of Sepang hosted its first GP the following year. The 5.543 km track succeeds in combining a series of spectacular corners and high safety standards with avant-guard facilities for teams and spectators.

HIGHLIGHTS

After his splendid race in Melbourne, Fernando Alonso was again one of the outstanding protagonists of the Malaysian GP, but this time for his disappointing performance. In qualifying he ruined everything at the final curve by spinning off into the gravel, and as a result the Spanish driver lined up on the last row of the grid alongside Sato, who also went off. Then he made up ten places on lap 1, concluding the race in seventh place, picking up two points in the table. Not a bad result, but where might he have finished if he hadn't made a mistake in qualifying? Clearly the pressure of being Formula 1's rising star is starting to take its toll...

PHOTO PORTFOLIO
FOLLOWING PAGES

The front row had a strange look about it as Webber (Jaguar) lined up alongside the world champion. Celebrations in the BAR Team for Jenson Button's first-ever podium and a second win for Schumacher and Ferrari in two GPs.

CHAMPIONSHIPS POINTS	AUSTRALIAN GP	MALAYSIAN GP	BAHRAIN GP	SAN MARINO GP	SPANISH GP	MONACO GP	EUROPEAN GP	CANADIAN GP	UNITED STATES GP	FRENCH GP	BRITISH GP	GERMAN GP	HUNGARIAN GP	BELGIUM GP	ITALIAN GP	CHINA GP	JAPANESE GP	BRAZILIAN GP	TOTAL POINT
1 M. Schumacher	10	10																	20
2 R. Barrichello	8	5																	13
3 J.P. Montoya	4	8																	12
4 J. Button	3	6																	9
5 F. Alonso	6	2																	8
6 J. Trulli	2	4																	6
7 R. Schumacher	5	-																	5
8 D. Coulthard	1	3																	4
9 F. Massa	-	1																	1
10 C. Da Matta	-	-																	-
11 T. Sato	-	-																	-
12 G. Fisichella	-	-																	-
13 C. Klien	-	-																	-
14 O. Panis	-	-																	-
15 G. Pantano	-	-																	-
16 G. Bruni	-	-																	-
17 Z. Baumgartner	-	-																	-
18 K. Raikkonen	-	-																	-
19 M. Webber	-	-																	-
20 N. Heidfeld	-	-																	-

158

Sepang

Bahrain - 4 April 2004

Pole Position

2004 Michael Schumacher

Starting Grid

1 
- Michael Schumacher — Ferrari — 1'30"139 
- Rubens Barrichello — Ferrari — 1'30"530

2 
- Juan-Pablo Montoya — Williams — 1'30"581 
- Ralf Schumacher — Williams — 1'30"633

3 
- Takuma Sato — BAR — 1'30"827 
- Jenson Button — BAR — 1'30"856

4 
- Jarno Trulli — Renault — 1'30"971 
- Olivier Panis — Toyota — 1'31"686

5 
- Cristiano Da Matta — Toyota — 1'31"717 
- David Coulthard — McLaren — 1'31"719

6 
- Giancarlo Fisichella — Sauber — 1'31"731 
- Christian Klien — Jaguar — 1'32"332

7 
- Felipe Massa — Sauber — 1'32"536 
- Mark Webber — Jaguar — 1'32"625

8 
- Giorgio Pantano — Jordan — 1'34"105 
- Fernando Alonso — Renault — 1'34"130

9 
- Gianmaria Bruni — Minardi — 1'34"584 
- Nick Heidfeld — Jordan — 1'33"506*

10 
- Kimi Raikkonen — McLaren — No Time* 
- Zsolt Baumgartner — Minardi — 1'35"787*

Relegated to back of starting grid after engine change

Results

	Driver	Car	KPH	Gap
1	M. Schumacher	Ferrari	208,976	-
2	R. Barrichello	Ferrari	208,922	1"367
3	J. Button	BAR	207,932	26"687
4	J. Trulli	Renault	207,717	32"214
5	T. Sato	BAR	206,933	52"460
6	F. Alonso	Renault	206,906	53"156
7	R. Schumacher	Williams	206,714	58"155
8	M. Webber	Jaguar	205,138	1 lap
9	O. Panis	Toyota	205,061	1 lap
10	C. Da Matta	Toyota	204,589	1 lap
11	G. Fisichella	Sauber	204,551	1 lap
12	F. Massa	Sauber	204,373	1 lap
13	J.P. Montoya	Williams	203,984	1 lap
14	C. Klien	Jaguar	203,402	1 lap
15	N. Heidfeld	Jordan	202,619	1 lap
16	G. Pantano	Jordan	201,044	2 laps
17	G. Bruni	Minardi	187,620	5 laps

Retirements

Driver	Car	Lap	Reason
D. Coulthard	McLaren	50	Engine
Z. Baungartner	Minardi	44	Engine
K. Raikkonen	McLaren	7	Engine

The Race

Driver	Car	Lap	Fastest Lap	Top Speed
M. Schumacher	Ferrari	7	1'30"252	326,4
F. Alonso	Renault	39	1'30"654	323,8
R. Schumacher	Williams	56	1'30"781	332,4
R. Barrichello	Ferrari	29	1'30"876	330,1
J. Button	BAR	24	1'30"960	324,8
J.P. Montoya	Williams	28	1'30"977	323,0
T. Sato	BAR	55	1'31"101	328,6
J. Trulli	Renault	24	1'31"421	323,7
D. Coulthard	McLaren	19	1'31"851	322,9
M. Webber	Jaguar	19	1'32"277	326,4
C. Da Matta	Toyota	23	1'32"319	325,2
G. Fisichella	Sauber	40	1'32"329	328,5
O. Panis	Toyota	22	1'32"401	325,0
C. Klien	Jaguar	38	1'32"533	329,2
F. Massa	Sauber	44	1'32"690	328,8
N. Heidfeld	Jordan	56	1'33"284	322,7
K. Raikkonen	McLaren	7	1'33"527	324,0
G. Pantano	Jordan	9	1'34"032	318,5
Z. Baumgartner	Minardi	24	1'34"555	323,0
G. Bruni	Minardi	40	1'35"130	317,8

BAHRAIN GP

FERRARI LEAVES RIVALS FLOUNDERING IN THE DESERT

The first Grand Prix in history to be held in the Middle East proved to be a dry and arid affair … and that was just the final race result as the Ferraris cleared off into the desert sun from the front row of the grid and were never seen again! In qualifying, row 2 went to Williams behind the red Maranello cars, while the third row was an all-BAR lock-out, with Sato convincingly quicker than team-mate Button.

Trulli qualified on row 4 followed by the two Toyotas of Panis and Da Matta. The McLarens were a disaster, with Coulthard tenth on the grid and Raikkonen starting on the final row after being forced to change his 10-cylinder Mercedes engine.

Engine problems were in fact the biggest headache for Ron Dennis' team as both Coulthard and Raikkonen were unable to finish the race because of engine failure. At the lights the Ferraris powered into the lead while behind there was an early scrap between Ralf Schumacher and Sato.

On lap 6 the German late-braked into the first of the Esses, managed to get his front wheels ahead of the Japanese driver but forced him wide. Contact was inevitable and Ralf's Williams flew off the track and almost flipped over. After a stop in the pits to check his front suspension, almost mowing down his pit crew in the process, Ralf returned to the race but this time well down the field and he eventually finished seventh, only to receive a warning from race control for reckless driving.

Despite the clash with Ralf Schumacher, Sato continued an inspired race to claim fifth, the best result in his career. BAR's Japanese driver only made one mistake when he risked ruining everything by battling with his team-mate and damaging his front wing after violently running over a kerb.

So it was Jenson Button who again stepped up to the final podium place with his second third on the run, followed by Trulli. Alonso was sixth but once again ran a disappointing race, this time under the watchful eyes of King Juan Carlos of Spain.

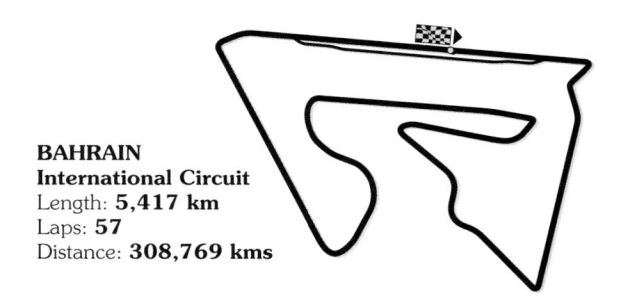

BAHRAIN
International Circuit
Length: **5,417 km**
Laps: **57**
Distance: **308,769 kms**

The most modern track on the calendar, featuring space-age structures, Bahrain is an oasis of luxury and comfort set in a desert landscape. Built in record time at a cost of over 150 million dollars, it was designed by Hermann Tilke, the same architect who planned the Sepang circuit, which it resembles in the design of the grandstands.

HIGHLIGHTS

The Sakhir Circuit, which had been designed and built in record time, gets our vote as the undisputed star of the weekend's proceedings even before the Formula 1 circus rolled into town … together with Bernie Ecclestone, the man who pioneered Formula 1's first foray into the Middle East desert. It is worth mentioning that the accord between Ecclestone and the King of Bahrain was only signed in September 2002 and that construction work began shortly afterwards on a design by Herman Tilke, the man who created the Sepang circuit and the one being built in Shanghai, China.

PHOTO PORTFOLIO
FOLLOWING PAGES

Different track, same result.
Ferrari scored their second 1-2 of the year, with Button again on the podium.
The new Bahrain circuit couldn't have had a better inauguration race.

	CHAMPIONSHIPS POINTS	AUSTRALIAN GP	MALAYSIAN GP	BAHRAIN GP	SAN MARINO GP	SPANISH GP	MONACO GP	EUROPEAN GP	CANADIAN GP	UNITED STATES GP	FRENCH GP	BRITISH GP	GERMAN GP	HUNGARIAN GP	BELGIUM GP	ITALIAN GP	CHINA GP	JAPANESE GP	BRAZILIAN GP	TOTAL POINT
1	M. Schumacher	10	10	10																30
2	R. Barrichello	8	5	8																21
3	J. Button	3	6	6																15
4	J.P. Montoya	4	8	-																12
5	F. Alonso	6	2	3																11
6	J. Trulli	2	4	5																11
7	R. Schumacher	5	-	2																7
8	T. Sato	-	-	4																4
9	D. Coulthard	1	3	-																4
10	F. Massa	-	1	-																1
11	M. Webber	-	-	1																1
12	C. Da Matta	-	-	-																-
13	O. Panis	-	-	-																-
14	G. Fisichella	-	-	-																-
15	C. Klien	-	-	-																-
16	G. Pantano	-	-	-																-
17	G. Bruni	-	-	-																-
18	N. Heidfeld	-	-	-																-
19	Z. Baumgartner	-	-	-																-
20	K. Raikkonen	-	-	-																-

GULF AIR طيران الخليج
GULF AIR
GULF AIR

MILD SEVEN
elf

SCHÜCO
West
Henkel
Mobil 1
Mercedes-Benz
SIEM
West
Mobil

BAHRAIN

IMOLA - 25 APRIL 2004

POLE POSITION

'90 A. Senna	'97 J. Villeneuve
'91 A. Senna	'98 D. Coulthard
'92 N. Mansell	'99 M. Hakkinen
'93 A. Prost	'00 M. Hakkinen
'94 A. Senna	'01 D. Coulthard
'95 M. Schumacher	'02 M. Schumacher
'96 M. Schumacher	'03 M. Schumacher

2004 JENSON BUTTON

	1°	2°	3°
'90	R. Patrese	G. Berger	A. Nannini
'91	A. Senna	G. Berger	J. Lehto
'92	N. Mansell	R. Patrese	A. Senna
'93	A. Prost	M. Schumacher	M. Brundle
'94	M. Schumacher	N. Larini	M. Hakkinen
'95	D. Hill	J. Alesi	G. Berger
'96	D. Hill	M. Schumacher	G. Berger
'97	H.H. Frentzen	M. Schumacher	E. irvine
'98	D. Coulthard	M. Schumacher	E. Irvine
'99	M. Schumacher	D. Coulthard	R. Barrichello
'00	M. Schumacher	M. Hakkinen	D. Coulthard
'01	R. Schumacher	D. Coulthard	R. Barrichello
'02	M. Schumacher	R. Barrichello	R. Schumacher
'03	M. Schumacher	K. Raikkonen	R. Barrichello

STARTING GRID

Pos	Driver	Team	Time		Driver	Team	Time
1	 Jenson Button	BAR	1'19"753		Michael Schumacher	Ferrari	1'20"011
2	 Juan-Pablo Montoya	Williams	1'20"212		 Rubens Barrichello	Ferrari	1'20"451
3	 Ralf Schumacher	Williams	1'20"538		 Fernando Alonso	Renault	1'20"895
4	 Takuma Sato	BAR	1'20"913		 Mark Webber	Jaguar	1'20"921
5	 Jarno Trulli	Renault	1'21"034		 Cristiano Da Matta	Toyota	1'21"087
6	 David Coulthard	McLaren	1'21"091		 Felipe Massa	Sauber	1'21"532
7	 Olivier Panis	Toyota	1'21"558		 Christian Klien	Jaguar	1'21"949
8	 Giorgio Pantano	Jordan	1'23"352		 Nick Heidfeld	Jordan	1'23"488
9	 Gianmaria Bruni	Minardi	1'26"899		 Giancarlo Fisichella	Sauber	No Time
10	 Zsolt Baumgartner	Minardi	1'46"299		 Kimi Raikkonen	McLaren	No Time

RESULTS

	Driver	Car	KPH	Gap
1	M. Schumacher	Ferrari	212,405	-
2	J. Button	BAR	212,008	9"702
3	J.P. Montoya	Williams	211,523	21"617
4	F. Alonso	Renault	211,440	23"654
5	J. Trulli	Renault	210,931	36"216
6	R. Barrichello	Ferrari	210,912	36"683
7	R. Schumacher	Williams	210,144	55"730
8	K. Raikkonen	McLaren	208,952	1 lap
9	G. Fisichella	Sauber	208,913	1 lap
10	F. Massa	Sauber	208,406	1 lap
11	O. Panis	Toyota	207,422	1 lap
12	D. Coulthard	McLaren	207,388	1 lap
13	M. Webber	Jaguar	207,028	1 lap
14	C. Klien	Jaguar	204,160	2 laps
15	Z. Baumgartner	Minardi	197,911	4 laps
16	T. Sato	BAR	209,173	6 laps

RETIREMENTS

Driver	Car	Lap	Reason
N. Heidfeld	Jordan	48	Axle-shaft
C. Da Matta	Toyota	32	Crashed
G. Bruni	Minardi	22	Brakes
G. Pantano	Jordan	6	Hydraulic circuit

THE RACE

Driver	Car	Lap	Fastest Lap	Top Speed
M. Schumacher	Ferrari	10	1'20"411	314,6
J. Button	BAR	28	1'21"201	313,7
F. Alonso	Renault	59	1'21"650	309,4
J. Trulli	Renault	11	1'21"666	305,6
R. Schumacher	Williams	30	1'21"689	315,0
J.P. Montoya	Williams	27	1'21"870	312,0
R. Barrichello	Ferrari	31	1'21"873	318,5
T. Sato	BAR	44	1'21"929	311,6
K. Raikkonen	McLaren	39	1'22"500	313,1
G. Fisichella	Sauber	60	1'22"654	312,8
O. Panis	Toyota	59	1'22"861	306,4
F. Massa	Sauber	36	1'22"895	314,5
M. Webber	Jaguar	55	1'22"931	308,7
D. Coulthard	McLaren	42	1'22"951	313,8
C. Da Matta	Toyota	25	1'23"108	307,7
N. Heidfeld	Jordan	44	1'23"381	310,7
C. Klien	Jaguar	27	1'23"647	306,4
G. Pantano	Jordan	6	1'25"457	304,3
Z. Baumgartner	Minardi	58	1'26"075	303,9
G. Bruni	Minardi	11	1'26"857	298,5

SAN MARINO GP

FOUR FOR FERRARI, THREE FOR BUTTON

After two successive podium finishes, both BAR and Jenson Button set the first pole position in their history .... ahead of Schumacher's Ferrari at the Imola circuit, dedicated to Enzo and Dino Ferrari!
The German actually made a mistake at the Variante Alta but, as he admitted afterwards, "even without that error I don't think I could have beaten Jenson, who made a fantastic lap."
Button has driven for Williams, Benetton and Renault in his 69 GPs and he moved to BAR in 2004 as replacement for the 1997 world champion, Jacques Villeneuve. The 24-year-old had promised in Australia that sooner or later both BAR and he himself would score some surprising results.
And the surprise came on a warm Saturday afternoon in April in climatic conditions that gave an advantage to the Michelin runners.
At the start of the race Jenson kept a cool head and powered into the lead. Schuey was behind, while Montoya in third attacked him on the outside of the Tosa, just like at the Nurburgring last year. This time Schumacher reacted, forcing the Colombian onto the gravel at the exit. Button meanwhile was powering away from the Ferrari at an amazing pace and led the race for the first eight laps.
The outcome was decided at the first round of pit-stops however as Schumacher stayed out on a clear track after Button had come in, the German succeeding in putting in a couple of laps at record-breaking pace. Schumacher then pitted and when he returned to the track, he was ahead of Button.
They went on to finish in that order, Schumacher scoring his fourth successive win and the young British driver claiming his third podium on the run. They were followed home by Montoya and the two Renaults of Alonso and Trulli. The Italian was fourth for a number of laps with Barrichello behind, but was then passed by his team-mate.
The Brazilian was a disappointing sixth after being blocked at the start by the two Williams and then got caught up in back-marker traffic, confirming that without a good start in modern-day F1, there is little hope of overtaking and moving up the field.
The rest were, quite frankly, nowhere, while a word apart must go to McLaren, whose crisis appears to worsen at every race.

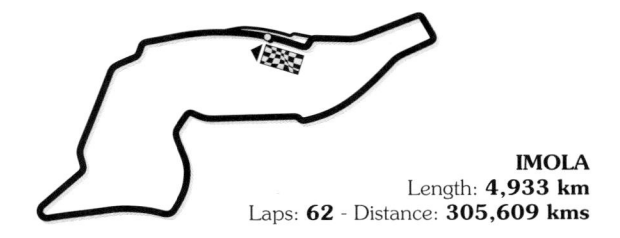

IMOLA
Length: **4,933 km**
Laps: **62** - Distance: **305,609 kms**

The most popular circuit for Ferrari fans was the venue for the Italian GP in 1980 and then every year without a break, for the San Marino GP. The track underwent its latest modifications after the tragic 1994 grand prix in which Senna and Ratzenberger lost their lives. Despite losing a lot of its spectacular nature, it gained in safety. The current length of the track is 4.933 km.

HIGHLIGHTS

McLaren's bleak period continued at Imola. First Raikkonen failed to finish the first three races of the year, then things went from bad to worse as the Finn started the Imola race from the back of the grid after engine problems; finally Kimi and Coulthard had two disappointing results in 8th and 12th respectively. The Scot's race was especially poor after he had made contact with Alonso on lap 1, which forced him to make a pit-stop to change the front nose.

PHOTO PORTFOLIO
FOLLOWING PAGES

Back to Europe and guess what? Another win for Schumacher at Imola, Ferrari's (and Minardi's) home track. First ever pole position for Button, who finished runner-up, while Montoya finished third after a bit of 'argy-bargy' with Schumacher on the opening lap.

CHAMPIONSHIPS POINTS	AUSTRALIAN GP	MALAYSIAN GP	BAHRAIN GP	SAN MARINO GP	SPANISH GP	MONACO GP	EUROPEAN GP	CANADIAN GP	UNITED STATES GP	FRENCH GP	BRITISH GP	GERMAN GP	HUNGARIAN GP	BELGIUM GP	ITALIAN GP	CHINA GP	JAPANESE GP	BRAZILIAN GP	TOTAL POINT
1 M. Schumacher	10	10	10	10															40
2 R. Barrichello	8	5	8	3															24
3 J. Button	3	6	6	8															23
4 J.P. Montoya	4	8	-	6															18
5 F. Alonso	6	2	3	5															16
6 J. Trulli	2	4	5	4															15
7 R. Schumacher	5	-	2	2															9
8 T. Sato	-	-	4	-															4
9 D. Coulthard	1	3	-	-															4
10 F. Massa	-	1	-	-															1
11 M. Webber	-	-	1	-															1
12 K. Raikkonen	-	-	-	1															1
13 G. Fisichella	-	-	-	-															-
14 C. Da Matta	-	-	-	-															-
15 O. Panis	-	-	-	-															-
16 C. Klien	-	-	-	-															-
17 G. Pantano	-	-	-	-															-
18 G. Bruni	-	-	-	-															-
19 Z. Baumgartner	-	-	-	-															-
20 N. Heidfeld	-	-	-	-															-

166

Imola

BARCELONA - 9 MAY 2004

POLE POSITION

2004 MICHAEL SCHUMACHER

'90	A. Senna	'97	J. Villeneuve
'91	G. Berger	'98	M. Hakkinen
'92	N. Mansell	'99	M. Hakkinen
'93	A. Prost	'00	M. Schumacher
'94	M. Schumacher	'01	M. Schumacher
'95	M. Schumacher	'02	M. Schumacher
'96	D. Hill	'03	M. Schumacher

STARTING GRID

1 
- Michael Schumacher — Ferrari — 1'15"022 
- Juan-Pablo Montoya — Williams — 1'15"639

2 
- Takuma Sato — BAR — 1'15"809 
- Jarno Trulli — Renault — 1'16"144

3 
- Rubens Barrichello — Ferrari — 1'16"272 
- Ralf Schumacher — Williams — 1'16"293

4 
- Olivier Panis — Toyota — 1'16"313 
- Fernando Alonso — Renault — 1'16"422

5 
- Mark Webber — Jaguar — 1'16"514 
- David Coulthard — McLaren — 1'16"636

6 
- Cristiano Da Matta — Toyota — 1'17"038 
- Giancarlo Fisichella — Sauber — 1'17"444

7 
- Kimi Raikkonen — McLaren — 1'17"445 
- Jenson Button — BAR — 1'17"575

8 
- Nick Heidfeld — Jordan — 1'17"802 
- Christian Klien — Jaguar — 1'17"812

9 
- Felipe Massa — Sauber — 1'17"866 
- Gianmaria Bruni — Minardi — 1'19"817

10 
- Giorgio Pantano — Jordan — 1'20"607 
- Zsolt Baumgartner — Minardi — 1'21"470

1° 2° 3°

'90	A. Prost	N. Mansell	A. Nannini
'91	N. Mansell	A. Prost	R. Patrese
'92	N. Mansell	M. Schumacher	J. Alesi
'93	A. Prost	A. Senna	M. Schumacher
'94	D. Hill	M. Schumacher	M. Brundell
'95	M. Schumacher	J. Herbert	G. Berger
'96	M. Schumacher	J. Alesi	J. Villeneuve
'97	J. Villeneuve	O. Panis	J. Alesi
'98	M. Hakkinen	D. Coulthard	M. Schumacher
'99	M. Hakkinen	D. Coulthard	M. Schumacher
'00	M. Hakkinen	D. Coulthard	R. Barrichello
'01	M. Schumacher	J.P. Montoya	J. Villeneuve
'02	M. Schumacher	J.P. Montoya	D. Coulthard
'03	M. Schumacher	F. Alonso	R. Barrichello

RESULTS

	DRIVER	CAR	KPH	GAP
1	M. Schumacher	Ferrari	209,205	-
2	R. Barrichello	Ferrari	208,677	13"290
3	J. Trulli	Renault	207,926	32"294
4	F. Alonso	Renault	207,900	32"952
5	T. Sato	BAR	207,532	42"327
6	R. Schumacher	Williams	206,306	73"804
7	G. Fisichella	Sauber	206,178	77"108
8	J. Button	BAR	205,732	1 lap
9	F. Massa	Sauber	205,082	1 lap
10	D. Coulthard	McLaren	204,416	1 lap
11	K. Raikkonen	McLaren	204,306	1 lap
12	M. Webber	Jaguar	204,295	1 lap
13	C. Da Matta	Toyota	204,075	1 lap

RETIREMENTS

G. Pantano	Jordan	51	Hydraulic circuit
J.P. Montoya	Williams	46	Brakes
C. Klien	Jaguar	43	Drive-by-wire
O. Panis	Toyota	33	Hydraulic circuit
N. Heidfeld	Jordan	33	Hydraulic circuit
G. Bruni	Minardi	31	Crashed
Z. Baumgartner	Minardi	17	Crashed

THE RACE

DRIVER	CAR	LAP	FASTEST LAP	TOP SPEED
M. Schumacher	Ferrari	12	1'17"450	328,9
J. Button	BAR	46	1'17"495	334,1
F. Alonso	Renault	27	1'17"556	323,0
T. Sato	BAR	47	1'17"678	333,8
R. Barrichello	Ferrari	18	1'17"887	330,3
J. Trulli	Renault	12	1'18"178	319,8
J.P. Montoya	Williams	28	1'18"262	333,6
R. Schumacher	Williams	27	1'18"548	331,5
M. Webber	Jaguar	11	1'18"617	328,5
F. Massa	Sauber	43	1'18"819	328,9
K. Raikkonen	McLaren	48	1'18"842	328,0
N. Heidfeld	Jordan	25	1'18"971	327,6
G. Fisichella	Sauber	37	1'19"062	329,0
C. Da Matta	Toyota	29	1'19"112	325,3
C. Klien	Jaguar	18	1'19"142	322,4
D. Coulthard	McLaren	38	1'19"175	323,7
O. Panis	Toyota	10	1'19"199	325,5
G. Pantano	Jordan	27	1'19"896	327,2
G. Bruni	Minardi	3	1'22"323	321,0
Z. Baumgartner	Minardi	8	1'23"390	314,9

SPANISH GP

A FULL HOUSE FOR FERRARI!

Ferrari were at the top of their game in Spain, with Schumacher and the team on maximum overdrive. What more is there to say about the world-beating Maranello squad and a car that dominated despite being potentially sidelined by a cracked exhaust after just 11 laps?
Some considerations are obvious: that the Formula 1 title race is over not even a third of the way into the championship and that it must find a solution to the monotonous, Ferrari-dominated racing. But it's not all Ferrari's fault: the Italian team is only doing its duty, reaping the benefits from fantastic team-work where nothing is left to chance. The damaged exhaust is clear proof of this. Schuey was immediately aware of the problem, it was confirmed by the telemetry and the reaction from the pits was swift. The German was told to drive as carefully as possible and just hope the car would last. And that was the way the race finished, with the red Maranello car picking up a fifth win on the trot.
But let's take a step backwards to Saturday morning when BAR confirmed its previous excellent form by setting quickest time around the Barcelona track. Then in official qualifying, Schumacher put in a perfect lap, forcing his rivals to play catch-up. Two-thirds of the way into his lap, Button was up on the split timing but then put his wheels on the grass and slipped down the classification. BAR team-mate Sato went much better, clinching third-quickest time, the best result ever for a Japanese driver in Formula 1.
Montoya lined up alongside the Ferrari driver while Trulli, with the Renault, was fourth quickest. Right behind him was local hero Alonso, whose presence was enough to guarantee a 200,000 circuit spectator figure over the weekend. Trulli got off to an electrifying start, nipping past Montoya and Schumacher and into the lead before the first turn. The Italian kept the lead until the first pitstop, when he was outfoxed by Schumacher and some superb team-work. Barrichello, thanks to two pitstops, was also able to bring his Ferrari home ahead of the Renault.
Fourth place went to Alonso, who drove a steady but rather unexciting race, maybe conditioned by the fear of putting a foot wrong in front of his home crowd and King Juan Carlos.
And what about Montoya? The only time he shone throughout the weekend was when he set second quickest time in qualifying. His disappointing race was interrupted twenty laps from the end after he suffered total brake failure.
Sato on the other hand put in a superb drive with his BAR, finishing fifth ahead of Ralf Schumacher and Fisichella.

BARCELONA
Length: **4,627 km**
Laps: **66** - Distance: **305,256 kms**

Spain hosted its first GP in 1951, but Formula 1 races have been held on an irregular basis at several different circuits including Jarama, Montjuich and Jerez, before settling at the Montmelò circuit in Barcelona in 1991, where it has remained ever since.

HIGHLIGHTS

The talking-point of the Spanish race was Takuma Sato, who qualified third on the grid and then finished fifth in the race. Sato made his F1 debut in the 2002 Australian GP for Jordan, and then replaced Jacques Villeneuve in the final race of the 2003 season in Japan, obtaining a well-deserved sixth place that earned him a drive for this season. It is also a great result for David Richards, who has been able to get the best out of his team and its two young drivers.

PHOTO PORTFOLIO
FOLLOWING PAGES

It was a great day for Jarno Trulli who blasted into the lead of the race at the start. The Italian finished third, scoring his first podium in 2004, followed by team-mate Alonso. King Juan Carlos greeted the drivers on the grid before the race.

CHAMPIONSHIPS POINTS	AUSTRALIAN GP	MALAYSIAN GP	BAHRAIN GP	SAN MARINO GP	SPANISH GP	MONACO GP	EUROPEAN GP	CANADIAN GP	UNITED STATES GP	FRENCH GP	BRITISH GP	GERMAN GP	HUNGARIAN GP	BELGIUM GP	ITALIAN GP	CHINA GP	JAPANESE GP	BRAZILIAN GP	TOTAL POINT
1 M. Schumacher	10	10	10	10	10														50
2 R. Barrichello	8	5	8	3	8														32
3 J. Button	3	6	6	8	1														24
4 F. Alonso	6	2	3	5	5														21
5 J. Trulli	2	4	5	4	6														21
6 J.P. Montoya	4	8	-	6	-														18
7 R. Schumacher	5	-	2	2	3														12
8 T. Sato	-	-	4	-	4														8
9 D. Coulthard	1	3	-	-	-														4
10 G. Fisichella	-	-	-	-	2														2
11 F. Massa	-	1	-	-	-														1
12 M. Webber	-	-	1	-	-														1
13 K. Raikkonen	-	-	-	1	-														1
14 C. Da Matta	-	-	-	-	-														-
15 O. Panis	-	-	-	-	-														-
16 C. Klien	-	-	-	-	-														-
17 G. Pantano	-	-	-	-	-														-
18 G. Bruni	-	-	-	-	-														-
19 Z. Baumgartner	-	-	-	-	-														-
20 N. Heidfeld	-	-	-	-	-														-

170

Barcelona

Monte Carlo - 23 May 2004

Pole Position

2004 JARNO TRULLI

'90	A. Senna	'97	H.H. Frentzen
'91	A. Senna	'98	M. Hakkinen
'92	N. Mansell	'99	M. Hakkinen
'93	A. Prost	'00	M. Schumacher
'94	M. Schumacher	'01	D. Coulthard
'95	D. Hill	'02	J.P. Montoya
'96	M. Schumacher	'03	R. Schumacher

Starting Grid

Pos	Left	Time	Right	Time
1	Jarno Trulli – Renault	1'13"985	Jenson Button – BAR	1'14"396
2	Fernando Alonso – Renault	1'14"408	Michael Schumacher – Ferrari	1'14"516
3	Kimi Raikkonen – McLaren	1'14"592	Rubens Barrichello – Ferrari	1'14"716
4	Takuma Sato – BAR	1'14"827	David Coulthard – McLaren	1'14"951
5	Juan-Pablo Montoya – Williams	1'15"039	Giancarlo Fisichella – Sauber	1'15"352
6	Mark Webber – Jaguar	1'15"725	Ralf Schumacher – Williams	1'14"345 *
7	Olivier Panis – Toyota	1'15"859	Christian Klien – Jaguar	1'15"919
8	Cristiano Da Matta – Toyota	1'16"169	Felipe Massa – Sauber	1'16"248
9	Nick Heidfeld – Jordan	1'16"488	Giorgio Pantano – Jordan	1'17"443
10	Zsolt Baumgartner – Minardi	1'20"060	Gianmaria Bruni – Minardi	1'20"115

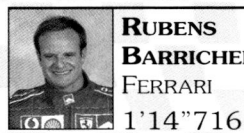

* Relegated to back of starting grid after engine change

Podium

	1°	2°	3°
'90	A. Senna	J. Alesi	G. Berger
'91	A. Senna	N. Mansell	J. Alesi
'92	A. Senna	N. Mansell	R. Patrese
'93	A. Senna	D. Hill	J. Alesi
'94	M. Schumacher	M. Brundle	G. Berger
'95	M. Schumacher	D. Hill	G. Berger
'96	O. Panis	D. Coulthard	J. Herbert
'97	M. Schumacher	R. Barrichello	E. Irvine
'98	M. Hakkinen	G. Fisichella	E. Irvine
'99	M. Schumacher	E. Irvine	M. Hakkinen
'00	D. Coulthard	R. Barrichello	G. Fisichella
'01	M. Schumacher	R. Barrichello	E. Irvine
'02	D. Coulthard	M. Schumacher	R. Schumacher
'03	J.P. Montoya	K. Raikkonen	M. Schumacher

Results

	Driver	Car	KPH	Gap
1	J. Trulli	Renault	145,880	-
2	J. Button	BAR	145,869	0"497
3	R. Barrichello	Ferrari	144,159	1'15"766
4	J.P. Montoya	Williams	143,439	1 lap
5	F. Massa	Sauber	142,370	1 lap
6	C. Da Matta	Toyota	142,367	1 lap
7	N. Heidfeld	Jordan	140,505	2 laps
8	O. Panis	Toyota	139,196	3 laps
9	Z. Baumgartner	Minardi	134,411	6 laps

Retirements

Driver	Car	Lap	Reason
R. Schumacher	Williams	69	Gearbox
M. Schumacher	Ferrari	45	Accident
F. Alonso	Renault	41	Accident
K. Raikkonen	McLaren	27	Engine
G. Bruni	Minardi	15	Gearbox
G. Pantano	Jordan	12	Gearbox
M. Webber	Jaguar	11	Transmission
T. Sato	BAR	2	Engine
D. Coulthard	McLaren	2	Accident
G. Fisichella	Sauber	2	Accident
C. Klien	Jaguar	0	Accident

The Race

Driver	Car	Lap	Fastest Lap	Top Speed
M. Schumacher	Ferrari	23	1'14"439	303,0
J. Trulli	Renault	22	1'14"870	299,5
J. Button	BAR	40	1'15"220	298,5
F. Alonso	Renault	23	1'15"226	299,4
J.P. Montoya	Williams	41	1'15"395	299,2
R. Barrichello	Ferrari	16	1'15"763	301,6
K. Raikkonen	McLaren	15	1'16"203	299,3
C. Da Matta	Toyota	22	1'16"232	298,8
O. Panis	Toyota	57	1'16"494	286,0
F. Massa	Sauber	23	1'17"151	300,0
M. Webber	Jaguar	11	1'17"466	294,5
R. Schumacher	Williams	18	1'17"588	295,0
N. Heidfeld	Jordan	35	1'18"262	295,1
G. Pantano	Jordan	10	1'19"415	294,9
D. Coulthard	McLaren	2	1'20"560	294,6
G. Fisichella	Sauber	2	1'20"804	290,5
T. Sato	BAR	2	1'21"368	276,9
G. Bruni	Minardi	10	1'21"592	276,9
Z. Baumgartner	Minardi	2	1'21"886	290,7
C. Klien	Jaguar	-	-	-

MONACO GP

TRULLI TAKES FIRST F1 CAREER POLE AND WIN

The Monaco weekend was an unforgettable one for the Italian driver who, after 116 races, scored the first pole position of his career and repeated the performance on Sunday with a well-deserved victory.
In addition to Trulli's superb lap, Saturday qualifying was also notable for Button setting an encouraging third-quickest time and Schuey down in a disappointing fifth place. Second place on the grid initially went to Ralf Schumacher, but the German was bumped down to twelfth place for changing his engine after Thursday practice.
There was the usual massive crowd and parade of VIPs on Sunday in the new pit garages as the tension mounted before the race and then the first start was aborted as Panis stalled his Toyota's engine on the grid.
On the restart, Trulli blasted away followed by Alonso, Button and an amazing Sato who barged his way between Schumacher and Montoya. The Japanese driver's race however came to an end at the Tabac corner on lap 3 when his engine blew in a cloud of impenetrable white smoke. Coulthard braked hard and Fisichella hurtled straight into him, launching his Sauber into a roll and into the guard-rail, but luckily the Italian emerged unhurt from the overturned wreck. The safety-car came out and the group reformed, with Trulli again shadowed by Button.
On lap 43, Alonso lapped Ralf Schumacher around the outside in the Loews tunnel on the dirty part of the track, but the lack of grip at that point pushed him against the barrier and his Renault was destroyed.
Out came the safety-car once again and several drivers, including Trulli and Button, took advantage to nip into the pits for a second pit stop. Schumacher lined up behind the safety car followed by the lapped Montoya and by Trulli, but as the cars were about to emerge from the tunnel, the German decided to brake suddenly, probably to warm up his brakes for the restart.
Montoya was caught out by the manoeuvre and made contact with Schumacher's Ferrari, which spun and slammed against the barrier, almost taking out the left front suspension of the car.
When the safety car peeled off again Trulli was back in the lead and went on to take the chequered flag despite coming under intense pressure from Button in the last few laps.
Third place went to an increasingly disappointing Barrichello, followed by Montoya, Massa, Da Matta, Heidfeld and Panis, the latter three scoring points for the first time in 2004.

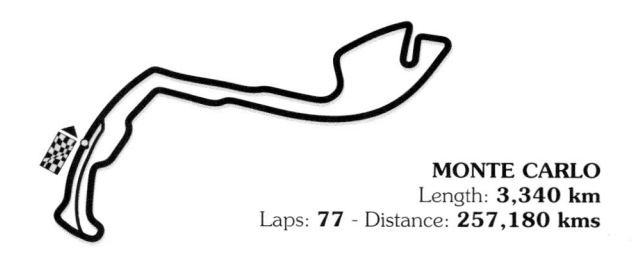

MONTE CARLO
Length: **3,340 km**
Laps: **77** - Distance: **257,180 kms**

The tightest, most twisty and, at 3.340 km the shortest track on the calendar, the Monte Carlo street circuit winds its way around the fascinating Principality of Monaco. Characterised by having the slowest average speed, it is a torture for drivers because of the high number of gear changes required during the race, approximately 3,700. The first GP to be held in Monte Carlo dates back to 1950.

HIGHLIGHTS

After 116 GPs, Jarno Trulli finally won his first-ever F1 race. He also scored his first-ever pole position, becoming the only Italian driver ever to set pole at the Monaco GP.
Trulli was born in Pescara in 1975 and is currently in his eighth season of F1, his third with Renault. He drove for Minardi in 1997, Prost in '98 and '99 and Jordan in 2000 and 2001.

PHOTO PORTFOLIO
FOLLOWING PAGES

New pits and a parade of VIPs for the most famous grand prix of the year. Naomi Campbell, Lionel Ritchie, Roger Moore and George Clooney were all there to celebrate Jarno Trulli's first F1 win and to watch Fisichella, Alonso and Schumacher's spectacular crashes.

	CHAMPIONSHIPS POINTS	AUSTRALIAN GP	MALAYSIAN GP	BAHRAIN GP	SAN MARINO GP	SPANISH GP	MONACO GP	EUROPEAN GP	CANADIAN GP	UNITED STATES GP	FRENCH GP	BRITISH GP	GERMAN GP	HUNGARIAN GP	BELGIUM GP	ITALIAN GP	CHINA GP	JAPANESE GP	BRAZILIAN GP	TOTAL POINT
1	M. Schumacher	10	10	10	10	10	-													50
2	R. Barrichello	8	5	8	3	8	6													38
3	J. Button	3	6	6	8	1	8													32
4	J. Trulli	2	4	5	4	6	10													31
5	J.P. Montoya	4	8	-	6	-	5													23
6	F. Alonso	6	2	3	5	5	-													21
7	R. Schumacher	5	-	2	2	3	-													12
8	T. Sato	-	-	4	-	4	-													8
9	F. Massa	-	1	-	-	-	4													5
10	D. Coulthard	1	3	-	-	-	-													4
11	C. Da Matta	-	-	-	-	-	3													3
12	G. Fisichella	-	-	-	-	2	-													2
13	N. Heidfeld	-	-	-	-	-	2													2
14	O. Panis	-	-	-	-	-	1													1
15	K. Raikkonen	-	-	-	1	-	-													1
16	M. Webber	-	-	1	-	-	-													1
17	C. Klien	-	-	-	-	-	-													-
18	G. Pantano	-	-	-	-	-	-													-
19	G. Bruni	-	-	-	-	-	-													-
20	Z. Baumgartner	-	-	-	-	-	-													-

173

174

MONTE CARLO

NÜRBURGRING - 30 MAY 2004

POLE POSITION

2004 MICHAEL SCHUMACHER

- '90 -
- '91 -
- '92 A. Prost
- '93 A. Prost
- '94 M. Schumacher
- '95 D. Coulthard
- '96 D. Hill
- '97 J. Villeneuve
- '98 -
- '99 H.H. Frentzen
- '00 D. Coulthard
- '01 M. Schumacher
- '02 J.P. Montoya
- '03 K. Raikkonen

STARTING GRID

Row 1
- Michael Schumacher — Ferrari — 1'28"351
- Takuma Sato — BAR — 1'28"986

Row 2
- Jarno Trulli — Renault — 1'29"135
- Kimi Raikkonen — McLaren — 1'29"137

Row 3
- Jenson Button — BAR — 1'29"245
- Fernando Alonso — Renault — 1'29"313

Row 4
- Rubens Barrichello — Ferrari — 1'29"353
- Juan-Pablo Montoya — Williams — 1'29"354

Row 5
- Ralf Schumacher — Williams — 1'29"459
- Olivier Panis — Toyota — 1'29"697

Row 6
- Cristiano Da Matta — Toyota — 1'29"706
- Christian Klien — Jaguar — 1'31"431

Row 7
- Nick Heidfeld — Jordan — 1'31"604
- Mark Webber — Jaguar — 1'31"797 *

Row 8
- Giorgio Pantano — Jordan — 1'31"979
- Felipe Massa — Sauber — 1'31"982

Row 9
- Zsolt Baumgartner — Minardi — 1'34"398 **
- Giancarlo Fisichella — Sauber — No Time ***

Row 10
- Gianmaria Bruni — Minardi — No Time ****
- David Coulthard — McLaren — No Time ***

* ONE SECOND PENALTY FOR IGNORING YELLOW FLAGS
** RELEGATED TO BACK OF STARTING GRID AFTER ENGINE CHANGE
*** DID NOT COMPLETE QUALIFYING
**** RELEGATED FOR COMING OUT OF PITS ON RED LIGHT

ALLIANZ GRAND PRIX OF EUROPE NÜRBURGRING 2004

	1°	2°	3°
'90	-	-	-
'91	-	-	-
'92	-	-	-
'93	A. Senna	D. Hill	A. Prost
'94	M. Schumacher	D. Hill	M. Hakkinen
'95	M. Schumacher	J. Alesi	D. Coulthard
'96	J. Villeneuve	M. Schumacher	D. Coulthard
'97	M. Hakkinen	D. Coulthard	J. Villeneuve
'98			
'99	J. Herbert	J. Trulli	R. Barrichello
'00	M. Schumacher	M. Hakkinen	D. Coulthard
'01	M. Schumacher	J.P. Montoya	D. Coulthard
'02	R. Barrichello	M. Schumacher	K. Raikkonen
'03	R. Schumacher	J.P. Montoya	R. Barrichello

RESULTS

	DRIVER	CAR	KPH	GAP
1	M. Schumacher	Ferrari	200,159	-
2	R. Barrichello	Ferrari	199,513	17"989
3	J. Button	BAR	199,350	22"533
4	J. Trulli	Renault	198,244	53"673
5	F. Alonso	Renault	197,985	1'00"987
6	G. Fisichella	Sauber	197,547	1'13"448
7	M. Webber	Jaguar	197,450	1'16"206
8	J.P. Montoya	Williams	196,410	1 lap
9	F. Massa	Sauber	195,355	1 lap
10	N. Heidfeld	Jordan	195,343	1 lap
11	O. Panis	Toyota	194,421	1 lap
12	C. Klien	Jaguar	194,167	1 lap
13	G. Pantano	Jordan	192,416	2 laps
14	G. Bruni	Minardi	188,344	3 laps
15	Z. Baumgartner	Minardi	187,596	3 laps

RETIREMENTS

Driver	Car	Lap	Reason
T. Sato	BAR	47	Engine
D. Coulthard	McLaren	25	Engine
K. Raikkonen	McLaren	9	Engine
R. Schumacher	Williams	0	Accident
C. Da Matta	Toyota	0	Accident

THE RACE

DRIVER	CAR	LAP	FASTEST LAP	TOP SPEED
M. Schumacher	Ferrari	7	1'29"468	321,2
T. Sato	BAR	11	1'30"004	315,5
R. Barrichello	Ferrari	14	1'30"101	320,7
J. Button	BAR	13	1'30"457	312,7
F. Alonso	Renault	29	1'31"065	311,8
J. Trulli	Renault	30	1'31"131	312,5
G. Fisichella	Sauber	23	1'31"413	316,1
J.P. Montoya	Williams	43	1'31"424	317,6
K. Raikkonen	McLaren	2	1'31"670	314,3
M. Webber	Jaguar	37	1'31"893	317,4
N. Heidfeld	Jordan	55	1'32"121	317,1
D. Coulthard	McLaren	14	1'32"337	316,9
O. Panis	Toyota	12	1'32"506	312,2
F. Massa	Sauber	37	1'32"729	315,6
G. Pantano	Jordan	27	1'32"772	318,4
C. Klien	Jaguar	14	1'32"804	314,2
Z. Baumgartner	Minardi	46	1'34"666	309,8
G. Bruni	Minardi	7	1'35"555	313,7
R. Schumacher	Williams	-	-	-
C. Da Matta	Toyota	-	-	-

EUROPEAN GP

ANOTHER FERRARI 1-2!

The home atmosphere of the Nurburgring (Schumacher was born just a few miles away at Kerpen) must have been an advantage for the world champion who easily clinched the 60th pole position of his career in qualifying.
Right behind Schumacher, probably still mulling over the incident at Monaco one week earlier, was BAR's Japanese sensation, Takuma Sato. Next up was Monaco winner Trulli, so fireworks were guaranteed at the start because the Japanese driver is not one to give way easily and Trulli's Renault has always proved to be a rocket-ship off the line. The first corner at the Nurburgring, the Castrol Kurve, is a tight right-hander that nearly always causes a massive pile-up and considerable tyre-smoking on the first lap.
Schumacher saw this risk and decided to get the hammers down immediately, but things got chaotic behind as Montoya, maybe following a contact with Panis, knocked his team-mate Ralf Schumacher off the track.
The race was over for Ralf but also for Da Matta, who was involved in the incident, while Montoya returned to the pits to replace his damaged nosecone. Schumacher was powering ahead up front, taking advantage of a low fuel load, and was increasing his lead over Raikkonen by more than 2 seconds a lap.
The German ran a lonely race, with the only danger coming from Webber and Panis who found themselves in his way between the exit of the pit-lane and the entrance to the Castrol Kurve when they came out of the pits.
Sato was on superb form and after Raikkonen's retirement, found himself in third position and gaining on Barrichello. The Japanese caught him and tried to pass him at the end of the straight but clipped the Ferrari. Sato came off the worst and had to pit to change the nosecone of his BAR. He came back out again in third place but thirteen laps from the end his engine exploded in a cloud of smoke on the pit straight.
BAR team-mate Jenson Button took over where Sato had left off and scored his fifth podium of the year, while the remaining points went to Trulli, Alonso, Fisichella, Webber and Montoya in that order.
Controversy raged after the race, with Barrichello furious with Sato, while Montoya and Ralf Schumacher were by now hardly on speaking terms with each other.

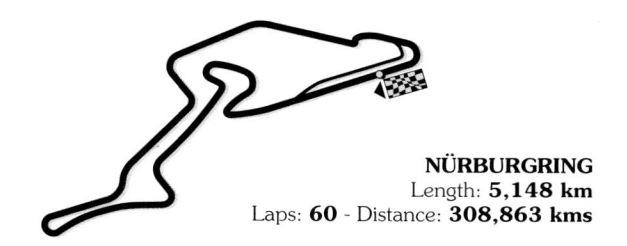

NÜRBURGRING
Length: **5,148 km**
Laps: **60** - Distance: **308,863 kms**

The original Nürburgring circuit measured 22 km in length and was immersed in the hills and forests around Adenau Castle. Faced with the need to improve safety standards at all circuits, the FIA required a new, shorter track (5.148 km) to be built and this used very little of the old circuit.

HIGHLIGHTS

Unlike Sato who is considered to be somewhat of a reckless driver, Fisichella on the contrary is one who uses his 'head'. After starting from the back of the grid for missing Saturday qualifying, the Rome-born driver recovered to finish sixth with a full fuel load. That result meant three more precious points for Sauber, which has now moved ahead of bigger and richer teams such as McLaren, Toyota and Jaguar in the manufacturers' standings.

PHOTO PORTFOLIO
FOLLOWING PAGES

Schummy gets the best start in his home GP, while behind it was disaster for the two Williams, with Montoya crashing into his team-mate and knocking him off the track.
For Ferrari it was another 1-2 win.

CHAMPIONSHIPS POINTS	AUSTRALIAN GP	MALAYSIAN GP	BAHRAIN GP	SAN MARINO GP	SPANISH GP	MONACO GP	EUROPEAN GP	CANADIAN GP	UNITED STATES GP	FRENCH GP	BRITISH GP	GERMAN GP	HUNGARIAN GP	BELGIUM GP	ITALIAN GP	CHINA GP	JAPANESE GP	BRAZILIAN GP	TOTAL POINT
1 M. Schumacher	10	10	10	10	10	-	10												60
2 R. Barrichello	8	5	8	3	8	6	8												46
3 J. Button	3	6	6	8	1	8	6												38
4 J. Trulli	2	4	5	4	6	10	5												36
5 F. Alonso	6	2	3	5	5	-	4												25
6 J.P. Montoya	4	8	-	6	-	5	1												24
7 R. Schumacher	5	-	2	2	3	-	-												12
8 T. Sato	-	-	4	-	4	-	-												8
9 F. Massa	-	1	-	-	-	4	-												5
10 G. Fisichella	-	-	-	-	2	-	3												5
11 D. Coulthard	1	3	-	-	-	-	-												4
12 C. Da Matta	-	-	-	-	-	3	-												3
13 M. Webber	-	-	1	-	-	-	2												3
14 N. Heidfeld	-	-	-	-	-	2	-												2
15 O. Panis	-	-	-	-	-	1	-												1
16 K. Raikkonen	-	-	-	1	-	-	-												1
17 C. Klien	-	-	-	-	-	-	-												-
18 G. Pantano	-	-	-	-	-	-	-												-
19 G. Bruni	-	-	-	-	-	-	-												-
20 Z. Baumgartner	-	-	-	-	-	-	-												-

Allianz
Allianz
HONDA

Allianz
NiQuitin CQ
hp

Allianz
PETROBRAS
Castrol

NÜRBURGRING

MONTREAL - 13 JUNE 2004

POLE POSITION

'90	A. Senna	'97	M. Schumacher
'91	R. Patrese	'98	D. Coulthard
'92	A. Senna	'99	M. Schumacher
'93	A. Prost	'00	M. Schumacher
'94	M. Schumacher	'01	M. Schumacher
'95	M. Schumacher	'02	J.P. Montoya
'96	D. Hill	'03	R. Schumacher

2004 RALF SCHUMACHER

STARTING GRID

1 
- Ralf Schumacher — Williams — 1'12"275
- Jenson Button — BAR — 1'12"341 

2 
- Jarno Trulli — Renault — 1'13"023
- Juan-Pablo Montoya — Williams — 1'13"072 

3 
- Fernando Alonso — Renault — 1'13"308
- Michael Schumacher — Ferrari — 1'13"355

4 
- Rubens Barrichello — Ferrari — 1'13"562
- Kimi Raikkonen — McLaren — 1'13"595 

5 
- David Coulthard — McLaren — 1'13"681
- Christian Klien — Jaguar — 1'14"532 

6 
- Giancarlo Fisichella — Sauber — 1'14"674
- Cristiano Da Matta — Toyota — 1'14"851 

7 
- Olivier Panis — Toyota — 1'14"891
- Mark Webber — Jaguar — 1'15"148 

8 
- Nick Heidfeld — Jordan — 1'15"321
- Timo Glock — Jordan — 1'16"323 

9 
- Felipe Massa — Sauber — No Time
- Zsolt Baumgartner — Minardi — 1'17"064 

10 
- Gianmaria Bruni — Minardi — No Time
- Takuma Sato — BAR — 1'17"004 

Podium

	1°	2°	3°
'90	A. Senna	N. Piquet	N. Mansell
'91	N. Piquet	S. Modena	R. Patrese
'92	G. Berger	M. Schumacher	J. Alesi
'93	A. Prost	M. Schumacher	D. Hill
'94	M. Schumacher	D. Hill	J. Alesi
'95	J. Alesi	R. Barrichello	E. Irvine
'96	D. Hill	J. Villeneuve	J. Alesi
'97	M. Schumacher	J. Alesi	G. Fisichella
'98	M. Schumacher	G. Fisichella	E. Irvine
'99	M. Hakkinen	G. Fisichella	E. Irvine
'00	M. Schumacher	R. Barrichello	G. Fisichella
'01	R. Schumacher	M. Schumacher	M. Hakkinen
'02	M. Schumacher	D. Coulthard	R. Barrichello
'03	M. Schumacher	R. Schumacher	J.P. Montoya

RESULTS

	DRIVER	CAR	KPH	GAP
1	M. Schumacher	Ferrari	207,165	-
2	R. Barrichello	Ferrari	206,966	5"108
3	J. Button	BAR	206,371	20"409
4	G. Fisichella	Sauber	203,433	1 lap
5	K. Raikkonen	McLaren	202,663	1 lap
6	D. Coulthard	McLaren	202,418	1 lap
7	T. Glock	Jordan	199,538	2 laps
8	N. Heidfeld	Jordan	199,525	2 laps
9	C. Klien	Jaguar	196,860	3 laps
10	Z. Baumgartner	Minardi	193,104	4 laps

RETIREMENTS

F. Massa	Sauber	62	Accident
T. Sato	BAR	48	Engine
F. Alonso	Renault	44	Axle-shaft
G. Bruni	Minardi	30	Gearbox
M. Webber	Jaguar	6	Accident
J. Trulli	Renault	0	Axle-shaft
R. Schumacher	Williams	-	Disqualified
J.P. Montoya	Williams	-	Disqualified
C. Da Matta	Toyota	-	Disqualified
O. Panis	Toyota	-	Disqualified

THE RACE

DRIVER	CAR	LAP	FASTEST LAP	TOP SPEED
R. Barrichello	Ferrari	68	1'13"622	347,9
M. Schumacher	Ferrari	18	1'13"630	344,6
F. Alonso	Renault	41	1'14"179	335,7
J. Button	BAR	68	1'14"246	334,7
K. Raikkonen	McLaren	44	1'14"752	333,8
T. Sato	BAR	25	1'15"076	334,6
G. Fisichella	Sauber	47	1'15"078	342,3
D. Coulthard	McLaren	55	1'15"478	339,9
F. Massa	Sauber	25	1'15"660	344,9
C. Klien	Jaguar	45	1'15"731	331,2
N. Heidfeld	Jordan	18	1'15"890	333,7
M. Webber	Jaguar	6	1'16"739	324,0
T. Glock	Jordan	42	1'16"900	332,3
Z. Baumgartner	Minardi	64	1'17"516	332,3
G. Bruni	Minardi	25	1'18"025	332,0
J. Trulli	Renault	-	-	-
R. Schumacher	Williams	-	-	-
J.P. Montoya	Williams	-	-	-
C. Da Matta	Toyota	-	-	-
O. Panis	Toyota	-	-	-

CANADIAN GP

WILLIAMS AND TOYOTA DISQUALIFIED!

Ralf Schumacher set pole position at the circuit dedicated to the late Gilles Villeneuve, ahead of Button in the BAR. Brother Michael was only sixth in the Ferrari while the two Renaults occupied the third and fifth places on the grid. The Montreal circuit clearly suited the German driver, who was also on pole the previous year, while for Williams it was the first pole position of the 2004 season. With five Michelin runners in the top 5 places it was clear that the French tyres, thanks to a track temperature that rarely exceeded 45°, were coming out on top this time.

One person who failed to take advantage of the tyre factor was Sato, BAR's Japanese driver, who was up on the final split on his quick lap. Sato had a spectacular spin coming out of the final chicane but avoided making contact with the wall and crossed the line with the fourth last time.

It all seemed to be going according to plan for Williams but the surprises, this time negative, were not over.

At the start Ralf powered away into the lead while Trulli, who had set an excellent third-quickest time in qualifying, managed to complete just a few metres before retiring from the race. The Williams driver came into the pits a few laps later for an early refuelling stop, which showed that the car had started with a low fuel load. Alonso took over the lead of the race, passing it provisionally to Schumacher before the German relinquished it to his younger brother in the hectic round of pit stops.

But at the midway point it was Ferrari who had moved into the lead of the race, and Schumacher easily went on to record his seventh win in eight races. He was followed home by brother Ralf and Barrichello.

But a further surprise was just around the corner. A few hours later, following post-race checks, the two Williams and the Toyotas were disqualified for using oversized brake ducts. Button was then moved up to third place while for the first time in 2004 both Jordans finished in the points with rookie Glock and Heidfeld, who took seventh and eighth at the flag.

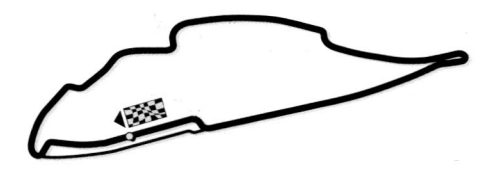

MONTREAL
Length: **4,361 km**
Laps: **70** - Distance: **305,270 kms**

This track is an artificial street circuit built on the island of Notre Dame in the centre of Montreal. It hosted its first Formula 1 grand prix in 1978. In 1984 it was named after the Canadian driver Gilles Villeneuve, who lost his life two years before. It is a fast circuit on which cars can reach speeds of over 340 km/h on the straights, which are combined with violent braking points and a number of tight S-bends.

HIGHLIGHTS

Timo Glock, the Jordan test-driver, made his Formula 1 debut in the Canadian GP, reputed to be one of the toughest circuits on the calendar. It was a lucky debut because thanks to the disqualification of Williams and Toyota, he was able to finish seventh, ahead of his expert team-mate Heidfeld. With two cars at the finish and three points in the title race, Jordan moved ahead of Toyota and Jaguar in the Constructors' standings.

PHOTO PORTFOLIO
FOLLOWING PAGES

Coulthard made contact with Klien (Jaguar) at the start, spun and ended up at the back of the field. It was a negative day for Renault, with Trulli out on lap 1 and Alonso on lap 44, both with driveshaft failure.
Ferrari scored a 1-2 with Schumacher taking his seventh win in Canada.

CHAMPIONSHIPS POINTS	AUSTRALIAN GP	MALAYSIAN GP	BAHRAIN GP	SAN MARINO GP	SPANISH GP	MONACO GP	EUROPEAN GP	CANADIAN GP	UNITED STATES GP	FRENCH GP	BRITISH GP	GERMAN GP	HUNGARIAN GP	BELGIUM GP	ITALIAN GP	CHINA GP	JAPANESE GP	BRAZILIAN GP	TOTAL POINT
1 M. Schumacher	10	10	10	10	10	-	10	10											70
2 R. Barrichello	8	5	8	3	8	6	8	8											54
3 J. Button	3	6	6	8	1	8	6	6											44
4 J. Trulli	2	4	5	4	6	10	5	-											36
5 F. Alonso	6	2	3	5	5	-	4	-											25
6 J.P. Montoya	4	8	-	6	-	5	1	-											24
7 R. Schumacher	5	-	2	2	3	-	-	-											12
8 G. Fisichella	-	-	-	-	2	-	3	5											10
9 T. Sato	-	-	4	-	4	-	-	-											8
10 D. Coulthard	1	3	-	-	-	-	-	3											7
11 F. Massa	-	1	-	-	-	4	-	-											5
12 K. Raikkonen	-	-	-	1	-	-	-	4											5
13 C. Da Matta	-	-	-	-	-	3	-	-											3
14 M. Webber	-	-	1	-	-	-	2	-											3
15 N. Heidfeld	-	-	-	-	-	2	-	1											3
16 T. Glock	/	/	/	/	/	/	/	2											2
17 O. Panis	-	-	-	-	-	1	-	-											1
18 C. Klien	-	-	-	-	-	-	-	-											-
19 G. Pantano	-	-	-	-	-	-	-	-											-
20 G. Bruni	-	-	-	-	-	-	-	-											-
21 Z. Baumgartner	-	-	-	-	-	-	-	-											-

181

Mobil 1
MICHELIN

8
FERNANDO ALON
MICHELIN

TRAK
elf
8
Telefónica
MICHELIN

Montreal

INDIANAPOLIS - 20 JUNE 2004

POLE POSITION

'00	M. Schumacher	'02	M. Schumacher
'01	M. Schumacher	'03	K. Raikkonen

2004
RUBENS BARRICHELLO

1°	2°	3°
'00 M. Schumacher	R. Barrichello	H.H. Frentzen
'01 M. Hakkinen	M. Schumacher	D. Coulthard
'02 R. Barrichello	M. Schumacher	D. Coulthard
'03 M. Schumacher	K. Raikkonen	H.H. Frentzen

STARTING GRID

1
- Rubens Barrichello — Ferrari — 1'10"223
- Michael Schumacher — Ferrari — 1'10"400

2
- Takuma Sato — BAR — 1'10"601
- Jenson Button — BAR — 1'10"820

3
- Juan-Pablo Montoya — Williams — 1'11"062
- Ralf Schumacher — Williams — 1'11"106

4
- Kimi Raikkonen — McLaren — 1'11"137
- Olivier Panis — Toyota — 1'11"167

5
- Fernando Alonso — Renault — 1'11"185
- Mark Webber — Jaguar — 1'11"286

6
- Cristiano Da Matta — Toyota — 1'11"691
- David Coulthard — McLaren — 1'12"026

7
- Christian Klien — Jaguar — 1'12"170
- Giancarlo Fisichella — Sauber — 1'12"470

8
- Felipe Massa — Sauber — 1'12"721
- Nick Heidfeld — Jordan — 1'13"147

9
- Giorgio Pantano — Jordan — 1'13"375
- Gianmaria Bruni — Minardi — 1'14"010

10
- Zsolt Baumgartner — Minardi — 1'14"812
- Jarno Trulli — Renault — No Time

RESULTS

	DRIVER	CAR	KPH	GAP
1	M. Schumacher	Ferrari	182,698	-
2	R. Barrichello	Ferrari	182,609	2"950
3	T. Sato	BAR	182,033	22"036
4	J. Trulli	Renault	181,658	34"544
5	O. Panis	Toyota	181,568	37"534
6	K. Raikkonen	McLaren	179,369	1 lap
7	D. Coulthard	McLaren	178,578	1 lap
8	Z. Baumgartner	Minardi	174,757	3 laps

RETIREMENTS

G. Fisichella	Sauber	65	Hydraulic circuit
M. Webber	Jaguar	60	Hydraulic circuit
N. Heidfeld	Jordan	43	Engine
J. Button	BAR	26	Gearbox
C. Da Matta	Toyota	17	Gearbox
R. Schumacher	Williams	9	Wheel
F. Alonso	Renault	8	Wheel
C. Klien	Jaguar	0	Accident
F. Massa	Sauber	0	Accident
G. Pantano	Jordan	0	Accident
G. Bruni	Minardi	0	Accident
J.P. Montoya	Williams	-	Disqualified

THE RACE

DRIVER	CAR	LAP	FASTEST LAP	TOP SPEED
R. Barrichello	Ferrari	7	1'10"399	356,4
M. Schumacher	Ferrari	8	1'10"412	348,4
T. Sato	BAR	47	1'10"727	349,9
O. Panis	Toyota	46	1'10"933	344,3
J. Button	BAR	22	1'11"025	353,6
J. Trulli	Renault	45	1'11"187	355,3
F. Alonso	Renault	8	1'11"236	346,0
K. Raikkonen	McLaren	59	1'11"248	355,6
R. Schumacher	Williams	8	1'11"982	354,7
G. Fisichella	Sauber	44	1'12"129	356,6
M. Webber	Jaguar	46	1'12"140	349,9
D. Coulthard	McLaren	44	1'12"155	354,7
C. Da Matta	Toyota	8	1'12"872	343,8
N. Heidfeld	Jordan	37	1'13"095	348,0
Z. Baumgartner	Minardi	39	1'14"097	338,8
C. Klien	Jaguar	-	-	-
F. Massa	Sauber	-	-	-
G. Pantano	Jordan	-	-	-
G. Bruni	Minardi	-	-	-
J.P. Montoya	Williams	-	-	-

UNITED STATES GP

AN INCIDENT-PACKED US GP

You've got to feel sorry for Ralf Schumacher. From the joy of his first pole of the season to the dismay of being disqualified in Canada and then his horrific crash at Indianapolis, which left the spectators, as well as the riders themselves, with bated breath as the Williams driver remained immobile in the cockpit of his wrecked car in the middle of the track.
Luckily the injuries suffered by the German driver were not serious but he will be forced to miss the upcoming French GP.
But back to the race weekend. On Saturday Barrichello, who had gone well on the first day of qualifying, put in a perfect lap to take pole position ahead of his team-mate and the two BARs. The two Williams drivers were next up, with Montoya ahead of Ralf, the Colombian enjoying massive support from his numerous fans. Trulli was again unlucky due to a gearbox problem in qualifying and the Italian would line up on the last row of the grid.
Rubens got off to a good start, but not as good as Alonso who powered from ninth on the grid to third at the first corner, right behind Schumacher. Behind it was total chaos, with four drivers - Klien (Jaguar), Massa (Sauber), Bruni (Minardi) and the returning Pantano (Jordan) – already eliminated after 300 metres. The next incident came on lap 8. At the end of the start-finish straight Alonso spun and crashed against the guard-rail when he punctured a tyre. On the next lap it was the turn of Ralf Schumacher to crash, also due to a puncture from debris left on the track.
The rear of his Williams slammed into the wall and what was left of the car came to a rest in the middle of the track and was just missed by the following cars. For almost two minutes Schumacher Jr. remained stationary in the cockpit and it seemed to take an eternity for the rescue trucks to arrive.
Meanwhile the race was continuing, with Schumacher setting the pace followed by Barrichello and a fantastic Sato, who ran a faultless race to step on to the podium for the first time in his career.
The same could also be said of Trulli who finished fourth after starting from the last row of the grid, the Italian even holding third place in the final stages of the race.
Eighth place for Hungarian Baumgartner with a Minardi was a great result for the Italian team, but the real scandal came three laps from the chequered flag when the track marshals black-flagged Montoya because the Williams team had failed to move his car in time from the starting-grid .... one and a half hours before!

INDIANAPOLIS
Length: 4,192 km
Laps: 73 - Distance: 306,016 kms

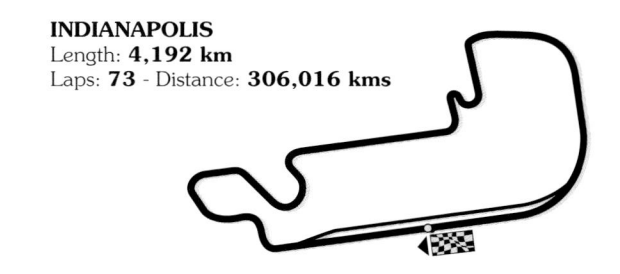

The circuit on which the Formula 1 GP is held is situated on the inside of the famous Indianapolis oval. It uses the start-finish straight and part of the banked curve that precedes it. The current track was inaugurated in 2000 with a win for Schumacher and Ferrari.

HIGHLIGHTS

After a gap of 14 years another Japanese driver made the podium in a Formula 1 grand prix race. The first to do so was Aguri Suzuki who finished third behind the two Benettons of Piquet and Moreno in the 1990 Japanese GP with a Larrousse. Takuma Sato, BAR's aggressive driver, had already come close to the podium on a couple of occasions in 2004.

PHOTO PORTFOLIO
FOLLOWING PAGES

The US GP was packed with incidents, almost all caused by punctures. The most serious was Ralf Schumacher's on lap 9, when his Williams slammed into the wall along the start-finish straight. The medical team took an eternity to reach him, while the rest of the field lined up behind the safety car, passing the Williams wreckage for several laps. Japan's Takuma Sato had cause to celebrate, with third place on the grid and a podium finish with the two Ferrari drivers.

	CHAMPIONSHIPS POINTS	AUSTRALIAN GP	MALAYSIAN GP	BAHRAIN GP	SAN MARINO GP	SPANISH GP	MONACO GP	EUROPEAN GP	CANADIAN GP	UNITED STATES GP	FRENCH GP	BRITISH GP	GERMAN GP	HUNGARIAN GP	BELGIUM GP	ITALIAN GP	CHINA GP	JAPANESE GP	BRAZILIAN GP	TOTAL POINT
1	M. Schumacher	10	10	10	10	10	-	10	10	10										80
2	R. Barrichello	8	5	8	3	8	6	8	8	8										62
3	J. Button	3	6	6	8	1	8	6	6	-										44
4	J. Trulli	2	4	5	4	6	10	5	-	5										41
5	F. Alonso	6	2	3	5	5	-	4	-	-										25
6	J.P. Montoya	4	8	-	6	-	5	1	-	-										24
7	T. Sato	-	-	4	-	4	-	-	-	6										14
8	R. Schumacher	5	-	2	2	3	-	-	-	-										12
9	G. Fisichella	-	-	-	-	2	-	3	5	-										10
10	D. Coulthard	1	3	-	-	-	-	-	3	2										9
11	K. Raikkonen	-	-	-	1	-	-	-	4	3										8
12	F. Massa	-	1	-	-	-	4	-	-	-										5
13	O. Panis	-	-	-	-	-	1	-	-	4										5
14	C. Da Matta	-	-	-	-	-	3	-	-	-										3
15	N. Heidfeld	-	-	-	-	-	2	-	1	-										3
16	M. Webber	-	-	1	-	-	-	2	-	-										3
17	T. Glock	/	/	/	/	/	/	/	2	/										2
18	Z. Baumgartner	-	-	-	-	-	-	-	-	1										1
19	C. Klien	-	-	-	-	-	-	-	-	-										-
20	G. Pantano	-	-	-	-	-	-	-	-	-										-
21	G. Bruni	-	-	-	-	-	-	-	-	-										-

185

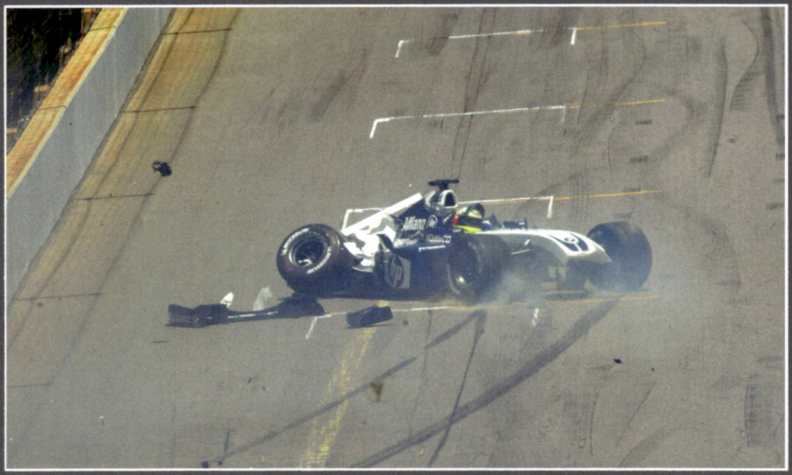

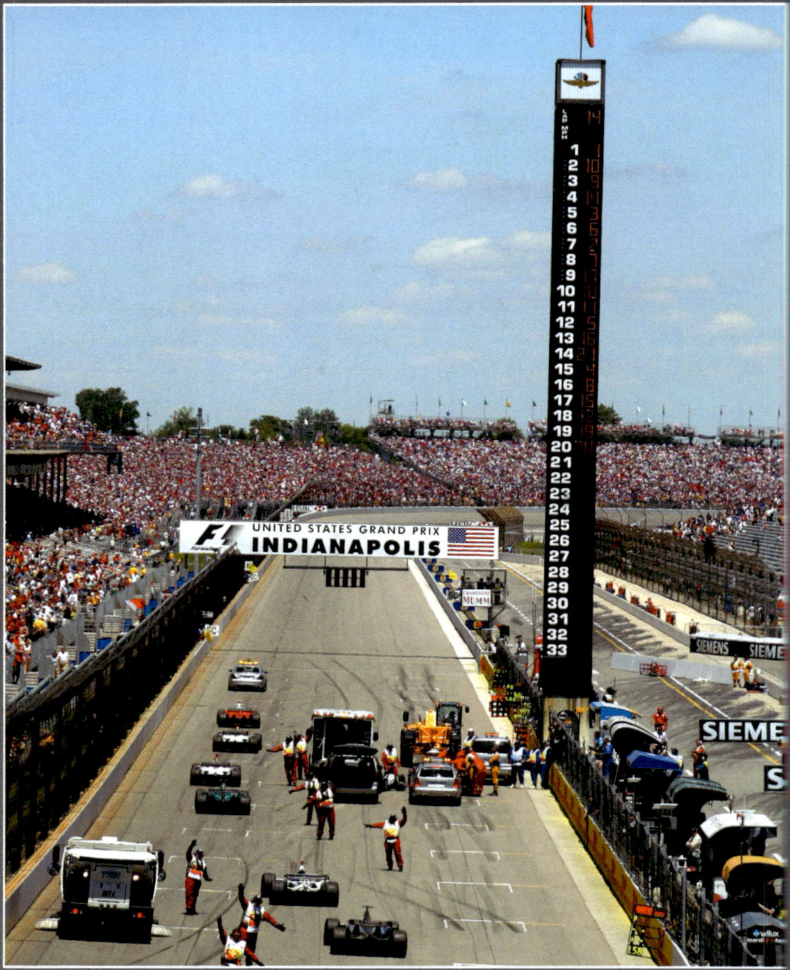
UNITED STATES GRAND PRIX
INDIANAPOLIS

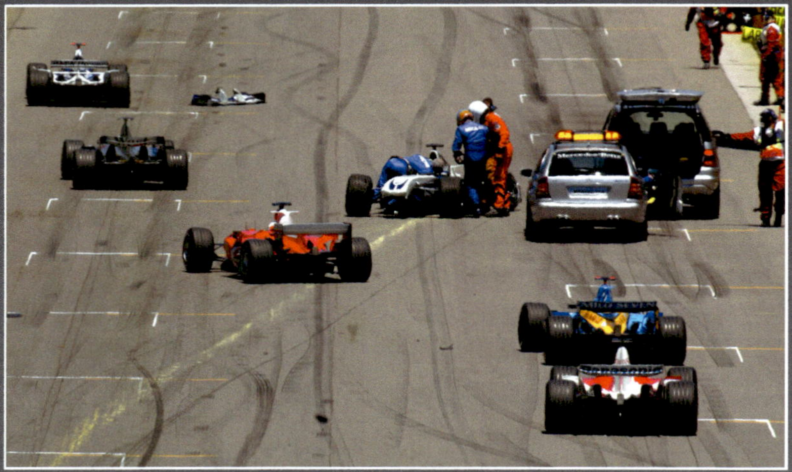

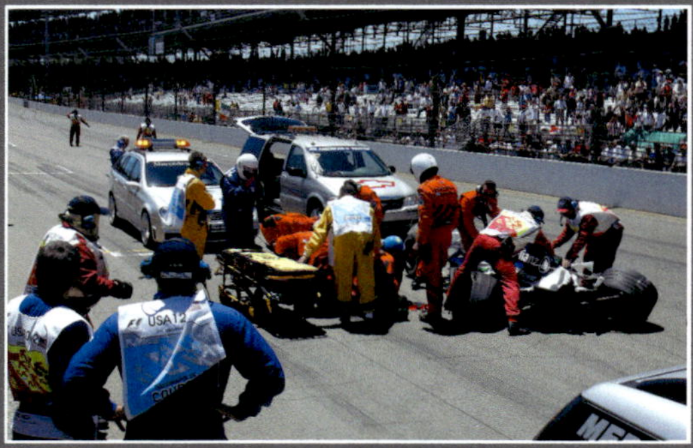

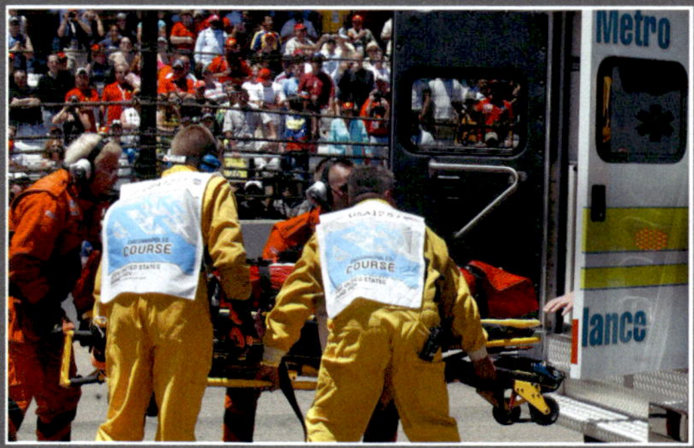
Metro

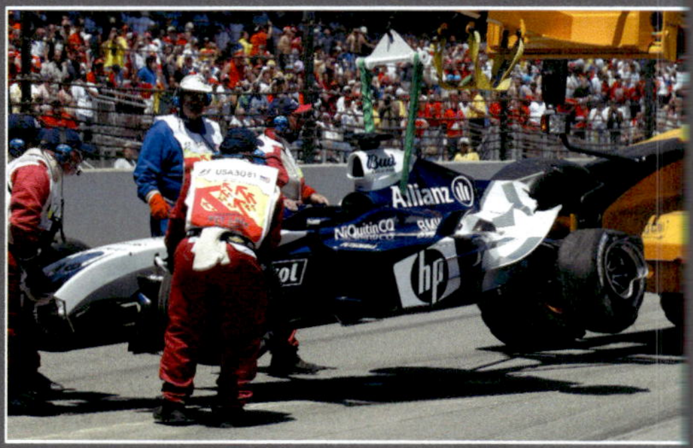
Allianz

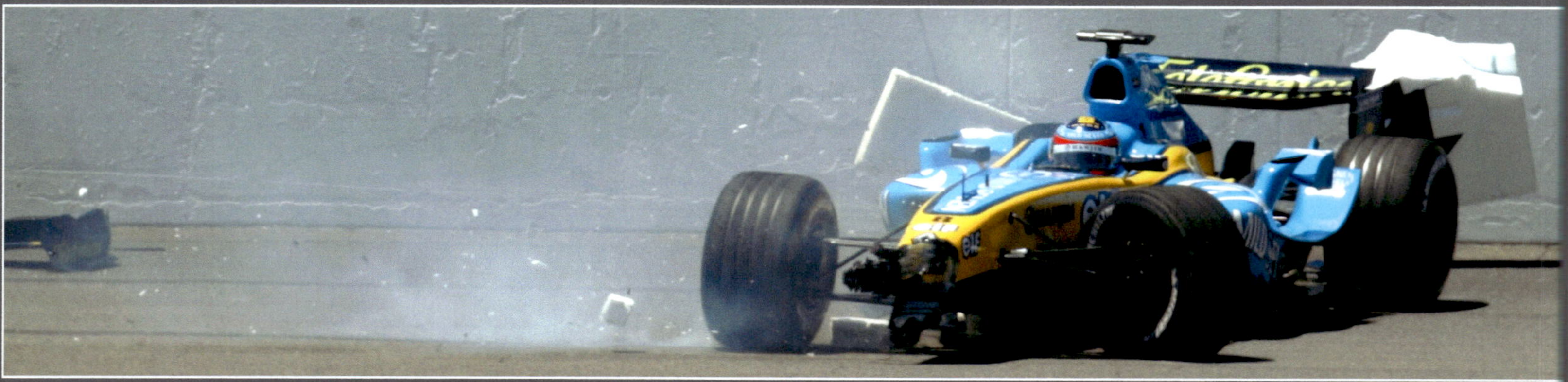

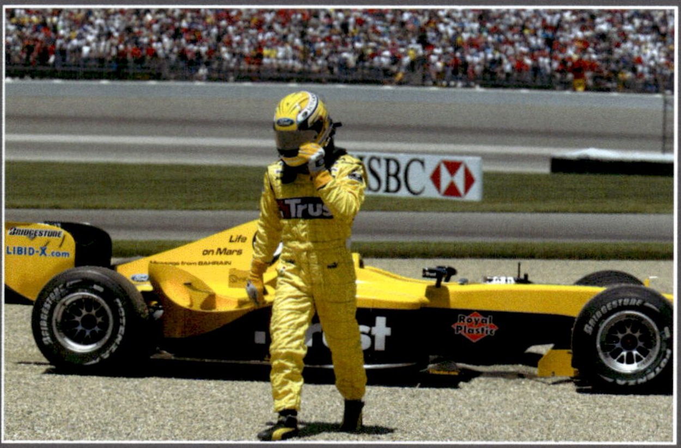

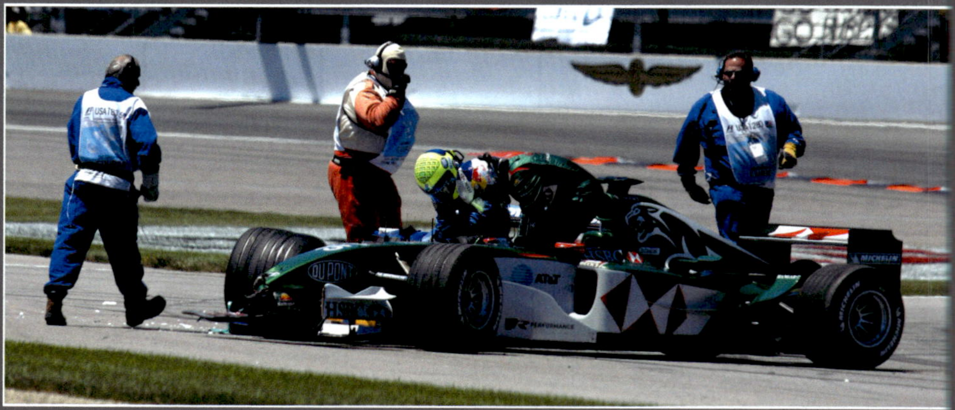

INDIANAPOLIS

187

MAGNY-COURS - 4 JULY 2004

POLE POSITION

- '90 N. Mansell
- '91 R. Patrese
- '92 N. Mansell
- '93 D. Hill
- '94 D. Hill
- '95 D. Hill
- '96 M. Schumacher
- '97 M. Schumacher
- '98 M. Hakkinen
- '99 R. Barrichello
- '00 M. Schumacher
- '01 R. Schumacher
- '02 J.P. Montoya
- '03 R. Schumacher

2004 FERNANDO ALONSO

STARTING GRID

1 
- Fernando Alonso — Renault — 1'13"698
- Michael Schumacher — Ferrari — 1'13"971

2 
- David Coulthard — McLaren — 1'13"987 
- Jenson Button — BAR — 1'13"995

3 
- Jarno Trulli — Renault — 1'14"070 
- Juan-Pablo Montoya — Williams — 1'14"172

4 
- Takuma Sato — BAR — 1'14"240 
- Marc Gene' — Williams — 1'14"275

5 
- Kimi Raikkonen — McLaren — 1'14"346
- Rubens Barrichello — Ferrari — 1'14"478

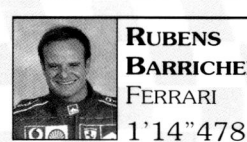

6 
- Cristiano Da Matta — Toyota — 1'14"553 
- Mark Webber — Jaguar — 1'14"798

7 
- Christian Klien — Jaguar — 1'15"065 
- Olivier Panis — Toyota — 1'15"130

8 
- Giancarlo Fisichella — Sauber — 1'16"177 
- Felipe Massa — Sauber — 1'16"200

9 
- Nick Heidfeld — Jordan — 1'16"807 
- Giorgio Pantano — Jordan — 1'17"462

10 
- Gianmaria Bruni — Minardi — 1'17"913 
- Zsolt Baumgartner — Minardi — 1'18"247

Podium

	1°	2°	3°
'90	A. Prost	I. Capelli	A. Senna
'91	N. Mansell	A. Prost	A. Senna
'92	N. Mansell	A. Prost	M. Brundle
'93	A. Prost	D. Hill	M. Schumacher
'94	M. Schumacher	D. Hill	G. Berger
'95	M. Schumacher	D. Hill	D. Coulthard
'96	D. Hill	J. Villeneuve	J. Alesi
'97	M. Schumacher	H.H. Frentzen	E. Irvine
'98	M. Schumacher	E. Irvine	M. Hakkinen
'99	H.H. Frentzen	M. Hakkinen	R. Barrichello
'00	D. Coulthard	M. Hakkinen	R. Barrichello
'01	M. Schumacher	R. Schumacher	R. Barrichello
'02	M. Schumacher	K. Raikkonen	D. Coulthard
'03	R. Schumacher	J.P. Montoya	M. Schumacher

RESULTS

#	DRIVER	CAR	KPH	GAP
1	M. Schumacher	Ferrari	205,035	-
2	F. Alonso	Renault	204,720	8"329
3	R. Barrichello	Ferrari	203,845	31"622
4	J. Trulli	Renault	203,828	32"082
5	J. Button	BAR	203,813	32"484
6	D. Coulthard	McLaren	203,700	35"520
7	K. Raikkonen	McLaren	203,673	36"230
8	J.P. Montoya	Williams	203,405	43"419
9	M. Webber	Jaguar	203,071	52"394
10	M. Genè	Williams	202,857	58"166
11	C. Klien	Jaguar	201,728	1 lap
12	G. Fisichella	Sauber	200,690	1 lap
13	F. Massa	Sauber	200,182	1 lap
14	C. Da Matta	Toyota	199,833	1 lap
15	O. Panis	Toyota	198,423	2 laps
16	N. Heidfeld	Jordan	196,849	2 laps
17	G. Pantano	Jordan	195,529	3 laps

RETIREMENTS

Driver	Car	Lap	Reason
G. Bruni	Minardi	65	Hydraulic circuit
Z. Baumgartner	Minardi	31	Crashed
T. Sato	BAR	15	Engine

THE RACE

DRIVER	CAR	LAP	FASTEST LAP	TOP SPEED
M. Schumacher	Ferrari	32	1'15"377	323,7
F. Alonso	Renault	34	1'15"551	314,6
K. Raikkonen	McLaren	30	1'15"791	319,9
M. Webber	Jaguar	53	1'15"956	322,2
J. Button	BAR	50	1'15"971	317,5
R. Barrichello	Ferrari	50	1'16"035	324,4
M. Genè	Williams	56	1'16"070	321,4
J.P. Montoya	Williams	48	1'16"140	320,6
J. Trulli	Renault	15	1'16"248	315,6
D. Coulthard	McLaren	11	1'16"303	322,9
G. Fisichella	Sauber	22	1'16"699	322,1
T. Sato	BAR	14	1'16"809	316,0
C. Klien	Jaguar	37	1'16"852	321,2
O. Panis	Toyota	53	1'17"069	318,4
F. Massa	Sauber	23	1'17"388	316,7
G. Pantano	Jordan	15	1'17"641	320,2
N. Heidfeld	Jordan	26	1'18"627	320,0
G. Bruni	Minardi	52	1'18"932	311,3
Z. Baumgartner	Minardi	13	1'19"659	312,8
C. Da Matta	Toyota	49	1'19"937	319,7

FRENCH GP

A TRIUMPH FOR FERRARI STRATEGY

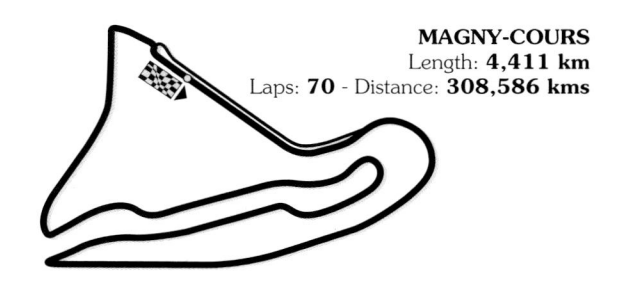

Fernando Alonso (Renault) set the French fans alight in the team's home GP after setting a superb pole position in front of world champions Ferrari. Behind them came Coulthard with the new McLaren, followed by Button (BAR) and Trulli with the second Renault.
Saturday's exploit looked as if it was going to be repeated on Sunday raceday as Alonso blasted away from Schumacher at the lights, while Trulli got an even better start from row 3, the Italian slotting in behind the Spaniard and the German at the first turn.
Things were looking good for Renault, but they hadn't counted on Ferrari's brilliant race strategy. After just 11 laps, Schumacher peeled away and came into the pits early for his first pit-stop. The rest of the field came in shortly after. Trulli stopped on lap 13 and Alonso on the following lap. It was obvious that all the teams were opting for a lighter fuel load strategy with, as a result, more pit-stops. The short Magny-Cours pit-lane also meant that time lost in the pits was limited to around eight seconds, in addition to the refuelling itself. Schumacher, who was already in the lead after his third, and apparently last pit-stop began to power ahead, increasing his lead over Alonso by a second a lap. In just a few laps, the German had an advantage of more than 20 seconds and it was clear that his Ferrari was running with a low fuel load and needed one more refuelling stop.
With this sort of lead, a win for Schumacher looked a foregone conclusion unless something went wrong during the pit-stop.
Schuey came in on lap 58, 12 from the end, refuelled without a hitch and he returned to the track with a big enough lead over Alonso to keep the Spanish driver at bay.
Third place went to Barrichello, who after battling with Button for several laps finally passed him for fourth place with a third of the race still to go and then set about chasing Trulli.
He was rewarded at the final curve of the last lap, when Trulli messed up his entry and Rubens dived into the inside of the turn before powering to the finish line amidst the cheers of his mechanics and the disappointment of Briatore.

MAGNY-COURS
Length: **4,411 km**
Laps: **70** - Distance: **308,586 kms**

The project was an ambitious one: to recreate the most famous curves of the other world championship circuits on this track. Magny-Cours, located in central France, took the place of Paul Ricard in 1991 and has been modified several times over the years. The last change was in 2003 when the chicane before the start-finish straight was modified.

HIGHLIGHTS

Barrichello is the only driver to score points in the first 10 races, the Brazilian taking six second places and two thirds.
On the other end of the scale no points have yet been scored by Klien (Jaguar), Pantano (Jordan), Bruni (Minardi) and Marc Gené, who however only made his season debut in France with the Williams left vacant by Ralf Schumacher. Regarding the Williams driver, with German doctors advising a recovery period of two months it looks as if his season is already over.

PHOTO PORTFOLIO
FOLLOWING PAGES

Alonso set pole position but the Spanish driver had to settle for the runner-up slot at the chequered flag.
Sato's BAR suffered engine failure after just 15 laps. Fisichella steps out of his car after the Italian had crashed into the guard rail due to suspension failure.

CHAMPIONSHIPS POINTS		AUSTRALIAN GP	MALAYSIAN GP	BAHRAIN GP	SAN MARINO GP	SPANISH GP	MONACO GP	EUROPEAN GP	CANADIAN GP	UNITED STATES GP	FRENCH GP	BRITISH GP	GERMAN GP	HUNGARIAN GP	BELGIUM GP	ITALIAN GP	CHINA GP	JAPANESE GP	BRAZILIAN GP	TOTAL POINT
1	M. Schumacher	10	10	10	10	10	-	10	10	10	10									90
2	R. Barrichello	8	5	8	3	8	6	8	8	8	6									68
3	J. Button	3	6	6	8	1	8	6	6	-	4									48
4	J. Trulli	2	4	5	4	6	10	5	-	5	5									46
5	F. Alonso	6	2	3	5	5	-	4	-	-	8									33
6	J.P. Montoya	4	8	-	6	-	5	1	-	-	1									25
7	T. Sato	-	-	4	-	4	-	-	-	6	-									14
8	R. Schumacher	5	-	2	2	3	-	-	-	-	/									12
9	D. Coulthard	1	3	-	-	-	-	-	3	2	3									12
10	G. Fisichella	-	-	-	-	2	-	3	5	-	-									10
11	K. Raikkonen	-	-	-	1	-	-	-	4	3	2									10
12	F. Massa	-	1	-	-	-	4	-	-	-	-									5
13	O. Panis	-	-	-	-	-	1	-	-	4	-									5
14	C. Da Matta	-	-	-	-	-	3	-	-	-	-									3
15	N. Heidfeld	-	-	-	-	-	2	-	1	-	-									3
16	M. Webber	-	-	1	-	-	-	2	-	-	-									3
17	T. Glock	/	/	/	/	/	/	/	2	/	/									2
18	Z. Baumgartner	-	-	-	-	-	-	-	1	-	-									1
19	C. Klien	-	-	-	-	-	-	-	-	-	-									-
20	M. Gené	/	/	/	/	/	/	/	/	/	-									-
21	G. Pantano	-	-	-	-	-	-	-	-	-	-									-
22	G. Bruni	-	-	-	-	-	-	-	-	-	-									-

Mobil 1
Mobil 1
Mob
elf
8

HONDA

HONDA

Red Bull
CREDIT SUISSE
MALAYSIA
PETRONAS
POTENZA
DASSAULT SYSTEMES

MAGNY-COURS

Silverstone - 11 July 2004

Pole Position

'90	N. Mansell	'97	J. Villeneuve
'91	N. Mansell	'98	M. Hakkinen
'92	N. Mansell	'99	M. Hakkinen
'93	A. Prost	'00	R. Barrichello
'94	D. Hill	'01	M. Schumacher
'95	D. Hill	'02	J.P. Montoya
'96	D. Hill	'03	R. Barrichello

2004 KIMI RAIKKONEN

Starting Grid

1 
- Kimi Raikkonen — McLaren — 1'18"233
- Rubens Barrichello — Ferrari — 1'18"305 

2 
- Jenson Button — BAR — 1'18"580
- Michael Schumacher — Ferrari — 1'18"710

3 
- Jarno Trulli — Renault — 1'18"715
- David Coulthard — McLaren — 1'19"148 

4 
- Juan-Pablo Montoya — Williams — 1'19"378
- Takuma Sato — BAR — 1'19"688 

5 
- Mark Webber — Jaguar — 1'120"004
- Felipe Massa — Sauber — 1'20"202 

6 
- Marc Gene' — Williams — 1'20"335
- Cristiano Da Matta — Toyota — 1'20"545 

7 
- Christian Klien — Jaguar — 1'21"559
- Giorgio Pantano — Jordan — 1'22"458 

8 
- Nick Heidfeld — Jordan — 1'22"677
- Fernando Alonso — Renault — 1'18"811 ** 

9 
- Olivier Panis — Toyota — 1'20"335 *
- Gianmaria Bruni — Minardi — 1'23"437 ** 

10 
- Zsolt Baumgartner — Minardi — 1'24"117 **
- Giancarlo Fisichella — Sauber — No Time *** 

* Relegated for obstructing Massa during qualifying lap
** Relegated for engine change
*** Did not do qualifying lap

192

FOSTER'S BRITISH GRAND PRIX

	1°	2°	3°
'90	A. Prost	T. Boutsen	A. Senna
'91	N. Mansell	G. Berger	A. Prost
'92	N. Mansell	R. Patrese	M. Brundle
'93	A. Prost	M. Schumacher	R. Patrese
'94	D. Hill	M. Schumacher	J. Alesi
'95	J. Herbert	J. Alesi	D. Coulthard
'96	J. Villeneuve	G. Berger	M. Hakkinen
'97	J. Villeneuve	J. Alesi	A. Wurz
'98	M. Schumacher	M. Hakkinen	E. Irvine
'99	D. Coulthard	E. Irvine	R. Schumacher
'00	D. Coulthard	M. Hakkinen	M. Schumacher
'01	M. Hakkinen	M. Schumacher	R. Barrichello
'02	M. Schumacher	R. Barrichello	J.P. Montoya
'03	R. Barrichello	J.P. Montoya	K. Raikkonen

Results

	Driver	Car	KPH	Gap
1	M. Schumacher	Ferrari	218,403	-
2	K. Raikkonen	McLaren	218,311	2"130
3	R. Barrichello	Ferrari	218,269	3"114
4	J. Button	BAR	217,945	10"683
5	J.P. Montoya	Williams	217,881	12"173
6	G. Fisichella	Sauber	217,850	12"888
7	D. Coulthard	McLaren	217,561	19"668
8	M. Webber	Jaguar	217,389	23"701
9	F. Massa	Sauber	217,375	24"023
10	F. Alonso	Renault	217,341	24"835
11	T. Sato	BAR	216,963	33"736
12	M. Genè	Williams	216,939	34"303
13	C. Da Matta	Toyota	213,201	1 lap
14	C. Klien	Jaguar	213,156	1 lap
15	N. Heidfeld	Jordan	212,792	1 lap
16	G. Bruni	Minardi	202,652	4 laps

Retirements

G. Pantano	Jordan	47	Crashed
J. Trulli	Renault	39	Suspension
Z. Baumgartner	Minardi	29	Engine
O. Panis	Toyota	16	Fire-fighting system

The Race

Driver	Car	Lap	Fastest Lap	Top Speed
M. Schumacher	Ferrari	14	1'18"739	289,5
R. Barrichello	Ferrari	8	1'19"296	283,7
J. Button	BAR	10	1'19"488	279,2
K. Raikkonen	McLaren	10	1'19"554	284,1
G. Fisichella	Sauber	22	1'19"813	272,5
J.P. Montoya	Williams	26	1'19"968	287,7
M. Genè	Williams	58	1'20"434	282,7
F. Alonso	Renault	39	1'20"442	285,4
F. Massa	Sauber	58	1'20"484	277,4
D. Coulthard	McLaren	25	1'20"547	286,0
J. Trulli	Renault	34	1'20"655	282,3
M. Webber	Jaguar	11	1'20"768	279,8
C. Da Matta	Toyota	35	1'20"768	276,9
T. Sato	BAR	12	1'20"790	279,8
C. Klien	Jaguar	10	1'20"956	286,7
N. Heidfeld	Jordan	17	1'21"720	268,2
G. Pantano	Jordan	13	1'22"146	266,9
O. Panis	Toyota	4	1'23"131	266,4
G. Bruni	Minardi	33	1'24"296	266,6
Z. Baumgartner	Minardi	12	1'24"317	258,3

BRITISH GP

McLaren Resurrection

Saturday's first practice session at the ultra-fast Silverstone track was a farce, annoying both the circuit spectators and F1 boss Bernie Ecclestone himself, when it turned into a battle to see who could set the slowest lap time! The reason for this was an oncoming storm, which meant that the slowest drivers could start the next session first.
In the all-important pole session, it was Kimi Raikkonen with the new McLaren who was surprisingly quickest, ahead of Barrichello, local favourite Button, with a new helmet livery, and Schumacher. Coulthard, in the second McLaren, was sixth, just behind Trulli in the Renault. Although Alonso actually set the sixth quickest time, he was penalised ten positions for an engine change.
Giancarlo Fisichella lined up on the last row of the grid after failing to take part in qualifying. This was not the first time the Italian driver had missed the session but on numerous occasions he had then delighted the crowds with a superb race.
Raikkonen blasted away from the lights and attacked the track with an vehemence that hadn't been seen in a long time, the Finn pulling out over three seconds on Schumacher (in 4th) in the opening lap. Meanwhile both Alonso and Fisichella got off to good starts and began to work their way up the field; at the flag Fisichella was a fantastic sixth, a result that was further confirmation of his ability despite him not being in one of the top teams. His 2004 performances must surely put Fisichella amongst the candidates for a top drive next year.
Except for the usual round of pit-stops that allowed Schumacher to move into the lead of the race, nothing much happened until lap 40 when Trulli's Renault had a front suspension failure, pitching him into the barriers and then the gravel in a massive accident. The Renault was utterly destroyed but the Italian immediately gave everyone the thumbs-up to show he was OK.
Out came the Safety Car, followed by Schuey, while Raikkonen (and also Barrichello) took the opportunity to refuel and they lined up behind the leader for the sprint-finish to the flag. On the restart Schumacher was ready however and the German completed the last 13 laps in the lead, scoring his tenth win of the year and his eightieth career victory.
Second was the resurgent McLaren of Raikkonen and third, once again, was Barrichello. Schumacher totally deserved his win after the Ferrari driver had run a superb, calculated race in which he had opted for two pit-stops against his rivals' three.

SILVERSTONE
Length: **5,141 km**
Laps: **60** - Distance: **308,355 kms**

The first British Grand Prix was organised at Silverstone by the Royal Automobile Club in 1948 on a disused airfield. After alternating with Aintree and Brands Hatch over the years, Silverstone has been the permanent home of the British Grand Prix since 1987.

HIGHLIGHTS

Giancarlo Fisichella was once again the hero of the day, the Italian having a superb run to sixth. After starting from the back of the grid, Fisichella ran faultlessly lap after lap, making numerous passes and proving again to be one of the best drivers around.
After a total of 134 GPs, nine seasons in Formula 1 with Minardi, Jordan, Benetton and Sauber, and just one deserved win to his name (Brazil 2003, albeit awarded post-race), now is surely the time to see what Fisichella can do in a really competitive car.

PHOTO PORTFOLIO
FOLLOWING PAGES

Celebrations in the McLaren pit garage with Raikkonen smiling at photographers after setting pole position, while the Minardi garage is sadly empty out of mourning for team manager John Walton, who died the day before. Jarno Trulli's Renault was a write-off after a horrific crash and Schumacher powered to yet another win.

CHAMPIONSHIPS POINTS		AUSTRALIAN GP	MALAYSIAN GP	BAHRAIN GP	SAN MARINO GP	SPANISH GP	MONACO GP	EUROPEAN GP	CANADIAN GP	UNITED STATES GP	FRENCH GP	BRITISH GP	GERMAN GP	HUNGARIAN GP	BELGIUM GP	ITALIAN GP	CHINA GP	JAPANESE GP	BRAZILIAN GP	TOTAL POINT
1	M. Schumacher	10	10	10	10	10	-	10	10	10	10	10								100
2	R. Barrichello	8	5	8	3	8	6	8	8	8	6	6								74
3	J. Button	3	6	6	8	1	8	6	6	-	4	5								53
4	J. Trulli	2	4	5	4	6	10	5	-	5	5	-								46
5	F. Alonso	6	2	3	5	5	-	4	-	-	8	-								33
6	J.P. Montoya	4	8	-	6	-	5	1	-	-	1	4								29
7	K. Raikkonen	-	-	-	1	-	-	-	4	3	2	8								18
8	T. Sato	-	-	4	-	4	-	-	-	6	-	-								14
9	D. Coulthard	1	3	-	-	-	-	-	3	2	3	2								14
10	G. Fisichella	-	-	-	-	2	-	3	5	-	-	3								13
11	R. Schumacher	5	-	2	2	3	-	-	-	-	/	/								12
12	F. Massa	-	1	-	-	-	4	-	-	-	-	-								5
13	O. Panis	-	-	-	-	-	1	-	4	-	-	-								5
14	M. Webber	-	-	1	-	-	-	2	-	-	-	1								4
15	C. Da Matta	-	-	-	-	-	3	-	-	-	-	-								3
16	N. Heidfeld	-	-	-	-	-	2	-	1	-	-	-								3
17	T. Glock	/	/	/	/	/	/	/	2	/	/	/								2
18	Z. Baumgartner	-	-	-	-	-	-	-	-	1	-	-								1
19	C. Klien	-	-	-	-	-	-	-	-	-	-	-								-
20	M. Genè	/	/	/	/	/	/	/	/	/	-	-								-
21	G. Pantano	-	-	-	-	-	-	-	-	-	-	-								-
22	G. Bruni	-	-	-	-	-	-	-	-	-	-	-								-

193

wilux
minardi F1 team
COSWORTH
SIEMENS

Kimi
Mobil 1
BOSS
SIEMENS
WARSTEINER
Räikkönen

FOST
Go Button!
BBG
John Boy
BRIDGESTONE
POTENZA

FOSTER'S

vodafone

FOSTER'S
Mercedes-Benz
AMG

SILVERSTONE

HOCKENHEIM - 25 JULY 2004

POLE POSITION

'90	A. Senna	'97	G. Berger
'91	N. Mansell	'98	M. Hakkinen
'92	N. Mansell	'99	M. Hakkinen
'93	A. Prost	'00	D. Coulthard
'94	G. Berger	'01	J.P. Montoya
'95	D. Hill	'02	M. Schumacher
'96	D. Hill	'03	J.P. Montoya

2004 MICHAEL SCHUMACHER

STARTING GRID

1
- 1: MICHAEL SCHUMACHER — FERRARI — 1'13"306 
- 2: JUAN-PABLO MONTOYA — WILLIAMS — 1'13"668

2 
- KIMI RAIKKONEN — McLAREN — 1'13"690
- DAVID COULTHARD — McLAREN — 1'13"821 

3 
- FERNANDO ALONSO — RENAULT — 1'13"874
- JARNO TRULLI — RENAULT — 1'14"134 

4 
- RUBENS BARRICHELLO — FERRARI — 1'14"278
- TAKUMA SATO — BAR — 1'14"287

5 
- OLIVIER PANIS — TOYOTA — 1'14"368
- ANTONIO PIZZONIA — WILLIAMS — 1'14"556 

6 
- MARK WEBBER — JAGUAR — 1'14"802
- CHRISTIAN KLIEN — JAGUAR — 1'15"011 

7 
- JENSON BUTTON — BAR — 1'13"674 *
- GIANCARLO FISICHELLA — SAUBER — 1'15"395 

8 
- CRISTIANO DA MATTA — TOYOTA — 1'15"454
- FELIPE MASSA — SAUBER — 1'15"616 

9 
- GIORGIO PANTANO — JORDAN — 1'16"192
- NICK HEIDFELD — JORDAN — 1'16"310 

10 
- GIANMARIA BRUNI — MINARDI — 1'18"055
- ZSOLT BAUMGARTNER — MINARDI — 1'18"400 

RELEGATED FOR ENGINE CHANGE

Podium

	1°	2°	3°
'90	A. Senna	A. Nannini	G. Berger
'91	N. Mansell	R. Patrese	J. Alesi
'92	N. Mansell	A. Senna	M. Schumacher
'93	A. Prost	M. Schumacher	M. Brundell
'94	G. Berger	O. Panis	E. Bernard
'95	M. Schumacher	D. Coulthard	G. Berger
'96	D. Hill	J. Alesi	J. Villeneuve
'97	G. Berger	M. Schumacher	M. Hakkinen
'98	M. Hakkinen	D. Coulthard	J. Villeneuve
'99	E. Irvine	M. Salo	H.H. Frentzen
'00	R. Barrichello	M. Hakkinen	D. Coulthard
'01	R. Schumacher	R. Barrichello	J. Villeneuve
'02	M. Schumacher	J.P. Montoya	R. Schumacher
'03	J.P. Montoya	D. Coulthard	J. Trulli

RESULTS

	DRIVER	CAR	KPH	GAP
1	M. Schumacher	Ferrari	215,852	-
2	J. Button	BAR	215,493	8"388
3	F. Alonso	Renault	215,153	16"351
4	D. Coulthard	McLaren	215,030	19"231
5	J.P. Montoya	Williams	214,868	23"055
6	M. Webber	Jaguar	214,103	41"108
7	A. Pizzonia	Williams	214,068	41"956
8	T. Sato	BAR	213,862	46"842
9	G. Fisichella	Sauber	213,013	1'07"102
10	C. Klien	Jaguar	212,951	1'08"578
11	J. Trulli	Renault	212,881	1'10"258
12	R. Barrichello	Ferrari	212,756	1'13"252
13	F. Massa	Sauber	211,734	1 lap
14	O. Panis	Toyota	211,134	1 lap
15	G. Pantano	Jordan	205,888	3 laps
16	Z. Baumgartner	Minardi	202,278	4 laps
17	G. Bruni	Minardi	199,821	4 laps

RETIREMENTS

N. Heidfeld	Jordan	42	Suspension
C. Da Matta	Toyota	38	Wheel
K. Raikkonen	McLaren	13	Broken rear wing

THE RACE

DRIVER	CAR	LAP	FASTEST LAP	TOP SPEED
K. Raikkonen	McLaren	10	1'13"780	329,8
M. Schumacher	Ferrari	5	1'13"783	332,0
J. Button	BAR	11	1'14"117	339,0
O. Panis	Toyota	59	1'14"247	328,8
F. Alonso	Renault	8	1'14"265	330,4
J. Trulli	Renault	9	1'14"386	332,1
J.P. Montoya	Williams	10	1'14"446	336,2
D. Coulthard	McLaren	8	1'14"558	338,0
T. Sato	BAR	29	1'14"585	339,9
A. Pizzonia	Williams	65	1'14"586	335,7
M. Webber	Jaguar	65	1'14"883	334,8
R. Barrichello	Ferrari	59	1'14"963	337,1
C. Klien	Jaguar	33	1'15"045	333,4
C. Da Matta	Toyota	20	1'15"145	328,7
G. Fisichella	Sauber	39	1'15"635	340,5
G. Pantano	Jordan	63	1'16"058	336,0
F. Massa	Sauber	61	1'16"248	340,3
N. Heidfeld	Jordan	20	1'16"903	333,9
G. Bruni	Minardi	52	1'18"372	321,6
Z. Baumgartner	Minardi	18	1'18"760	327,1

German GP

SCHUMACHER SMASHES ALL RECORDS!

In qualifying Schummy put in a fantastic lap to claim pole ahead of Montoya. For the German it was the 61st pole position in 205 GPs (an incredible 30% ratio) and the hundredth time his Ferrari had started from the front row.
The records keep piling up and hardly any remain to be beaten because Ayrton Senna's 65 pole positions and Riccardo Patrese's 256 races are both now within striking distance.
At the start the Ferrari driver was quickest off the line, leaving Montoya standing. The Colombian was also swamped by a spectacular Alonso who from fifth place on the grid powered into second after just a few metres.
In the usual Nurburgring bottleneck at the end of the start-finish line, the driver who came off the worst (but it was mainly his fault) was Barrichello. The Brazilian made contact with Coulthard, damaged his front wing and as a result had to pit for a replacement.
This was the start of a spectacular race, one that had not been seen in F1 for some time, with plenty of overtaking moves and never-ending surprises. For the first time in 2004 Raikkonen had his hands on a competitive McLaren and was having no problems in keeping the pace of the Ferrari. But on lap 19, for no particular reason, his car lost its rear wing on the straight at more than 300 km/h. Kimi inevitably crashed into the tyre wall but luckily he was unhurt, to the evident relief of everyone watching from the pit garage and in particular his girlfriend who the following week was to become Mrs Raikkonen.
Meanwhile there was another driver setting the race alight. Jenson Button, who started thirteenth on the grid, was driving his BAR like a man possessed and moved into the lead, thanks to intelligent pit-stop work.
At the flag Button finished a superb runner-up ahead of Alonso, in third, who had slowed for a while due to a sudden and inexplicable problem with his Renault.
Alonso's clash with Button was really what made the race however and their repeated overtaking moves and 300 km/h battle curve after curve and side-by-side reminded us of times gone past.

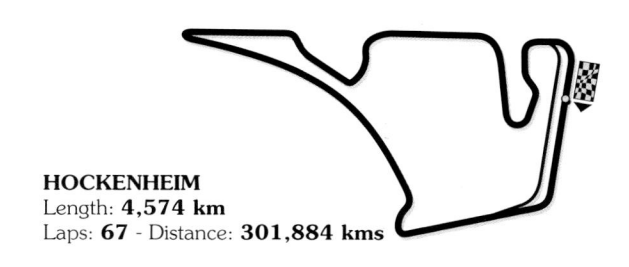

HOCKENHEIM
Length: **4,574 km**
Laps: **67** - Distance: **301,884 kms**

From 1951 onwards, the year in which the first German GP was held, the race alternated between the Nürburgring, the Avus and Hockenheim. In 1986 Hockenheim became the official home of the Formula 1 German GP. Inaugurated in 1939, the track has undergone several modifications over the years, the last of which in 2002.

HIGHLIGHTS

Once again Jenson Button gets the 'Driver of the Day' award. Starting thirteenth on the grid because he had to change his engine in qualifying, not only did the Brit finish runner-up, but he also sent the crowd wild with racing from another era. In particular his duel with Alonso stood out for the spectacular lines taken by both drivers, side-by-side, corner after corner.
A big thanks to Jenson and Fernando for putting on an exciting show, one that took them both onto the podium but above all finally succeeded in livening up Formula 1 for spectators worldwide.

PHOTO PORTFOLIO
FOLLOWING PAGES

Panis (Toyota) stops at the start due to electronic gremlins.
It was a disappointing day for Barrichello, who made contact with Coulthard on the opening lap and then punctured a tyre on the final lap, while Schumacher jumps for joy on the podium.

	CHAMPIONSHIPS POINTS	AUSTRALIAN GP	MALAYSIAN GP	BAHRAIN GP	SAN MARINO GP	SPANISH GP	MONACO GP	EUROPEAN GP	CANADIAN GP	UNITED STATES GP	FRENCH GP	BRITISH GP	GERMAN GP	HUNGARIAN GP	BELGIUM GP	ITALIAN GP	CHINA GP	JAPANESE GP	BRAZILIAN GP	TOTAL POINT
1	M. Schumacher	10	10	10	10	10	-	10	10	10	10	10	10							110
2	R. Barrichello	8	5	8	3	8	6	8	8	8	6	6	-							74
3	J. Button	3	6	6	8	1	8	6	6	-	4	5	8							61
4	J. Trulli	2	4	5	4	6	10	5	-	5	5	-	-							46
5	F. Alonso	6	2	3	5	5	-	4	-	-	8	-	6							39
6	J.P. Montoya	4	8	-	6	-	5	1	-	-	1	4	4							33
7	D. Coulthard	1	3	-	-	-	-	-	3	2	3	2	5							19
8	K. Raikkonen	-	-	-	1	-	-	-	4	3	2	8	-							18
9	T. Sato	-	-	4	-	4	-	-	-	6	-	-	1							15
10	G. Fisichella	-	-	-	-	2	-	3	5	-	-	3	-							13
11	R. Schumacher	5	-	2	2	3	-	-	-	-	/	/	/							12
12	M. Webber	-	-	1	-	-	-	2	-	-	-	1	3							7
13	F. Massa	-	1	-	-	-	4	-	-	-	-	-	-							5
14	O. Panis	-	-	-	-	-	1	-	-	4	-	-	-							5
15	C. Da Matta	-	-	-	-	-	-	3	-	-	-	-	-							3
16	N. Heidfeld	-	-	-	-	-	2	-	1	-	-	-	-							3
17	T. Glock	/	/	/	/	/	/	/	2	/	/	/	/							2
18	A. Pizzonia	/	/	/	/	/	/	/	/	/	/	/	2							2
19	Z. Baumgartner	-	-	-	-	-	-	-	1	-	-	-	-							1
20	C. Klien	-	-	-	-	-	-	-	-	-	-	-	-							-
21	M. Genè	/	/	/	/	/	/	/	/	/	/	/	/							-
22	G. Pantano	-	-	-	-	-	-	-	-	-	-	-	-							-
23	G. Bruni	-	-	-	-	-	-	-	-	-	-	-	-							-

197

Mobil 1
Mobil 1
Mobil 1
LUCKY STRIKE
Panasonic
BENSON&HEDGES

Mobil 1
Mobil 1

Marlboro

SCHÜCO
Henkel
Mobil 1
West
SIEMENS
vodafone

Hockenheim

BUDAPEST - 15 AUGUST 2004

POLE POSITION

'90	T. Boutsen	'97	M. Schumacher
'91	A. Senna	'98	M. Hakkinen
'92	R. Patrese	'99	M. Hakkinen
'93	A. Prost	'00	M. Schumacher
'94	M. Schumacher	'01	M. Schumacher
'95	D. Hill	'02	R. Barrichello
'96	M. Schumacher	'03	F. Alonso

2004 MICHAEL SCHUMACHER

STARTING GRID

1
- Michael Schumacher — Ferrari — 1'19"146 
- Rubens Barrichello — Ferrari — 1'19"323

2
- Takuma Sato — BAR — 1'19"693 
- Jenson Button — BAR — 1'19"700

3
- Fernando Alonso — Renault — 1'19"996 
- Antonio Pizzonia — Williams — 1'20"170

4
- Juan-Pablo Montoya — Williams — 1'20"199 
- Giancarlo Fisichella — Sauber — 1'20"324

5
- Jarno Trulli — Renault — 1'20"411 
- Kimi Raikkonen — McLaren — 1'20"570

6
- Mark Webber — Jaguar — 1'20"730 
- David Coulthard — McLaren — 1'20"897

7
- Olivier Panis — Toyota — 1'21"068 
- Christian Klien — Jaguar — 1'21"118

8
- Riccardo Zonta — Toyota — 1'21"135 
- Nick Heidfeld — Jordan — 1'22"180

9
- Giorgio Pantano — Jordan — 1'22"356 
- Zsolt Baumgartner — Minardi — 1'24"329

10
- Gianmaria Bruni — Minardi — 1'24"679
- Felipe Massa — Sauber — No Time 

	1°	2°	3°
'90	T. Boutsen	A. Senna	N. Piquet
'91	A. Senna	N. Mansell	R. Patrese
'92	A. Senna	N. Mansell	G. Berger
'93	D. Hill	R. Patrese	G. Berger
'94	M. Schumacher	D. Hill	J. Verstappen
'95	D. Hill	D. Coulthard	G. Berger
'96	J. Villeneuve	D. Hill	J. Alesi
'97	J. Villeneuve	D. Hill	J. Herbert
'98	M. Schumacher	D. Coulthard	J. Villeneuve
'99	M. Hakkinen	D. Coulthard	E. Irvine
'00	M. Hakkinen	M. Schumacher	D. Coulthard
'01	M. Schumacher	R. Barrichello	D. Coulthard
'02	R. Barrichello	M. Schumacher	R. Schumacher
'03	F. Alonso	K. Raikkonen	J.P. Montoya

RESULTS

	DRIVER	CAR	KPH	GAP
1	M. Schumacher	Ferrari	192,798	-
2	R. Barrichello	Ferrari	192,640	4"696
3	F. Alonso	Renault	191,307	44"599
4	J.P. Montoya	Williams	190,712	1'02"613
5	J. Button	BAR	190,553	1'07"439
6	T. Sato	BAR	190,027	1 lap
7	A. Pizzonia	Williams	189,990	1 lap
8	G. Fisichella	Sauber	189,136	1 lap
9	D. Coulthard	McLaren	189,068	1 lap
10	M. Webber	Jaguar	188,215	1 lap
11	O. Panis	Toyota	187,685	1 lap
12	N. Heidfeld	Jordan	186,220	2 laps
13	C. Klien	Jaguar	184,979	2 laps
14	G. Bruni	Minardi	179,260	4 laps
15	Z. Baumgartner	Minardi	177,838	5 laps

RETIREMENTS

G. Pantano	Jordan	48	Gearbox
J. Trulli	Renault	41	Engine
R. Zonta	Toyota	31	Electrical
F. Massa	Sauber	21	Brakes
K. Raikkonen	McLaren	13	Fuel injection

THE RACE

DRIVER	CAR	LAP	FASTEST LAP	TOP SPEED
M. Schumacher	Ferrari	29	1'19"071	313,8
R. Barrichello	Ferrari	29	1'19"213	313,6
F. Alonso	Renault	49	1'20"275	311,0
J. Button	BAR	47	1'20"425	303,7
A. Pizzonia	Williams	48	1'20"501	308,3
J. Trulli	Renault	10	1'20"705	306,2
J.P. Montoya	Williams	49	1'20"715	309,0
M. Webber	Jaguar	45	1'20"825	308,7
G. Fisichella	Sauber	53	1'21"022	309,4
T. Sato	BAR	10	1'21"030	304,2
D. Coulthard	McLaren	67	1'21"134	306,3
O. Panis	Toyota	50	1'21"310	304,6
N. Heidfeld	Jordan	68	1'21"518	305,1
K. Raikkonen	McLaren	6	1'21"678	307,3
F. Massa	Sauber	14	1'21"856	312,0
R. Zonta	Toyota	13	1'22"525	306,9
C. Klien	Jaguar	45	1'22"530	306,9
G. Pantano	Jordan	43	1'22"927	306,5
G. Bruni	Minardi	65	1'24"601	296,5
Z. Baumgartner	Minardi	63	1'24"855	298,0

HUNGARIAN GP

FERRARI WORLD CHAMPIONS!

Twelve wins out of 13 GPs, World Champions after just thirteen races. Pole position, fastest lap and another win after leading every lap of the Hungarian GP. For almost four years Schumacher's Ferrari has not suffered any mechanical failure (the last time was the German GP at Hockenheim on July 29, 2001), an overwhelming demonstration of the Italian engine's unrivalled reliability.

To conclude the Prancing Horse's triumphant weekend, Barrichello qualified on the front row of the grid and finished behind Schumacher in the race. This made it twenty-two times the German and the Brazilian have accumulated a 1-2 finish. Once again the BAR drivers had a superb qualifying session, but this time Sato was ahead of Button. The British driver was followed by Alonso and Pizzonia, who was surprisingly quicker than team-mate Montoya.

At the lights Schumacher got off the mark well ahead of Barrichello, who was able to slot in behind and protect the German from Alonso's attacks. The Renault has the best launch control system in F1 but this time Alonso was unable to do anything about Schumacher, who remained in the lead throughout the 70-lap race, despite making three pit stops.

Except for Button overtaking Sato, nothing much happened amongst the rest of the field, as always on the Budapest track where it is almost impossible to pass. One driver who did try was Felipe Massa, who was forced to start from the back of the grid after changing his engine in qualifying. Massa passed Pantano (Jordan) but had to slow and then stop because of a problem with his Sauber's brakes. Things went better for the other Sauber of Fisichella, who finished eighth in the race after qualifying eighth on the grid.

It was another disastrous race for Raikkonen, who was called into the pits after just 13 laps for an engine problem. The chequered flag saw the two Ferraris finish first and second, followed by Alonso and Montoya. The result was yet another double triumph for the Prancing Horse manufacturer, exactly sixteen years since the passing away of Enzo Ferrari.

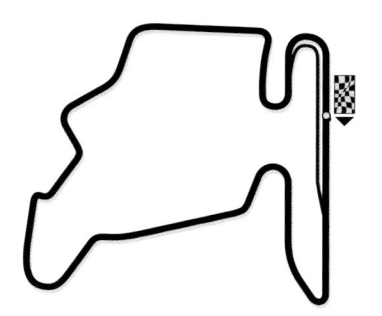

HUNGARORING
Length: **4,381 km**
Laps: **70**
Distance: **306,663 kms**

This twisty circuit was built and inaugurated in just eight months in 1986. Immersed in the Hungarian countryside and just 20 km from the capital Budapest, it is one of the slowest tracks on the F1 calendar. Overtaking is made difficult by the short straights and narrow track surface.

HIGHLIGHTS

Williams returned to a traditional nose after deciding to abandon the 'walrus' shape, invented by the young Italian designer Antonia Terzi which had caused such controversy at the start of the season. The change failed to bring about much improvement in the results however, as Montoya finished fourth and Pizzonia seventh.

PHOTO PORTFOLIO
FOLLOWING PAGES

Roberto Carlos, the Real Madrid defender and the Ecclestone family were the VIPs in the Budapest paddock.
Once again the race saw Ferrari take first and second place, but above all it conquered the World Constructors' title for the sixth time in six years.

CHAMPIONSHIPS POINTS	AUSTRALIAN GP	MALAYSIAN GP	BAHRAIN GP	SAN MARINO GP	SPANISH GP	MONACO GP	EUROPEAN GP	CANADIAN GP	UNITED STATES GP	FRENCH GP	BRITISH GP	GERMAN GP	HUNGARIAN GP	BELGIUM GP	ITALIAN GP	CHINA GP	JAPANESE GP	BRAZILIAN GP	TOTAL POINT
1 M. Schumacher	10	10	10	10	10	-	10	10	10	10	10	10	10						120
2 R. Barrichello	8	5	8	3	8	6	8	8	8	6	6	-	8						82
3 J. Button	3	6	6	8	1	8	6	6	-	4	5	8	4						65
4 J. Trulli	2	4	5	4	6	10	5	-	5	5	-	-	-						46
5 F. Alonso	6	2	3	5	5	-	4	-	-	8	-	6	6						45
6 J.P. Montoya	4	8	-	6	-	5	1	-	-	1	4	4	5						38
7 D. Coulthard	1	3	-	-	-	-	-	3	2	3	2	5	-						19
8 K. Raikkonen	-	-	-	1	-	-	-	4	3	2	8	-	-						18
9 T. Sato	-	-	4	-	4	-	-	-	6	-	-	1	3						18
10 G. Fisichella	-	-	-	-	2	-	3	5	-	-	3	-	1						14
11 R. Schumacher	5	-	2	2	3	-	-	-	-	/	/	/	/						12
12 M. Webber	-	-	1	-	-	-	2	-	-	-	1	3	-						7
13 F. Massa	-	1	-	-	-	4	-	-	-	-	-	-	-						5
14 O. Panis	-	-	-	-	-	1	-	-	4	-	-	-	-						5
15 A. Pizzonia	/	/	/	/	/	/	/	/	/	/	/	2	2						4
16 C. Da Matta	-	-	-	-	-	3	-	-	-	-	-	-	-						3
17 N. Heidfeld	-	-	-	-	-	2	-	1	-	-	-	-	-						3
18 T. Glock	/	/	/	/	/	/	/	2	/	/	/	/	/						2
19 Z. Baumgartner	-	-	-	-	-	-	-	-	1	-	-	-	-						1
20 C. Klien	-	-	-	-	-	-	-	-	-	-	-	-	-						-
21 M. Genè	/	/	/	/	/	/	/	/	-	/	/	-	/						-
22 G. Pantano	-	-	-	-	-	-	-	-	-	-	-	-	-						-
23 G. Bruni	-	-	-	-	-	-	-	-	-	-	-	-	-						-

202

BUDAPEST

Spa - 29 August 2004

Pole Position

2004 JARNO TRULLI

'90 A. Senna	'97 J. Villeneuve
'91 A. Senna	'98 M. Hakkinen
'92 N. Mansell	'99 M. Hakkinen
'93 A. Prost	'00 M. Hakkinen
'94 R. Barrichello	'01 J.P. Montoya
'95 G. Berger	'02 M. Schumacher
'96 J. Villeneuve	'03 -

Starting Grid

1
- Jarno Trulli — Renault — 1'56"232 
- Michael Schumacher — Ferrari — 1'56"304

2
- Fernando Alonso — Renault — 1'56"686 
- David Coulthard — McLaren — 1'57"990 

3
- Giancarlo Fisichella — Sauber — 1'58"040 
- Rubens Barrichello — Ferrari — 1'58"175

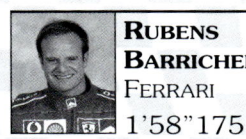

4
- Mark Webber — Jaguar — 1'58"729 
- Felipe Massa — Sauber — 1'59"008 

5
- Olivier Panis — Toyota — 1'59"552 
- Kimi Raikkonen — McLaren — 1'59"635 

6
- Juan-Pablo Montoya — Williams — 1'59"681 
- Jenson Button — BAR — 2'00"237 

7
- Christian Klien — Jaguar — 2'01"246 
- Antonio Pizzonia — Williams — 2'01"447 

8
- Takuma Sato — BAR — 2'01"813 
- Nick Heidfeld — Jordan — 2'02"645 

9
- Gianmaria Bruni — Minardi — 2'02"651 
- Zsolt Baumgartner — Minardi — 2'03"303 

10
- Giorgio Pantano — Jordan — 2'03"833 
- Riccardo Zonta — Toyota — 2'03"895 

Podium

	1°	2°	3°
'90	A. Senna	A. Prost	G. Berger
'91	A. Senna	G. Berger	N. Piquet
'92	M. Schumacher	N. Mansell	R. Patrese
'93	D. Hill	M. Schumacher	A. Prost
'94	D. Hill	M. Hakkinen	J. Verstappen
'95	M. Schumacher	D. Hill	M. Brundle
'96	M. Schumacher	J. Villeneuve	M. Hakkinen
'97	M. Schumacher	G. Fisichella	M. Hakkinen
'98	D. Hill	R. Schumacher	J. Alesi
'99	D. Coulthard	M. Hakkinen	H.H. Frentzen
'00	M. Hakkinen	M. Schumacher	R. Schumacher
'01	M. Schumacher	D. Coulthard	G. Fisichella
'02	M. Schumacher	R. Barrichello	J.P. Montoya
'03	-		

Results

	DRIVER	CAR	KPH	GAP
1	K. Raikkonen	McLaren	198,898	-
2	M. Schumacher	Ferrari	198,786	3"132
3	R. Barrichello	Ferrari	198,742	4"371
4	F. Massa	Sauber	198,452	12"504
5	G. Fisichella	Sauber	198,395	14"104
6	C. Klien	Jaguar	198,376	14"614
7	D. Coulthard	McLaren	198,257	17"970
8	O. Panis	Toyota	198,231	18"693
9	J. Trulli	Renault	198,110	22"115
10	N. Heidfeld	Jordan	180,039	4 laps

Retirements

R. Zonta	Toyota	41	Engine
J.P. Montoya	Williams	37	Wheel
A. Pizzonia	Williams	31	Gearbox
J. Button	BAR	29	Wheel
Z. Baumgartner	Minardi	28	Accident
F. Alonso	Renault	11	Hydraulic circuit
M. Webber	Jaguar	0	Accident
T. Sato	BAR	0	Accident
G. Bruni	Minardi	0	Accident
G. Pantano	Jordan	0	Accident

The Race

DRIVER	CAR	LAP	FASTEST LAP	TOP SPEED
K. Raikkonen	McLaren	42	1'45"108	318,7
M. Schumacher	Ferrari	28	1'45"503	320,0
R. Barrichello	Ferrari	43	1'45"666	313,2
F. Alonso	Renault	9	1'45"870	316,7
J. Trulli	Renault	9	1'45"898	311,0
J.P. Montoya	Williams	36	1'46"547	319,9
D. Coulthard	McLaren	11	1'46"579	320,2
A. Pizzonia	Williams	26	1'46"740	321,4
G. Fisichella	Sauber	11	1'46"758	314,7
J. Button	BAR	26	1'47"151	319,4
C. Klien	Jaguar	11	1'47"509	310,7
R. Zonta	Toyota	26	1'47"576	310,7
F. Massa	Sauber	29	1'47"624	311,2
O. Panis	Toyota	29	1'47"765	310,7
N. Heidfeld	Jordan	40	1'50"471	297,0
Z. Baumgartner	Minardi	25	1'51"031	305,9
M. Webber	Jaguar	0	-	-
T. Sato	BAR	0	-	-
G. Bruni	Minardi	0	-	-
G. Pantano	Jordan	0	-	-

BELGIAN GP

SCHUMACHER IN SEVENTH HEAVEN AT SPA

Jarno Trulli provided a ray of sunshine amidst the typically changeable Spa weather by claiming his second career pole for Renault. The Italian was pursued by Schumacher, who hit rain during his quick lap, and by Alonso, Coulthard, Fisichella and Barrichello.

When the lights flicked off, Alonso powered away to one of his usual superb starts ahead of the German, and dived in front of his Renault team-mate to take the lead. Coulthard also nipped past Schumacher, who moved wide at the first curve to avoid being knocked off. It was the same curve, tight and to the right, that was the cause of yet another of Spa's infamous multiple collisions. First Webber slammed into the rear of Barrichello, damaging his Jaguar and forcing the Brazilian into the pits for a lengthy stop. Further back, Baumgartner (Minardi) crashed into the back of team-mate Bruni and he was then hit by Pantano (Jordan), causing the Hungarian's Minardi to burst into flames. Out came the safety car.

At the restart, Raikkonen (McLaren) cut inside of the Ferrari of Schumacher and shortly after took his team-mate to move into third, immediately behind the two Renaults. When Trulli came in for his pit stop, Alonso took over at the front, but it wasn't to last long.

On lap 12, the young Spanish driver's Renault had an oil leak and he had two big spins before coming to a permanent rest in the gravel. After the boredom of Hungary, this race was turning into a classic. Half-way through, Montoya tried to pass Trulli at Les Combes with the same manoeuvre he had previously tried on Schumacher. This time round he arrived late however and hit the innocent Italian, who had to enter the pits.

Then Button's right rear tyre blew under braking for Les Combes, causing his BAR to spin and crash into Baumgartner's Minardi. The safety car came out again, bunching the group up, and the last ten laps of the race were a sprint to the finish, with Raikkonen leading, followed by Schummy, Montoya, Barrichello and Zonta.

The Finn managed to hold off his Ferrari rival to the flag to give McLaren its first win of the season. Second place went to Schumacher, who with this result became world champion for the seventh time, followed by Barrichello, who inherited third after Montoya retired with a blown rear tyre.

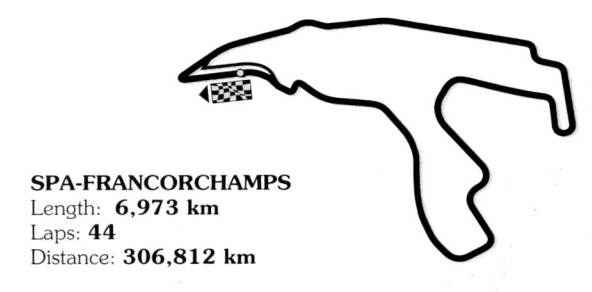

SPA-FRANCORCHAMPS
Length: **6,973 km**
Laps: **44**
Distance: **306,812 km**

Spa-Francorchamps, together with Monza, is the quickest circuit in Formula 1. After a year's break, in 2004 the Belgian GP returned to the Ardennes track, which is the longest (6.968 km) and most spectacular on the F1 calendar. Spa is also renowned for the Eau Rouge curve, a real test of courage for today's F1 drivers.

HIGHLIGHTS

The number of accidents caused by punctures is becoming one of the biggest talking-points of the 2004 season. Luckily the consequences have so far not been dramatic, the most serious being the one involving Ralf Schumacher at Indianapolis. At Spa, Coulthard, Button, Barrichello and Montoya were the next drivers to suffer from high-speed tyre blowouts. The race was also noteworthy for the excellent performance of Ricardo Zonta, who was running fourth with just a few laps to go when his engine blew.

PHOTO PORTFOLIO
FOLLOWING PAGES

A fortnight later and it was another triumph for Ferrari as Schumacher scooped his seventh world title, even though the honours in Belgium went to Finland's Kimi Raikkonen, who scored McLaren's first win of the year.

CHAMPIONSHIPS POINTS		AUSTRALIAN GP	MALAYSIAN GP	BAHRAIN GP	SAN MARINO GP	SPANISH GP	MONACO GP	EUROPEAN GP	CANADIAN GP	UNITED STATES GP	FRENCH GP	BRITISH GP	GERMAN GP	HUNGARIAN GP	BELGIAN GP	ITALIAN GP	CHINA GP	JAPANESE GP	BRAZILIAN GP	TOTAL POINT
1	M. Schumacher	10	10	10	10	10	-	10	10	10	10	10	10	10	8					128
2	R. Barrichello	8	5	8	3	8	6	8	8	8	6	6	-	8	6					88
3	J. Button	3	6	6	8	1	8	6	6	-	4	5	8	4	-					65
4	J. Trulli	2	4	5	4	6	10	5	-	5	5	-	-	-	-					46
5	F. Alonso	6	2	3	5	5	-	4	-	-	8	-	6	6	-					45
6	J.P. Montoya	4	8	-	6	-	5	1	-	-	1	4	4	5	-					38
7	K. Raikkonen	-	-	-	1	-	-	-	4	3	2	8	-	-	10					28
8	D. Coulthard	1	3	-	-	-	-	-	3	2	3	2	5	-	2					21
9	T. Sato	-	-	4	-	4	-	-	-	6	-	-	1	3	-					18
10	G. Fisichella	-	-	-	-	2	-	3	5	-	-	3	-	1	4					18
11	R. Schumacher	5	-	2	2	3	-	-	-	-	/	/	/	/	/					12
12	F. Massa	-	1	-	-	-	4	-	-	-	-	-	-	-	5					10
13	M. Webber	-	-	1	-	-	-	2	-	-	-	1	3	-	-					7
14	O. Panis	-	-	-	-	-	1	-	-	4	-	-	-	-	1					6
15	A. Pizzonia	/	/	/	/	/	/	/	/	/	/	/	2	2	-					4
16	C. Klien	-	-	-	-	-	-	-	-	-	-	-	-	-	3					3
17	C. Da Matta	-	-	-	-	3	-	-	-	-	-	-	-	-	-					3
18	N. Heidfeld	-	-	-	-	-	2	-	1	-	-	-	-	-	-					3
19	T. Glock	/	/	/	/	/	/	/	2	/	/	/	/	/	/					2
20	Z. Baumgartner	-	-	-	-	-	-	-	1	-	-	-	-	-	-					1
21	M. Genè	/	/	/	/	/	/	/	/	-	/	/	/	/	/					-
22	G. Pantano	-	-	-	-	-	-	-	-	-	-	-	-	-	-					-
23	G. Bruni	-	-	-	-	-	-	-	-	-	-	-	-	-	-					-
24	R. Zonta	/	/	/	/	/	/	/	/	/	/	/	/	/	-					-

206

SPA-FRANCORCHAMPS

207

MONZA - 12 SEPTEMBER 2004

POLE POSITION

'90 A. Senna	'97 J. Alesi
'91 A. Senna	'98 M. Schumacher
'92 N. Mansell	'99 M. Hakkinen
'93 A. Prost	'00 M. Schumacher
'94 J. Alesi	'01 J.P. Montoya
'95 D. Coulthard	'02 J.P. Montoya
'96 D. Hill	'03 M. Schumacher

2004 RUBENS BARRICHELLO

	1°	2°	3°
'90	A. Senna	A. Prost	G. Berger
'91	N. Mansell	A. Senna	A. Prost
'92	A. Senna	M. Brundle	M. Schumacher
'93	D. Hill	J. Alesi	M. Andretti
'94	D. Hill	G. Berger	M. Hakkinen
'95	J. Herbert	M. Hakkinen	H.H. Frentzen
'96	M. Schumacher	J. Alesi	M. Hakkinen
'97	D. Coulthard	J. Alesi	H.H. Frentzen
'98	M. Schumacher	E. Irvine	R. Schumacher
'99	H.H. Frentzen	R. Schumacher	M. Salo
'00	M. Schumacher	M. Hakkinen	R. Schumacher
'01	J.P. Montoya	R. Barrichello	R. Schumacher
'02	R. Barrichello	M. Schumacher	E. Irvine
'03	M. Schumacher	J.P. Montoya	R. Barrichello

STARTING GRID

1
- Rubens Barrichello — Ferrari — 1'20"089 
- Juan-Pablo Montoya — Williams — 1'20"620 

2
- Michael Schumacher — Ferrari — 1'20"637
- Fernando Alonso — Renault — 1'20"645 

3
- Takuma Sato — BAR — 1'20"715 
- Jenson Button — BAR — 1'20"786

4
- Kimi Raikkonen — McLaren — 1'20"877 
- Antonio Pizzonia — Williams — 1'20"888 

5
- Jarno Trulli — Renault — 1'21"027 
- David Coulthard — McLaren — 1'21"049 * 

6
- Riccardo Zonta — Toyota — 1'21"520 
- Mark Webber — Jaguar — 1'21"602 

7
- Olivier Panis — Toyota — 1'21"841 
- Christian Klien — Jaguar — 1'21"989 

8
- Giancarlo Fisichella — Sauber — 1'22"239 
- Felipe Massa — Sauber — 1'22"287 

9
- Giorgio Pantano — Jordan — 1'23"239 
- Gianmaria Bruni — Minardi — 1'24"940 

10
- Zsolt Baumgartner — Minardi — 1'25"808 ** 
- Nick Heidfeld — Jordan — 1'22"301 *** 

* STARTED FROM PITLANE
** PENALISED 1" FOR CUTTING CHICANE
*** RELEGATED AFTER ENGINE CHANGE

RESULTS

	DRIVER	CAR	KPH	GAP
1	R. Barrichello	Ferrari	244,374	-
2	M. Schumacher	Ferrari	244,301	1"347
3	J. Button	BAR	243,823	10"197
4	T. Sato	BAR	243,545	15"370
5	J.P. Montoya	Williams	242,636	32"352
6	D. Coulthard	McLaren	242,578	33"439
7	A. Pizzonia	Williams	242,562	33"752
8	G. Fisichella	Sauber	242,472	35"431
9	M. Webber	Jaguar	241,342	56"761
10	J. Trulli	Renault	240,839	1'06"316
11	R. Zonta	Toyota	239,990	1'22"531
12	F. Massa	Sauber	239,556	1 lap
13	C. Klien	Jaguar	238,608	1 lap
14	N. Heidfeld	Jordan	237,241	1 lap
15	Z. Baumgartner	Minardi	230,246	3 laps

RETIREMENTS

F. Alonso	Renault	40	Crashed
G. Pantano	Jordan	33	Crashed
G. Bruni	Minardi	29	Fire
K. Raikkonen	McLaren	13	Hydraulic circuit
O. Panis	Toyota	0	Crashed

THE RACE

DRIVER	CAR	LAP	FASTEST LAP	TOP SPEED
R. Barrichello	Ferrari	41	1'21"046	364,0
M. Schumacher	Ferrari	35	1'21"361	367,3
A. Pizzonia	Williams	32	1'22"246	369,9
G. Fisichella	Sauber	51	1'22"615	365,3
T. Sato	BAR	32	1'22"660	358,2
J. Button	BAR	13	1'22"671	356,3
J. Trulli	Renault	52	1'22"855	365,2
F. Alonso	Renault	31	1'22"881	365,7
D. Coulthard	McLaren	24	1'22"889	365,3
J.P. Montoya	Williams	32	1'22"929	363,6
F. Massa	Sauber	50	1'22"941	365,4
M. Webber	Jaguar	53	1'23"090	358,6
K. Raikkonen	McLaren	11	1'23"365	360,2
R. Zonta	Toyota	52	1'23"410	355,3
C. Klien	Jaguar	29	1'23"432	358,8
G. Pantano	Jordan	13	1'24"061	355,0
N. Heidfeld	Jordan	23	1'24"166	350,9
Z. Baumgartner	Minardi	31	1'26"356	359,4
G. Bruni	Minardi	24	1'26"371	352,9
O. Panis	Toyota	0	-	-

ITALIAN GP

SUPER BARRICHELLO!

"Despite having done literally hundreds of laps at Monza throughout my career, I've never done one as quick and precise as the one I did today" declared Rubens Barrichello after stepping out of his Ferrari at the end of Saturday qualifying. The Brazilian was on pole, half-a-second quicker than Montoya and his team-mate, Michael Schumacher, who had already been crowned 2004 world champion. The German was the first to congratulate Rubens, followed by an adoring Monza crowd and Ferrari president Luca di Montezemolo, who was present at the circuit with several members of the Agnelli family.

On Sunday the weather changed and a sudden downpour fell on the circuit late in the morning. The rain stopped shortly before the start but dark clouds were looming over the circuit, making tyre choice was a bit of a lottery. Rubens opted for intermediates while most drivers went for slicks.

At the lights the Brazilian got off to the best start and headed the field into the first chicane, followed by Alonso who was again quick off the mark. But the choice of intermediates proved to be the wrong one because it wasn't raining and the track was drying rapidly. Barrichello was forced to come in to change to slicks after just four laps.

It looked as if Monza was going to be another unlucky race for the number 2 Ferrari but Rubens was urged on by 100,000 tifosi and he was determined to break his Monza jinx. Meanwhile Schumacher, who got away to a cautious start, made a mistake during the opening lap, spinning at the second chicane and dropping down to 15th place. Clearly annoyed by the error he had committed in front of the Ferrari faithful, Schumacher also put on his own personal show as he put his head down and powered to the runner-up slot at the chequered flag. Third place went to Jenson Button, who again put on a superb performance, followed by team-mate Takuma Sato. The Japanese driver moved up a place after Alonso spun in the chicane before the straight leading to the Parabolica 13 laps from the end and finished with his rear wheels in the gravel.

Raikkonen (McLaren) had a disappointing race, the Finn going out with engine failure on lap 13, while Montoya (Williams) was penalised towards the end by a lengthy pit-stop and a gearbox problem. It was a real shame for the Colombian driver, who had set an extraordinary record lap at an average speed of over 260 km/h in Saturday's pre-qualifying session.

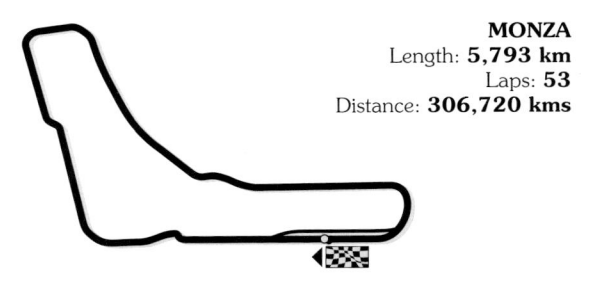

MONZA
Length: **5,793 km**
Laps: **53**
Distance: **306,720 kms**

Work on the Autodromo di Monza officially began on February 26, 1922 and the circuit was completed in August that same year. The track, situated in the parkland of Monza's Villa Reale, has undergone several modifications over the years, including the elimination of the high-speed banking in 1968.

HIGHLIGHTS

Things were not as tranquil at Renault as they had been in the previous races. Briatore had had a few unkind words to say about Jarno Trulli, whom he accused of not giving 100% and of already having his mind focussed on Toyota, the team the Italian will join in 2005. What is certain is that with third and fourth place at Monza, BAR are becoming serious candidates to clinch second place in this year's Constructors' championship.

PHOTO PORTFOLIO
FOLLOWING PAGES

Barrichello sets his first pole position of the year in front of 100,000 Ferrari tifosi in the Italian GP at Monza. Schumacher and Jenson Button stepped up to the podium with the Brazilian, who scored Ferrari's 13th win in 15 races.

CHAMPIONSHIPS POINTS		AUSTRALIAN GP	MALAYSIAN GP	BAHRAIN GP	SAN MARINO GP	SPANISH GP	MONACO GP	EUROPEAN GP	CANADIAN GP	UNITED STATES GP	FRENCH GP	BRITISH GP	GERMAN GP	HUNGARIAN GP	BELGIUM GP	ITALIAN GP	CHINA GP	JAPANESE GP	BRAZILIAN GP	TOTAL POINT
1	M. Schumacher	10	10	10	10	10	-	10	10	10	10	10	10	10	8	8				136
2	R. Barrichello	8	5	8	3	8	6	8	8	8	6	6	-	8	6	10				98
3	J. Button	3	6	6	8	1	8	6	6	-	4	5	8	4	-	6				71
4	J. Trulli	2	4	5	4	6	10	5	-	5	5	-	-	-	-	-				46
5	F. Alonso	6	2	3	5	5	-	4	-	-	8	-	6	6	-	-				45
6	J.P. Montoya	4	8	-	6	-	5	1	-	-	1	4	4	5	-	4				42
7	K. Raikkonen	-	-	-	1	-	-	-	4	3	2	8	-	-	10	-				28
8	D. Coulthard	1	3	-	-	-	-	3	2	3	2	5	-	2	3	-				24
9	T. Sato	-	-	4	-	4	-	-	-	6	-	-	1	3	-	5				23
10	G. Fisichella	-	-	-	-	2	-	3	5	-	-	3	-	1	4	1				19
11	R. Schumacher	5	-	2	2	3	-	-	-	/	/	/	/	/	/	/				12
12	F. Massa	-	1	-	-	-	4	-	-	-	-	-	-	-	5	-				10
13	M. Webber	-	-	1	-	-	-	2	-	-	-	1	3	-	-	-				7
14	O. Panis	-	-	-	-	-	1	-	-	4	-	-	-	-	1	-				6
15	A. Pizzonia	/	/	/	/	/	/	/	/	/	/	/	2	2	-	2				6
16	C. Klien	-	-	-	-	-	-	-	-	-	-	-	-	-	3	-				3
17	C. Da Matta	-	-	-	-	-	3	-	-	-	-	-	-	-	/	/				3
18	N. Heidfeld	-	-	-	-	-	2	-	1	-	-	-	-	-	-	-				3
19	T. Glock	/	/	/	/	/	/	/	2	/	/	/	/	/	/	/				2
20	Z. Baumgartner	-	-	-	-	-	-	1	-	-	-	-	-	-	-	-				1
21	M. Genè	/	/	/	/	/	/	/	/	-	-	-	/	/	/	/				
22	G. Pantano	-	-	-	-	-	-	-	-	-	-	-	-	-	-	-				
23	G. Bruni	-	-	-	-	-	-	-	-	-	-	-	-	-	-	-				
24	R. Zonta	/	/	/	/	/	/	/	/	/	/	/	/	/	-	-				

210

MONZA

Shanghai - 26 September 2004

Pole Position

2004 Rubens Barrichello

Starting Grid

1 
- Rubens Barrichello — Ferrari — 1'34"012 
- Kimi Raikkonen — McLaren — 1'34"178

2 
- Jenson Button — BAR — 1'34"295 
- Felipe Massa — Sauber — 1'34"759

3 
- Ralf Schumacher — Williams — 1'34"891 
- Fernando Alonso — Renault — 1'34"917

4 
- Giancarlo Fisichella — Sauber — 1'34"951 
- Olivier Panis — Toyota — 1'34"975

5 
- David Coulthard — McLaren — 1'35"029 
- Juan-Pablo Montoya — Williams — 1'35"245

6 
- Mark Webber — Jaguar — 1'35"286 
- Jacques Villeneuve — Renault — 1'35"384

7 
- Riccardo Zonta — Toyota — 1'35"410 
- Nick Heidfeld — Jordan — 1'36"507

8 
- Christian Klien — Jaguar — 1'36"535 
- Timo Glock — Jordan — 1'37"140

9 
- Gianmaria Bruni — Minardi — No Time 
- Takuma Sato — BAR — 1'34"993 *

10 
- Zsolt Baumgartner — Minardi — 1'40"240 *
- Michael Schumacher — Ferrari — No Time **

* Relegated after engine change
** Started from pitlane

Results

	Driver	Car	KPH	Gap
1	R. Barrichello	Ferrari	205,185	-
2	J. Button	BAR	205,145	1"035
3	K. Raikkonen	McLaren	205,128	1"469
4	F. Alonso	Renault	203,946	32"510
5	J.P. Montoya	Williams	203,467	45"193
6	T. Sato	BAR	203,106	54"791
7	G. Fisichella	Sauber	202,705	1'05"464
8	F. Massa	Sauber	202,160	1'20"080
9	D. Coulthard	McLaren	202,140	1'20"619
10	M. Webber	Jaguar	201,514	1 lap
11	J. Villeneuve	Renault	201,508	1 lap
12	M. Schumacher	Ferrari	201,147	1 lap
13	N. Heidfeld	Jordan	200,476	1 lap
14	O. Panis	Toyota	200,446	1 lap
15	T. Glock	Jordan	199,310	1 lap
16	Z. Baumgartner	Minardi	191,107	3 laps

Retirements

G. Bruni	Minardi	36	Accident
R. Schumacher	Williams	37	Accident
R. Zonta	Toyota	35	Gearbox
C. Klien	Jaguar	11	Accident

The Race

Driver	Car	Lap	Fastest Lap	Top Speed
M. Schumacher	Ferrari	55	1'32"238	337,6
R. Barrichello	Ferrari	28	1'32"455	338,0
K. Raikkonen	McLaren	53	1'32"876	330,3
J. Button	BAR	33	1'32"935	333,2
J.P. Montoya	Williams	34	1'33"108	338,1
F. Massa	Sauber	43	1'33"483	339,7
G. Fisichella	Sauber	25	1'33"520	340,8
T. Sato	BAR	36	1'33"533	331,8
R. Schumacher	Williams	31	1'33"546	335,9
F. Alonso	Renault	55	1'33"625	329,0
D. Coulthard	McLaren	26	1'33"727	330,6
R. Zonta	Toyota	24	1'34"268	338,2
O. Panis	Toyota	51	1'34"603	334,9
N. Heidfeld	Jordan	55	1'34"717	329,0
M. Webber	Jaguar	32	1'34"893	330,7
T. Glock	Jordan	54	1'34"931	330,0
J. Villeneuve	Renault	55	1'34"950	332,1
C. Klien	Jaguar	10	1'36"888	333,8
G. Bruni	Minardi	23	1'37"377	325,5
Z. Baumgartner	Minardi	51	1'37"578	329,5

CHINESE GP

BARRICHELLO, THE CHINESE DRAGON

Barrichello in pole position and Schumacher at the back of the starting-grid was the verdict after Saturday qualifying for the first-ever Chinese GP at the brand-new Shanghai circuit. Alongside the Brazilian's Ferrari was the McLaren of Raikkonen followed by Button (BAR), Massa (Sauber), the returning Ralf Schumacher (Williams) and Alonso in the Benetton. In qualifying, in the presence of Ferrari president Luca di Montezemolo, the German was the last driver to take to the track, as befits a multiple world champion. He powered down the start-finish straight and a few seconds later, amidst the incredulity of thousands of Chinese spectators lining the circuit and millions of TV viewers all over the world, the German was off the track. Schummy off the track at the first curve? Impossible…
Michael had to line up at the back of the grid but he opted for a pit lane start and would begin his race after all the others had got a clean getaway. Barrichello immediately blasted into the lead, shadowed by Raikkonen and Alonso, who made his usual superb getaway, this time slotting in between Massa and Button, to grab third.
What about Schumacher? On the second lap he was 15 seconds behind the leader Rubens, but he was powering through the field and by lap 10 was already in ninth place. The following lap he spun however and slipped down another three places, but the worst was yet to come. On lap 12 he made contact with Klien, then punctured his left rear tyre, eventually finishing the race in twelfth place, one lap down on the winner. It was a nightmare weekend for the newly-crowned world champion.
While Barrichello was safely in command, Ralf Schumacher and Coulthard were battling for the leading positions but they ended up by making contact. Ralf ruined his suspension and retired while the Scot went on to finish ninth in a McLaren that was far from perfect after the incident.
Barrichello took the chequered flag for his second win of the season, followed by Button in the BAR, a result that consolidated the Anglo-Japanese team's position in the Constructors' standings ahead of Renault, and by a rejuvenated Raikkonen.

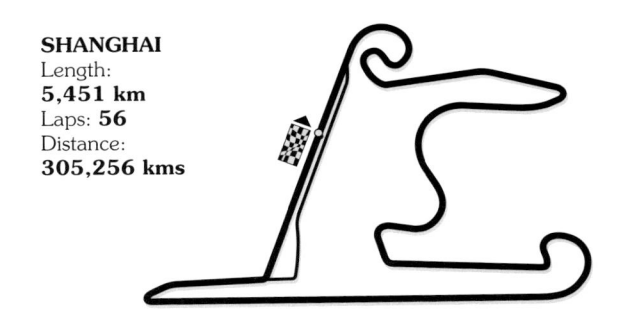

SHANGHAI
Length: **5,451 km**
Laps: **56**
Distance: **305,256 kms**

Formula 1 comes to China this year at the brand-new Shanghai circuit. Measuring 5.451 km, it is very twisty but has a long straight before the curve that leads back to the start.

HIGHLIGHTS

Jacques Villeneuve's return to Formula 1 in the ex-Trulli Renault did not exactly set the world on fire. Twelfth in qualifying, the Canadian finished the Chinese GP in eleventh position. The result was a disappointing one for the 1997 world champion (with Williams-Renault), but it is worth mentioning that Jacques had not raced an F1 car for a year and had not done much training for his return, a considerable handicap on an exhausting circuit like Shanghai.

PHOTO PORTFOLIO
FOLLOWING PAGES

Joy and misfortune in the first Chinese Grand Prix. Jacques Villeneuve returns to F1 with Renault after a year's absence. Jaguar instead announced its retirement from F1 at the end of the season. And finally the joy of the entire Ferrari team, with president Montezemolo on the podium with Barrichello.

	CHAMPIONSHIPS POINTS	AUSTRALIAN GP	MALAYSIAN GP	BAHRAIN GP	SAN MARINO GP	SPANISH GP	MONACO GP	EUROPEAN GP	CANADIAN GP	UNITED STATES GP	FRENCH GP	BRITISH GP	GERMAN GP	HUNGARIAN GP	BELGIUM GP	ITALIAN GP	CHINA GP	JAPANESE GP	BRAZILIAN GP	TOTAL POINT
1	M. Schumacher	10	10	10	10	10	-	10	10	10	10	10	10	10	8	8	-			136
2	R. Barrichello	8	5	8	3	8	6	8	8	8	6	6	-	5	8	4	-	8	6	10	10			108
3	J. Button	3	6	6	8	1	8	6	6	-	4	5	8	4	-	6	8			79
4	F. Alonso	6	2	3	5	5	-	4	-	-	8	-	6	6	-	-	5			50
5	J. Trulli	2	4	5	4	6	10	5	-	5	5	-	-	-	-	-	/			46
6	J.P. Montoya	4	8	-	6	-	5	1	-	-	1	4	4	5	-	4	4			46
7	K. Raikkonen	-	-	-	1	-	-	-	4	3	2	8	-	-	10	-	6			34
8	T. Sato	-	-	4	-	4	-	-	-	6	-	-	1	3	-	5	3			26
9	D. Coulthard	1	3	-	-	-	-	3	2	3	2	5	-	2	3	-			24
10	G. Fisichella	-	-	-	-	2	-	3	5	-	-	3	-	1	4	1	2			21
11	R. Schumacher	5	-	2	2	3	-	-	-	-	/	/	/	/	/	/	-			12
12	F. Massa	-	1	-	-	-	4	-	-	-	-	-	-	-	5	-	1			11
13	M. Webber	-	-	1	-	-	-	2	-	-	-	1	3	-	-	-	-			7
14	O. Panis	-	-	-	-	-	1	-	-	4	-	-	-	-	1	-	-			6
15	A. Pizzonia	/	/	/	/	/	/	/	/	/	/	2	2	-	2	/			6
16	C. Klien	-	-	-	-	-	-	-	-	-	-	-	-	3	-	-	-			3
17	C. Da Matta	-	-	-	-	3	-	-	-	-	-	-	-	/	/	/	/			3
18	N. Heidfeld	-	-	-	-	2	-	1	-	-	-	-	-	-	-	-	-			3
19	T. Glock	/	/	/	/	/	/	/	2	/	/	/	/	/	/	/	/			2
20	Z. Baumgartner	-	-	-	-	-	-	-	1	-	-	-	-	/	/	/	/			1
21	M. Genè	-	-	-	-	-	-	-	-	-	-	-	-	-	-	/	-			-
22	G. Pantano	-	-	-	-	-	-	-	-	-	-	-	-	-	-	-	/			-
23	G. Bruni	-	-	-	-	-	-	-	-	-	-	-	-	-	-	-	-			-
24	R. Zonta	/	/	/	/	/	/	/	/	/	/	/	/	/	/	/	-			-
25	J. Villeneuve	/	/	/	/	/	/	/	/	/	/	/	/	/	/	/	-			-

213

214

SHANGHAI

Suzuka - 10 October 2004

Pole Position

'90 A. Senna	'97 J. Villeneuve
'91 G. Berger	'98 M. Schumacher
'92 N. Mansell	'99 M. Schumacher
'93 A. Prost	'00 M. Schumacher
'94 M. Schumacher	'01 M. Schumacher
'95 M. Schumacher	'02 M. Schumacher
'96 J. Villeneuve	'03 R. Barrichello

2004 Michael Schumacher

Starting Grid

1 
- Michael Schumacher — Ferrari — 1'33"542 
- Ralf Schumacher — Williams — 1'34"032

2 
- Mark Webber — Jaguar — 1'34"571 
- Takuma Sato — BAR — 1'34"897

3 
- Jenson Button — BAR — 1'35"157 
- Jarno Trulli — Toyota — 1'35"213

4 
- Giancarlo Fisichella — Sauber — 1'36"136 
- David Coulthard — McLaren — 1'36"156

5 
- Jacques Villeneuve — Renault — 1'36"274 
- Olivier Panis — Toyota — 1'36"420

6 
- Fernando Alonso — Renault — 1'36"663 
- Kimi Raikkonen — McLaren — 1'36"820

7 
- Juan-Pablo Montoya — Williams — 1'37"653 
- Christian Klien — Jaguar — 1'38"258

8 
- Rubens Barrichello — Ferrari — 1'38"637 
- Nick Heidfeld — Jordan — 1'41"953

9 
- Timo Glock — Jordan — 1'43"533 
- Gianmaria Bruni — Minardi — 1'48"069

10 
- Felipe Massa — Sauber — No Time 
- Zsolt Baumgartner — Minardi — No Time

	1°	2°	3°
'90	N. Piquet	R. Moreno	A. Suzuki
'91	G. Berger	A. Senna	R. Patrese
'92	R. Patrese	G. Berger	M. Brundle
'93	A. Senna	A. Prost	M. Hakkinen
'94	D. Hill	M. Schumacher	J. Alesi
'95	M. Schumacher	M. Hakkinen	J. Herbert
'96	D. Hill	M. Schumacher	M. Hakkinen
'97	M. Schumacher	H.H. Frentzen	E. Irvine
'98	M. Hakkinen	E. Irvine	D. Coulthard
'99	M. Hakkinen	M. Schumacher	E. Irvine
'00	M. Schumacher	M. Hakkinen	D. Coulthard
'01	M. Schumacher	J.P. Montoya	D. Coulthard
'02	M. Schumacher	R. Barrichello	K. Raikkonen
'03	R. Barrichello	K. Raikkonen	D. Coulthard

Results

	DRIVER	CAR	KPH	GAP
1	M. Schumacher	Ferrari	218,524	-
2	R. Schumacher	Williams	217,918	14"098
3	J. Button	BAR	217,680	19"662
4	T. Sato	BAR	217,162	31"781
5	F. Alonso	Renault	216,908	37"767
6	K. Raikkonen	McLaren	216,840	39"362
7	J.P. Montoya	Williams	216,163	55"347
8	G. Fisichella	Sauber	216,124	56"276
9	F. Massa	Sauber	214,725	1'29"656
10	J. Villeneuve	Renault	214,315	1 lap
11	J. Trulli	Toyota	214,039	1 lap
12	C. Klien	Jaguar	212,968	1 lap
13	N. Heidfeld	Jordan	212,612	1 lap
14	O. Panis	Toyota	210,107	2 laps
15	T. Glock	Jordan	208,548	2 laps
16	G. Bruni	Minardi	203,977	3 laps

Retirements

Z. Baumgartner	Minardi	41	Crashed
D. Coulthard	McLaren	38	Accident
R. Barrichello	Ferrari	38	Accident
M. Webber	Jaguar	20	Hydraulic circuit

The Race

DRIVER	CAR	LAP	FASTEST LAP	TOP SPEED
R. Barrichello	Ferrari	30	1'32"730	313,3
M. Schumacher	Ferrari	41	1'32"796	312,1
R. Schumacher	Williams	23	1'33"467	309,3
F. Massa	Sauber	40	1'33"614	314,6
T. Sato	BAR	28	1'33"742	304,1
J.P. Montoya	Williams	30	1'33"779	314,3
J. Button	BAR	33	1'33"819	305,6
G. Fisichella	Sauber	44	1'33"850	310,9
D. Coulthard	McLaren	14	1'33"917	307,3
K. Raikkonen	McLaren	35	1'33"920	306,6
M. Webber	Jaguar	13	1'34"229	299,7
F. Alonso	Renault	29	1'34"279	307,0
O. Panis	Toyota	11	1'34"438	297,1
J. Trulli	Toyota	52	1'34"626	298,4
C. Klien	Jaguar	32	1'35"261	293,7
J. Villeneuve	Renault	28	1'35"290	306,5
N. Heidfeld	Jordan	25	1'35"524	298,0
T. Glock	Jordan	14	1'36"667	299,2
G. Bruni	Minardi	27	1'39"352	285,9
Z. Baumgartner	Minardi	26	1'39"434	285,2

JAPANESE GP

ALL IN ONE DAY!

Never before in Formula 1 had qualifying and the race taken place in the same day, just a few hours apart. As a result, never before had a driver obtained pole position and the win in the same day. Who better to obtain this new record than the king of record-breakers himself, Michael Schumacher! This situation came about because of the appalling weather conditions in Japan. On Friday the heavens opened and this was the first warning sign, together with a few earth tremors, that Typhoon Ma-On was on its way. For safety reasons the circuit was closed on Saturday and official qualifying was rescheduled for Sunday morning. Schumacher immediately set the pole, followed by his brother Ralf, Webber (Jaguar) and Sato (BAR), who was rapidly becoming the idol of the Japanese fans. There was just enough time for a few interviews and they all lined up on the grid at the start.

When the red lights went out, Schumacher powered away followed by his brother and the two BARs, with Button passing his team-mate Sato as they went into turn 1. Trulli, for the first time behind the wheel of a Toyota, followed the group while on lap 2, Fisichella dived past Villeneuve in the Renault for eighth place. Alonso was immediately up behind his team-mate whom he passed easily on lap 6 and then started to chase after the Sauber, while Sato gave way to his team-mate Button on the same lap. Meanwhile further down the field there was a great battle between Montoya, Barrichello and Raikkonen.

After these frenetic opening laps, things settled down in this order and as always it was only the pit-stops that modified the final results. Two-thirds of the way into the race Barrichello and Coulthard, who were fighting for fifth place, provided some action when they made contact at the chicane. Rubens ruined his front suspension and the Scot was forced to retire. The two Schumacher brothers finished on the podium at Suzuka, with Button taking third place and Sato an excellent fourth, after being penalised by a three pit-stop strategy against his team-mate's two.

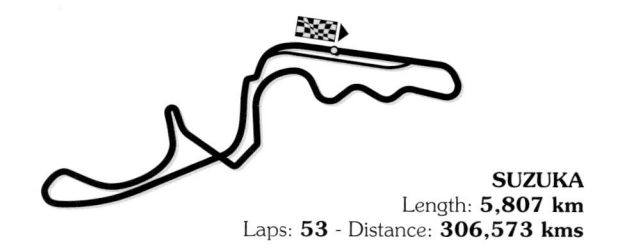

SUZUKA
Length: **5,807 km**
Laps: **53** - Distance: **306,573 kms**

The Suzuka track hosted its first F1 race in 1987. The futuristic structure, built in the 1960s, is situated in the middle of an enormous amusement park. The circuit has an unusual figure-of-eight layout and is fast and difficult, albeit with several points for overtaking.

HIGHLIGHTS

Jarno Trulli got an early drive for his 2005 team when he took to the track in Toyota colours. In qualifying he immediately went quicker than his team-mate Panis, despite the latter having more familiarity with the Japanese car, and lined up on the third row.
Trulli then was running in an excellent fifth position until his first pit-stop. The Italian would eventually finish in eleventh position due to excessive tyre wear, a problem that has always afflicted the Toyota.

PHOTO PORTFOLIO
FOLLOWING PAGES

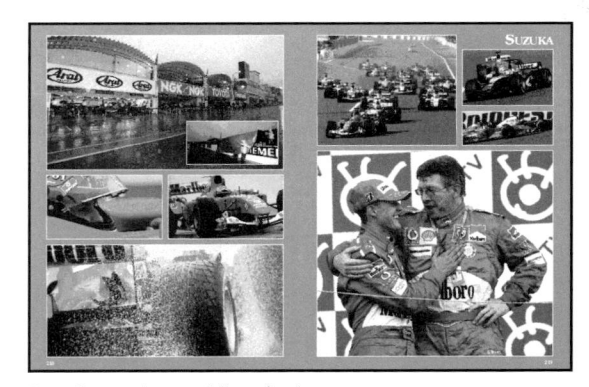

Suzuka in the middle of a hurricane with the paddock and pits flooded and the circuit closed on Saturday.
Barrichello ruined his race when he made contact with Coulthard, while Schumacher celebrates his 13th win in 2004 with Ross Brawn.

	CHAMPIONSHIPS POINTS	AUSTRALIAN GP	MALAYSIAN GP	BAHRAIN GP	SAN MARINO GP	SPANISH GP	MONACO GP	EUROPEAN GP	CANADIAN GP	UNITED STATES GP	FRENCH GP	BRITISH GP	GERMAN GP	HUNGARIAN GP	BELGIUM GP	ITALIAN GP	CHINA GP	JAPANESE GP	BRAZILIAN GP	TOTAL POINT
1	M. Schumacher	10	10	10	10	10	-	10	10	10	10	10	10	10	8	8	-	10		146
2	R. Barrichello	8	5	8	3	8	6	8	8	8	6	6	-	8	6	10	10	-		108
3	J. Button	3	6	6	8	1	8	6	6	-	4	5	8	4	-	6	8	6		85
4	F. Alonso	6	2	3	5	5	-	4	-	-	8	-	6	6	-	-	5	4		54
5	J.P. Montoya	4	8	-	6	-	5	1	-	-	1	4	4	5	-	4	4	2		48
6	J. Trulli	2	4	5	4	6	10	5	-	5	5	-	-	-	-	/	-			46
7	K. Raikkonen	-	-	-	1	-	-	-	4	3	2	8	-	-	10	-	6	3		37
8	T. Sato	-	-	4	-	4	-	-	-	6	-	-	-	1	3	-	5	3	5	31
9	D. Coulthard	1	3	-	-	-	4	-	-	3	2	3	2	5	-	2	3	-	-	24
10	G. Fisichella	-	-	-	-	2	-	3	5	-	-	3	-	1	4	1	2	1		22
11	R. Schumacher	5	-	2	2	3	-	-	/	/	/	/	/	/	/	-	8			20
12	F. Massa	-	1	-	-	-	4	-	-	-	-	-	-	5	-	1	-			11
13	M. Webber	-	-	1	-	-	-	2	-	-	-	1	3	-	-	-	-	-		7
14	O. Panis	-	-	-	-	-	1	-	-	4	-	-	-	-	1	-	-	-		6
15	A. Pizzonia	/	/	/	/	/	/	/	/	/	/	/	2	2	-	2	/	/		6
16	C. Klien	-	-	-	-	-	-	-	-	-	-	-	-	-	3	-	-	-		3
17	C. Da Matta	-	-	-	-	3	-	-	-	-	-	-	-	-	/	/	/			3
18	N. Heidfeld	-	-	-	-	2	-	1	-	-	-	-	-	-	-	-	-	-		3
19	T. Glock	/	/	/	/	/	/	/	2	/	/	/	/	/	/	/	-	-		2
20	Z. Baumgartner	-	-	-	-	-	-	1	-	-	-	-	-	-	-	-	-	-		1
21	M. Genè	/	/	/	/	/	/	/	/	/	/	/	-	-	-	-	/	/		-
22	G. Pantano	-	-	-	-	-	-	-	-	-	-	-	-	-	-	/	/			-
23	G. Bruni	-	-	-	-	-	-	-	-	-	-	-	-	-	-	-	-	-		-
24	R. Zonta	/	/	/	/	/	/	/	/	/	/	/	-	-	-	-	/	/		-
25	J. Villeneuve	/	/	/	/	/	/	/	/	/	/	/	/	/	/	-	-	-		-

218

SUZUKA

INTERLAGOS - 24 OCTOBER 2004

POLE POSITION

'90 A. Senna	'97 J. Villeneuve
'91 A. Senna	'98 M. Hakkinen
'92 N. Mansell	'99 M. Hakkinen
'93 A. Prost	'00 M. Hakkinen
'94 A. Senna	'01 M. Schumacher
'95 D. Hill	'02 J.P. Montoya
'96 D. Hill	'03 R. Barrichello

2004 RUBENS BARRICHELLO

STARTING GRID

1 
- Rubens Barrichello — Ferrari — 1'10"646 
- Juan-Pablo Montoya — Williams — 1'10"850

2 
- Kimi Raikkonen — McLaren — 1'10"892 
- Felipe Massa — Sauber — 1'10"922

3 
- Jenson Button — BAR — 1'11"092 
- Takuma Sato — BAR — 1'11"120

4 
- Ralf Schumacher — Williams — 1'11"131 
- Fernando Alonso — Renault — 1'11"454

5 
- Jarno Trulli — Toyota — 1'11"483 
- Giancarlo Fisichella — Sauber — 1'11"571

6 
- Mark Webber — Jaguar — 1'11"665 
- David Coulthard — McLaren — 1'11"750

7 
- Jacques Villeneuve — Renault — 1'11"836 
- Riccardo Zonta — Toyota — 1'11"974

8 
- Christian Klien — Jaguar — 1'12"211 
- Nick Heidfeld — Jordan — 1'12"829

9 
- Timo Glock — Jordan — 1'13"502 
- Michael Schumacher — Ferrari — 1'11"386 *

10 
- Gianmaria Bruni — Minardi — No Time ** 
- Zsolt Baumgartner — Minardi — 1'13"550 *

* RELEGATED AFTER ENGINE CHANGE
** STARTED FROM PITLANE

GRANDE PRÊMIO DO BRASIL

	1°	2°	3°
'90	A. Prost	G. Berger	A. Senna
'91	A. Senna	R. Patrese	G. Berger
'92	N. Mansell	R. Patrese	M. Schumacher
'93	A. Senna	D. Hill	M. Schumacher
'94	M. Schumacher	D. Hill	J. Alesi
'95	G. Berger	M. Hakkinen	J. Alesi
'96	D. Hill	J. Alesi	M. Schumacher
'97	J. Villeneuve	G. Berger	O. Panis
'98	M. Hakkinen	D. Coulthard	M. Schumacher
'99	M. Hakkinen	M. Schumacher	H.H. Frentzen
'00	M. Schumacher	G. Fisichella	H.H. Frentzen
'01	D. Coulthard	M. Schumacher	N. Heidfeld
'02	M. Schumacher	R. Schumacher	D. Coulthard
'03	K. Raikkonen	G. Fisichella	F. Alonso

RESULTS

	DRIVER	CAR	KPH	GAP
1	J.P. Montoya	Williams	208,516	-
2	K. Raikkonen	McLaren	208,476	1"022
3	R. Barrichello	Ferrari	207,569	24"099
4	F. Alonso	Renault	206,603	48"908
5	R. Schumacher	Williams	206,571	49"740
6	T. Sato	BAR	206,551	50"248
7	M. Schumacher	Ferrari	206,537	50"626
8	F. Massa	Sauber	206,085	1'02"310
9	G. Fisichella	Sauber	206,026	1'03"842
10	J. Villeneuve	Renault	205,452	1 lap
11	D. Coulthard	McLaren	204,902	1 lap
12	J. Trulli	Toyota	204,389	1 lap
13	R. Zonta	Toyota	203,467	1 lap
14	C. Klien	Jaguar	202,233	2 laps
15	T. Glock	Jordan	200,288	2 laps
16	Z. Baumgartner	Minardi	196,743	4 laps
17	G. Bruni	Minardi	196,134	4 laps

RETIREMENTS

M. Webber	Jaguar	23	Accident
N. Heidfeld	Jordan	15	Gearbox
J. Button	BAR	3	Engine

THE RACE

DRIVER	CAR	LAP	FASTEST LAP	TOP SPEED
J.P. Montoya	Williams	49	1'11"473	320,3
K. Raikkonen	McLaren	52	1'11"562	323,8
R. Barrichello	Ferrari	22	1'11"672	323,4
M. Schumacher	Ferrari	49	1'11"763	326,8
R. Schumacher	Williams	23	1'11"764	323,8
G. Fisichella	Sauber	69	1'11"877	325,9
T. Sato	BAR	51	1'11"941	322,3
F. Massa	Sauber	68	1'12"066	326,8
F. Alonso	Renault	42	1'12"118	324,5
J. Villeneuve	Renault	68	1'12"210	322,0
J. Trulli	Toyota	65	1'12"435	318,8
D. Coulthard	McLaren	40	1'12"522	319,7
C. Klien	Jaguar	49	1'12"891	317,4
R. Zonta	Toyota	69	1'12"961	320,9
M. Webber	Jaguar	20	1'13"197	323,5
T. Glock	Jordan	68	1'13"905	316,7
Z. Baumgartner	Minardi	45	1'14"743	318,7
G. Bruni	Minardi	50	1'14"756	314,9
N. Heidfeld	Jordan	11	1'15"855	303,7
J. Button	BAR	2	1'24"440	270,8

BRAZILIAN GP

MONTOYA, FAREWELL MY WILLIAMS!

With the two world titles already sewn up, the main interest in the Brazilian GP was whether or not the local fans would be celebrating the victory of their idol Barrichello, or at the very least one of the South American drivers on the grid. Saturday's qualifying went some way to confirming their best hopes: first Barrichello, with a determined Montoya alongside, followed by Felipe Massa (Sauber) in fourth place. Michael Schumacher was relegated to the back of the starting-grid after his nasty crash in the morning's free practice session. The German flew off at Ferradura, destroying his Ferrari in the process (with flames licking out of the rear) and was forced to change his car.
Things were back to normal on Sunday, when a light rain convinced most of the riders on the grid to opt for intermediate tyres. The GP got underway and Barrichello was immediately passed by Raikkonen while Button and Montoya latched on to their exhausts, but Ruben was determined to offer some spectacle to his fellow Brazilians and two laps later passed the Finn again at the end of the start-finish straight. On the same lap Button stopped with engine failure while shortly before, Schumacher, who had started like a rocket from the last row of the grid, ruined everything by spinning at the Senna curves and slipping down the field. A run of chaotic pit-stops then got underway as the drivers all came in to change to slicks seeing as it wasn't raining anymore and the track was drying out. Raikkonen and Montoya even came in together and left again side-by-side in the pit lane! At the exit Kimi had the best line but Montoya passed him a few metres later. Barrichello also came in for a pit stop but dropped down to eighth place and Alonso (who had started on dry-weather tyres) took a temporary lead before he eventually came into the pits. One-third of the way into the race the two Jaguars slammed into each other and Webber had to retire.
It couldn't have been a worse way to say goodbye to Formula 1.
Montoya moved into the lead followed by Raikkonen, his future team-mate, but the Finn was unable to attack JPM as his McLaren was not as quick as the Williams. Immediately behind them Ferrari's Brazilian driver was getting the best of a battle for third place with four other drivers, Alonso, who was having a great race, Sato and the two Schumacher brothers.
The Williams driver went on to take the chequered flag, the Colombian dedicating the win to his mechanics, followed by Raikkonen and Barrichello, who finally stepped onto his home podium after ten years of trying.
It was not a particularly positive end to the season for Ferrari, which had given the impression of an overwhelming superiority throughout the year. It was also another missed opportunity for the Brazilian driver, who was clearly disappointed with third place.

INTERLAGOS
Length: **4,309 km**
Laps: **71**
Distance: **305,909 kms**

The Interlagos circuit, situated on the outskirts of Sao Paolo, held its first F1 race in 1973. It was then replaced by Jacarepaguà in 1981 because it was deemed to be unsafe. After restructuring work, Interlagos obtained the go-ahead from the FIA in 1990 to again hold the Brazilian GP. Together with Imola, it is the only track to run in an anti-clockwise direction.

HIGHLIGHTS

Formula 1 said farewell to Jaguar after five years of mediocre performances. The results of the prestigious British marque, which is owned by Ford and which has always been a symbol of power and class in the automobile sector, certainly did not live up to expectations.
It was a sad goodbye, underlined by the incredible incident involving both cars in the team's last race.

	CHAMPIONSHIPS POINTS	AUSTRALIAN GP	MALAYSIAN GP	BAHRAIN GP	SAN MARINO GP	SPANISH GP	MONACO GP	EUROPEAN GP	CANADIAN GP	UNITED STATES GP	FRENCH GP	BRITISH GP	GERMAN GP	HUNGARIAN GP	BELGIUM GP	ITALIAN GP	CHINA GP	JAPANESE GP	BRAZILIAN GP	TOTAL POINT
1	M. Schumacher	10	10	10	10	10	-	10	10	10	10	10	10	10	8	8	-	10	2	148
2	R. Barrichello	8	5	8	3	8	6	8	8	8	6	6	-	8	6	10	10	-	6	114
3	J. Button	3	6	6	8	1	8	6	6	-	4	5	8	4	-	6	8	6	-	85
4	F. Alonso	6	2	3	5	5	-	4	-	-	8	-	6	6	-	-	5	4	5	59
5	J.P. Montoya	4	8	-	6	-	5	1	-	-	1	4	4	5	-	4	4	2	10	58
6	J. Trulli	2	4	5	4	6	10	5	-	5	5	-	-	-	-	-	/	-	-	46
7	K. Raikkonen	-	-	-	1	-	-	-	4	3	2	8	-	-	10	-	6	3	8	45
8	T. Sato	-	-	4	-	4	-	-	-	6	-	-	1	3	-	5	3	5	3	34
9	D. Coulthard	1	3	-	-	-	-	-	3	2	3	2	5	-	2	3	-	-	-	24
10	R. Schumacher	5	-	2	2	3	-	-	-	-	/	/	/	/	/	/	-	8	4	24
11	G. Fisichella	-	-	-	-	2	-	3	5	-	-	3	-	1	4	1	2	1	-	22
12	F. Massa	-	1	-	-	-	4	-	-	-	-	-	-	-	5	-	1	-	1	12
13	M. Webber	-	-	1	-	-	-	2	-	-	-	1	3	-	-	-	-	-	-	7
14	O. Panis	-	-	-	-	-	1	-	-	4	-	-	-	1	-	-	-	/	-	6
15	A. Pizzonia	/	/	/	/	/	/	/	/	/	/	2	2	-	2	-	/	/	/	6
16	C. Klien	-	-	-	-	-	-	-	-	-	-	-	-	3	-	-	-	-	-	3
17	C. Da Matta	-	-	-	3	-	-	-	-	-	-	-	-	-	/	/	/	-	-	3
18	N. Heidfeld	-	-	-	-	2	-	1	-	-	-	-	-	-	-	-	-	-	-	3
19	T. Glock	/	/	/	/	/	/	2	/	/	/	/	/	/	/	/	/	-	-	2
20	Z. Baumgartner	-	-	-	-	-	-	1	-	-	-	-	-	-	-	-	-	-	-	1
21	M. Genè	/	/	/	/	/	/	/	/	/	/	/	-	/	/	/	/	/	/	-
22	G. Pantano	-	-	-	-	-	-	-	-	-	-	-	-	-	-	-	/	/	/	-
23	G. Bruni	-	-	-	-	-	-	-	-	-	-	-	-	-	-	-	-	-	-	-
24	R. Zonta	/	/	/	/	/	/	/	/	/	/	/	-	/	/	/	-	-	-	-
25	J. Villeneuve	/	/	/	/	/	/	/	/	/	/	/	/	/	/	/	-	-	-	-

PHOTO PORTFOLIO
FOLLOWING PAGES

Weekend to forget for Schummy who lost control of his car in Saturday's free practice, destroying the Ferrari.
Button also had an unfortunate weekend with engine failure for his BAR.
On the top of the podium, a happy Juan Pablo Montoya, who said goodbye to Williams with a fantastic win.

221

Marlboro

Mercedes-Benz
F1
FIA Formula 1
WORLD CHAMPIONSHIP

HONDA
LUCKY STRIKE

POTENZA
PETROBRAS
FedEx
FedEx
West
SIEMENS

SAO PAULO (INTERLAGOS)

223

2004 World Championship: Drivers & Constructors

Drivers	Australian GP	Malaysian GP	Bahrain GP	San Marino GP	Spanish GP	Monaco GP	European GP	Canadian GP	United States GP	French GP	British GP	German GP	Hungarian GP	Belgium GP	Italian GP	China GP	Japanese GP	Brazilian GP	Total Point
M. Schumacher	10	10	10	10	10	-	10	10	10	10	10	10	10	8	8	-	10	2	148
R. Barrichello	8	5	8	3	8	6	8	8	8	6	6	-	8	6	10	10	-	6	114
J. Button	3	6	6	8	1	8	6	6	-	4	5	8	4	-	6	8	6	-	85
F. Alonso	6	2	3	5	5	-	4	-	-	8	-	6	6	-	-	5	4	5	59
J.P. Montoya	4	8	-	6	-	5	1	-	-	1	4	4	5	-	4	4	2	10	58
J. Trulli	2	4	5	4	6	10	5	-	5	5	-	-	-	-	-	-	-	-	46
K. Raikkonen	-	-	-	1	-	-	-	4	3	2	8	-	-	10	-	6	3	8	45
T. Sato	-	-	4	-	4	-	-	6	-	-	1	3	-	5	3	5	3	-	34
D. Coulthard	1	3	-	-	-	-	3	2	3	2	5	-	2	3	-	-	-	-	24
R. Schumacher	5	-	2	2	3	-	-	-	-	-	-	-	-	-	-	8	4	-	24
G. Fisichella	-	-	-	-	2	-	3	5	-	-	3	-	1	4	1	2	1	-	22
F. Massa	-	1	-	-	-	4	-	-	-	-	-	5	-	-	1	1	-	-	12
M. Webber	-	-	1	-	-	2	-	-	-	1	3	-	-	-	-	-	-	-	7
O. Panis	-	-	-	-	1	-	-	4	-	-	-	-	-	1	-	-	-	-	6
A. Pizzonia	/	/	/	/	/	/	/	/	/	-	2	2	-	2	-	/	/	/	6
C. Klien	-	-	-	-	-	-	-	-	-	-	-	3	-	-	-	-	-	-	3
C. Da Matta	-	-	-	-	3	-	-	-	-	-	-	-	-	-	-	-	-	-	3
N. Heidfeld	-	-	-	-	2	-	1	-	-	-	-	-	-	-	-	-	-	-	3
T. Glock	-	-	-	-	-	-	2	-	-	-	-	-	-	-	-	-	-	-	2
Z. Baumgartner	-	-	-	-	-	-	-	-	1	-	-	-	-	-	-	-	-	-	1
M. Genè	-	-	-	-	-	-	-	-	-	-	-	-	-	-	-	-	-	-	0
G. Pantano	-	-	-	-	-	-	-	-	-	-	-	-	-	-	-	-	-	-	0
G. Bruni	-	-	-	-	-	-	-	-	-	-	-	-	-	-	-	-	-	-	0
R. Zonta	/	/	/	/	/	/	/	/	/	-	-	-	-	-	-	/	/	/	0
J. Villeneuve	/	/	/	/	/	/	/	/	/	/	/	/	/	/	/	-	-	-	0

Constructors	Australian GP	Malaysian GP	Bahrain GP	San Marino GP	Spanish GP	Monaco GP	European GP	Canadian GP	United States GP	French GP	British GP	German GP	Hungarian GP	Belgium GP	Italian GP	China GP	Japanese GP	Brazilian GP	Total Point
Ferrari	18	15	18	13	18	6	18	18	18	16	16	10	18	14	18	10	10	8	262
BAR	3	6	10	8	5	8	6	6	-	6	4	5	9	7	-	11	11	3	119
Renault	8	6	8	9	11	10	9	-	5	13	-	6	6	-	-	5	4	5	105
Williams	9	8	2	8	3	5	1	-	-	1	4	6	7	-	6	4	10	14	88
McLaren	1	3	-	1	-	-	7	5	5	10	5	-	12	3	6	3	8	69
Sauber	-	1	-	2	4	3	5	-	-	3	-	1	9	1	3	1	1	34
Jaguar	-	-	1	-	-	2	-	-	-	1	3	-	3	-	-	-	-	-	10
Toyota	-	-	-	-	4	-	4	-	-	-	-	-	1	-	-	-	-	-	9
Jordan	-	-	-	-	-	-	2	-	3	-	-	-	-	-	-	-	-	-	5
Minardi	-	-	-	-	-	-	-	-	1	-	-	-	-	-	-	-	-	-	1

	N° GP	N° Pole Position	N° Fastest Lap	N° Retirements	Australian GP	Malaysian GP	Bahrain GP	San Marino GP	Spanish GP	Monaco GP	European GP	Canadian GP	United States GP	French GP	British GP	German GP	Hungarian GP	Belgium GP	Italian GP	China GP	Japanese GP	Brazilian GP
M. Schumacher	18	8	10	2	1	1	1	1	1	R	1	1	1	1	1	1	1	2	2	R	1	7
R. Barrichello	18	4	4	1	2	4	2	6	2	3	2	2	2	3	3	12	2	3	1	1	R	3
J. Button	18	1	-	3	6	3	3	2	8	2	3	3	R	5	4	2	5	R	3	2	3	R
F. Alonso	18	1	-	5	3	7	6	4	4	R	5	R	R	2	10	3	3	R	R	4	5	4
J.P. Montoya	18	-	2	2	5	2	13	3	R	4	8	Sq.	Sq.	8	5	5	4	R	5	5	7	1
J. Trulli	17	2	-	3	7	5	4	5	3	1	4	R	4	4	R	11	R	9	10	-	11	12
K. Raikkonen	18	1	2	8	R	R	R	8	11	R	R	5	6	7	2	R	R	1	R	3	R	2
T. Sato	18	-	-	5	9	15	5	16	5	R	R	R	3	R	11	8	6	R	4	6	R	6
D. Coulthard	18	-	-	4	8	6	R	12	10	R	R	6	7	6	7	4	9	7	6	9	R	11
G. Fisichella	18	-	-	1	10	11	11	9	7	R	6	R	9	12	6	9	8	5	8	7	R	9
R. Schumacher	12	-	1	4	4	R	7	7	6	10	R	Sq.	1	R	-	-	-	-	-	R	5
F. Massa	18	-	-	4	R	8	12	10	9	5	9	R	R	13	9	13	R	4	12	8	9	8
M. Webber	18	-	-	8	R	R	8	13	12	R	7	R	9	8	6	10	R	9	10	R	R
O. Panis	17	-	-	3	13	12	9	11	R	8	11	Sq.	5	15	R	14	11	8	R	14	13	-
A. Pizzonia	4	-	-	1	-	-	-	-	-	-	-	-	-	-	7	7	R	7	-	-	-	-
C. Klien	18	-	-	4	11	10	14	14	R	R	12	R	R	11	14	10	13	6	13	R	12	14
C. Da Matta	13	-	-	5	12	9	10	R	13	6	R	Sq.	R	14	13	R	R	-	-	-	-	-
N. Heidfeld	18	-	-	7	R	R	15	R	R	7	10	8	R	16	15	R	12	11	14	13	13	R
T. Glock	4	-	-	-	-	-	-	-	-	-	-	7	-	-	-	-	-	-	-	15	15	15
Z. Baumgartner	18	-	-	7	R	16	R	15	R	9	15	10	8	R	R	16	15	R	15	16	R	16
R. Zonta	4	-	-	1	-	-	-	-	-	-	-	-	-	-	-	-	-	10	11	R	-	13
J. Villeneuve	3	-	-	-	-	-	-	-	-	-	-	-	-	-	-	-	-	-	-	11	10	10
M. Genè	2	-	-	-	-	-	-	-	-	-	-	-	-	-	-	10	12	-	-	-	-	-
G. Pantano	15	-	-	9	14	13	16	R	R	R	13	R	R	17	R	15	R	R	-	-	-	-
G. Bruni	18	-	-	9	R	14	17	R	R	R	14	R	R	18	16	17	14	R	R	16	R	17

- R: retired   Sq.: disqualified

World Champions 1950-2004

N. Farina	(I - Alfa Romeo)	1950	
J.M. Fangio	(RA - Alfa Romeo)	1951	
A. Ascari	(I - Ferrari)	1952	
A. Ascari	(I - Ferrari)	1953	
J.M. Fangio	(RA - Maserati, Mercedes)	1954	
J.M. Fangio	(RA - Mercedes)	1955	
J.M. Fangio	(RA - Ferrari)	1956	
J.M. Fangio	(RA - Maserati)	1957	
M. Hawthorn	(GB - Ferrari)	1958	Vanwall
J. Brabham	(AUS - Cooper)	1959	Cooper
J. Brabham	(AUS - Cooper)	1960	Cooper
P. Hill	(USA - Ferrari)	1961	Ferrari
G. Hill	(GB - Brm)	1962	Brm
J. Clark	(GB - Lotus)	1963	Lotus
J. Surtees	(GB - Ferrari)	1964	Ferrari
J. Clark	(GB - Lotus)	1965	Lotus
J. Brabham	(AUS - Brabham)	1966	Brabham
D. Hulme	(NZ - Brabham)	1967	Brabham
G. Hill	(GB - Lotus)	1968	Lotus
J. Stewart	(GB - Matra)	1969	Matra
J. Rindt	(A - Lotus)	1970	Lotus
J. Stewart	(GB - Tyrrell)	1971	Tyrrell
E. Fittipaldi	(BR - Lotus)	1972	Lotus
J. Stewart	(GB - Tyrrell)	1973	Lotus
E. Fittipaldi	(BR - McLaren)	1974	McLaren
N. Lauda	(A - Ferrari)	1975	Ferrari
J. Hunt	(GB - McLaren)	1976	Ferrari
N. Lauda	(A - Ferrari)	1977	Ferrari
M. Andretti	(USA - Lotus)	1978	Lotus
J. Scheckter	(ZA - Ferrari)	1979	Ferrari
A. Jones	(AUS - Williams)	1980	Williams
N. Piquet	(BR - Brabham)	1981	Williams
K. Rosberg	(SF - Williams)	1982	Ferrari
N. Piquet	(BR - Brabham)	1983	Ferrari
N. Lauda	(A - McLaren)	1984	McLaren
A. Prost	(F - McLaren)	1985	McLaren
A. Prost	(F - McLaren)	1986	Williams
N. Piquet	(BR - Williams)	1987	Williams
A. Senna	(BR - McLaren)	1988	McLaren
A. Prost	(F - McLaren)	1989	McLaren
A. Senna	(BR - McLaren)	1990	McLaren
A. Senna	(BR - McLaren)	1991	McLaren
N. Mansell	(GB - Williams)	1992	Williams
A. Prost	(F - Williams)	1993	Williams
M. Schumacher	(D - Benetton)	1994	Williams
M. Schumacher	(D - Benetton)	1995	Benetton
D. Hill	(GB - Williams)	1996	Williams
J. Villeneuve	(CDN - Williams)	1997	Williams
M. Hakkinen	(FIN - McLaren)	1998	McLaren
M. Hakkinen	(FIN - McLaren)	1999	Ferrari
M. Schumacher	(D - Ferrari)	2000	Ferrari
M. Schumacher	(D - Ferrari)	2001	Ferrari
M. Schumacher	(D - Ferrari)	2002	Ferrari
M. Schumacher	(D - Ferrari)	2003	Ferrari
M. Schumacher	(D - Ferrari)	2004	Ferrari

F1 2004

Fotografia / *Photography* / Foto / *Fotografie*	BRYN WILLIAMS - FRITS VAN ELDIK - PAOLO D'ALESSIO
Disegni tecnici / *Cutaways* / Illustrationen / *Illustraties*	PAOLO D'ALESSIO
Realizzazione grafica / *Graphic realization* / Grafische gestaltung / *Grafische vormgeving*	DIEGO GALBIATI
Traduzioni / *Translations* / Übersetzung / *Vertaling*	JULIAN THOMAS RICK WINKELMAN BEATE HERBERICH
Stampa / *Printing* / Druck / *Druck*	EDITORIALE LLOYD - TRIESTE (ITALY)
Legatoria / *Binding* / Buchbinderei / *Binder*	LEGATORIA FRIULIA - MANIAGO-PN (ITALY)
Realizzazione / *Editorial production* / Herstellungskoordination / *Redactie en samenstelling*	© 2004 WORLDWIDE SEP EDITRICE - CASSINA DE PECCHI (MILANO - ITALY) www.sepeditrice.com

Member of the
World Sportpublisher's Association

Printed in Italy - November 2004

© 2004 SEP Editrice - Cassina de Pecchi (Milano - ITALY)
ISBN 88-87110-48-4

© 2004 Nederlands Taalgebied Ars Scribendi BV - Etten-Leur
ISBN 90-5566-014-0

© 2004 Race Report - Hilversum
ISBN 90-5566-015-9

Si ringrazia
AUTOSPRINT
settimanale di automobilismo sportivo leader in Italia,
fonte inesauribile di informazioni e dati statistici ripresi per questo libro.

F1 2004